GRACE FLANAGAN
(203) 505-1913

What is actually happening...
↳ questioning, asking critical questions
there might be something else going on

All God's Animals

key Things to Remember (probably for exam)

Thomistic Framework → p16 (Thomas Aquinas)   (Chapter 1)

1) animals serve us

2) we have no obligation towards them

3) we shouldn't mistreat them because it goes against our morality/reason

3 Arguments for Theodicy of Evolution (chapter 2)

1) good is unavoidably tied to evil → "The Only Way" argument; only way God could have created a world with such beauty/diversity

2) universe is incomplete, developing into something greater → God trying to bring about something more wonderful

3) universe giving rise to human freedom should itself develop thru own autonomous processes
↳ if God wanted to create autonomous beings, then the universe also had to be autonomous

Why is there suffering? 3 arguments → allows to shape in spontaneous/free way

Why choose evolution? Millions of yrs predation/prey? Why would this be the way?

How animals relate to → Imago Dei, The Fall, and to Dominion

Theodicy → how does it explain animal suffering?

TRANSHUMANIST perspective
↳ transcend present human limitations

Causal Joint Theory of God's...
↳ joint comm. God intervenes w/ cosmic ties to get creation to move in certain direction

Metaphysical Causality
↳ Being behind the form
whatever causality God is doing isn't
be a matter of ... ; whatever God is doing
is second level ... underneath it all, and
shapes form but not in a way that affects causality

THE FALL → Human and nonhuman creation have both been affected by sin (humans sin)
so, also, when God intervenes, God would save them, too; it follows

God made a choice in light of the sin that would arise the whole world is somehow not how it is supposed to be; cosmic fall

SELECTED TITLES FROM THE MORAL TRADITIONS SERIES
David Cloutier, Darlene Weaver, and Andrea Vicini, SJ, Editors

The Acting Person and Christian Moral Life
Darlene Fozard Weaver

Aquinas on Virtue: A Causal Reading
Nicholas Austin, SJ

Catholic Moral Theology in the United States: A History
Charles E. Curran

Creative Conformity: The Feminist Politics of US Catholic and Iranian Shi'i Women
Elizabeth M. Bucar

The Critical Calling: Reflections on Moral Dilemmas since Vatican II
Richard A. McCormick

Diverse Voices in Modern US Moral Theology
Charles E. Curran

Family Ethics: Practices for Christians
Julie Hanlon Rubio

Hope for Common Ground: Mediating the Personal and the Political in a Divided Church
Julie Hanlon Rubio

Keeping Faith with Human Rights
Linda Hogan

Kinship across Borders: A Christian Ethic of Immigration
Kristin E. Heyer

Moral Evil
Andrew Michael Flescher

The Origins of War: A Catholic Perspective
Matthew A. Shadle

Overcoming Our Evil: Human Nature and Spiritual Exercises in Xunzi and Augustine
Aaron Stalnaker

Prophetic and Public: The Social Witness of US Catholicism
Kristin E. Heyer

Reconsidering Intellectual Disability: L'Arche, Medical Ethics, and Christian Friendship
Jason Reimer Greig

The Sexual Person: Toward a Renewed Catholic Anthropology
Todd A. Salzman and Michael G. Lawler

Theological Bioethics: Participation, Justice, and Change
Lisa Sowle Cahill

The Vice of Luxury: Economic Excess in a Consumer Age
David Cloutier

What makes humans distinct? ⟹ are there things that put us in a distinct category?
↳ higher order thinking (religion, mathematics, seeking)
↳ built a society, create, explore, develop, problem solve
↳ empathy, compassion that isn't instinctual, necessarily
↳ think and reason w/ things that don't necessarily have matter thinking "abstractly"...
↳ can animals be moral beings in any sort of way? Do

All God's Animals

they reflect on actions as to whether they're good or bad and then choose?

humans = special object of God's distinction...
but not radically diff. than animals

A Catholic Theological
Framework for Animal Ethics

↳ Animals = God's creation = treat them as we'd treat one another

CHRISTOPHER STECK, SJ

Georgetown University Press / Washington, DC

The publisher is not responsible for third-party websites or their content. URL links were active at time of publication.

Library of Congress Cataloging-in-Publication Data

Names: Steck, Christopher W., author.
Title: All God's Animals : A Catholic Theological Framework for Animal Ethics / Christopher Steck, SJ.
Other titles: Moral Traditions series.
Description: Washington, DC : Georgetown University Press, 2019. | Series: The moral traditions series | Includes bibliographical references and index.
Identifiers: LCCN 2019004747 (print) | LCCN 2019008940 (ebook) | ISBN 9781626167148 (hardcover : alk. paper) | ISBN 9781626167155 (pbk. : alk. paper) | ISBN 9781626167162 (ebook : alk. paper)
Subjects: LCSH: Animal welfare—Religious aspects—Catholic Church. | Animal welfare—Moral and ethical aspects.
Classification: LCC HV4708 .S6423 2019 (print) | LCC HV4708 (ebook) | DDC 241/.693—dc23
LC record available at https://lccn.loc.gov/2019004747
♾ This book is printed on acid-free paper meeting the requirements of the American National Standard for Permanence in Paper for Printed Library Materials.

20 19   9 8 7 6 5 4 3 2

Printed in the United States of America.

Cover design by Nathan Putens.
Cover image from the Booth Family Center for Special Collections, Lauinger Library, Georgetown University, Washington, DC.
The image depicts *Edge of the Forest at Fontainebleau, Setting Sun*, etching after Theodore Rousseau.

When the bow appears in the clouds, I will see it and remember the everlasting covenant between God and every living creature—every mortal being that is on earth.

—Genesis 9:16

To John S. "Jack" Carroll
with hope in the covenant
between God and all creatures.

CONTENTS

Acknowledgments
xi

INTRODUCTION
Animals as Fellow Creatures of the Covenant
1

CHAPTER 1
Tradition: Learning to See Animals
8

CHAPTER 2
Creation: The *Imago Dei* and a Covenantal Anthropocentrism
56

CHAPTER 3
Redemption: The Divine *Magis* and Animals
95

CHAPTER 4
Sanctification: The Spirit's Cosmic Embrace
133

CHAPTER 5
Ethics: Ministers of the Eschatological Covenant
171

CONTENTS

Bibliography
213

Index
237

About the Author
249

ACKNOWLEDGMENTS

ALL SCHOLARLY works build on the labors of others, but some do so more than others. This is one such work. For decades now, Christian theologians and ethicists have worked to advance the Christian tradition beyond its former neglect of nonhuman creation. I have benefited greatly from their groundbreaking work and am most grateful for it.

I was fortunate to have scout leaders as parents. They gave up many weekends and long stretches during the summer so that a group of Kool-Aid–fueled kids could experience our amazing world up close. Whatever respect and care I have for nature and the creatures within it are due significantly to their example and the many experiences of nature that their generosity made possible.

A research leave from Georgetown University in the spring of 2017 allowed me to make significant progress on this book. I spent the first part of that semester at the Jesuit Spirituality Center in Grand Coteau, Louisiana. It was good to be back among the stately oaks and Spanish moss. My thanks to the members of the community for their warm welcome, with a particular note of gratitude to Derrick Weingartner, SJ, the community's rector, and Mark Thibodeaux, SJ, who was then the novice master and is still a dear friend.

The second part of the semester was spent at a fairly secluded home made available to me, then and many times after, by Georgetown alumni Kevin and Nancy Clark. It was a beautiful setting for writing about God's creatures. I cannot thank them enough for their kindness and friendship.

This book is significantly better because of the input I received from many friends. Otto Hentz, SJ and Brian McDermott, SJ corrected numerous textual errors and helped me clarify a number of theological points, including the nature/grace discussion in chapter 3. This is the second round for Otto, after his having also read a draft of my book on Hans Urs von Balthasar's ethics, so I really owe him. David Clough, a classmate from Yale and good friend, met with me several hours one Sunday afternoon at a bookstore café in Portland, Oregon. He carefully went over the manuscript with me, giving invaluable feedback that was at once helpfully critical and encouraging—a great experience of collegiality. Jack Segelstein, a Georgetown alumnus (COL '18) and former student, did yeoman's work in helping to copyedit an early draft of the manuscript and its final proofs. My heartfelt thanks to all these friends for their assistance.

Early on in the process, Carole Sargent of Georgetown's Office of Scholarly Publications and Richard Brown, then director of Georgetown University Press, helped me understand the ins and outs of writing and publishing a book. I was fortunate that Georgetown University Press agreed to publish the manuscript; its staff has been very helpful in assisting me in the publishing process. I am grateful to them all.

Finally, my thanks to my family, friends, brother Jesuits, and colleagues who have helped in many other ways with this book, often by patiently listening while I recounted various researching and writing experiences. Their enthusiastic encouragement has been much appreciated.

INTRODUCTION

Animals as Fellow Creatures of the Covenant

c o v e n a n t

Creation looks toward the covenant, but the covenant completes creation.

—Joseph Cardinal Ratzinger

THE INITIAL idea for this book began to germinate when I was rereading a section of Lisa Sowle Cahill's work on the pacifist and just war traditions, which she examines in the context of the kingdom of God.[1] The kingdom of God has been inaugurated in Jesus's life, and the Christian is now called to witness to it through practices that reflect its ideals. I believe that what has come to be termed the "already / not yet" of the kingdom (i.e., the idea that the kingdom has already begun in Jesus Christ but its fulfillment is yet to come) is a valuable framework for Christian ethics. It gives Christianity its peculiar stereoscopic vision: looking to a future that is already in-breaking within the present order, even if obscured by it. Though the Christian community cannot hope to do more than offer an imaginative portrayal of that transformed future, it believes that Christ has revealed the fundamental values that will animate it. Witnessing to these values (e.g., peacemaking, forgiveness, justice, liberation) is the responsibility of all Christians, a task that will sometimes require a countercultural response at odds with more prudential judgments about what is "realistic." The kingdom disrupts conventional ethics. Yet, because the kingdom is not here in its fullness, our moral lives will often, sometimes unavoidably so, fall short of the kingdom's ideals.

Much of the literature on the connection between Christian ethics and the kingdom focuses on a set of similar themes, which are all related to the renewal of social harmony in a broken world. But I began to wonder how the task of witnessing to the kingdom might relate to nonhuman creatures. What would ethical care for animals look like if framed by the already / not yet of the kingdom? If animals are to share in the eschaton with us, must our treatment of them, like all acts prescribed by Christian ethics, be attentive to the ideals of the kingdom?

My initial attempt to write on this topic led me in an unexpected direction: to speak about a "kingdom ethics" for animals requires that they somehow be part of that kingdom. That is, I felt that I first needed to defend including animals in the eschaton before I could argue that they deserved to be treated, in the present age, as co-sharers in it. Developing a case for their inclusion led me more deeply into contemporary theological debates about the eschaton, evolution, the environment, and Christian views of creation. These conversations have progressed substantially over the last several decades and are now quite developed in their scope, perspectives, and interdisciplinarity. Nonetheless, what is missing from them, I came to believe, is a comprehensive, Catholic theology of animals that brings together in a systematic form recent magisterial teachings and the insights of contemporary theology.

The result is this book. The first four chapters develop a theology of animals, with the aim of making the case that at least some of them share in an eschatological destiny. The final chapter, the aim of my original endeavor, explores the ethical implications of this theology. Though I believe much of what I develop in this book can be applied to other non-human creatures, my focus is on animals, specifically those creatures that are cognitively sophisticated enough to have something like a sense of self that endures across time (and perhaps also have other qualities, such as a sense of the past and future as *their* past and future, a capacity for having affection for one another, empathy, a conscious awareness of themselves and the world around them, and a rudimentary capacity to reason). In the pages that follow, I argue that these qualities are central to God's goal in creating and redeeming, and thus we can hope that animals endowed with some or all such qualities will also be included in God's renewal of the world.

My use of the term "animal" is intentionally fluid and includes more than land-based creatures (e.g., birds and sea creatures). I do not use it to delineate a clear boundary between creatures, but only as a designation for a domain of creatures that, I believe, provides the best case for developing Catholic thought with regard to nonhuman life, the eschaton, and ethics. My argument is intentionally restricted in order to critique the view that, to use colloquial language, "animals don't go to heaven" by arguing that at least some do, and thus I focus on the most likely candidates for such a redemptive embrace. Again, however, my argument is not meant to preclude the possibility that other (or even all) creatures will also be welcomed into the age to come.

Chapter 1 explores how historical Catholic attitudes toward animals were shaped by what I call the "Thomistic framework." It comprises three commitments: animals have no rights, animals are meant to serve humanity, and cruelty to animals is wrong, not because it does them an injustice but because it adversely affects the human agent's character. Since Vatican II, these views have been modified if not discarded. Still, I examine the history of Catholic views on animals, especially as it has unfolded in the last several centuries, because we need to learn from it. Specifically, this history suggests that Catholic attitudes toward animals have too often been distorted by a complacent unwillingness to attend to them and genuinely perceive them for what they are: creatures loved by God, with their own distinctive subjectivities, emotions, and abilities to experience joy and sorrow. I conclude by raising a concern that this historical resistance to "seeing" animals is not just a deficiency of our past but also a failure in the present.

Chapter 2 begins the case for a theological reinterpretation of animals. Among the current pressures urging us to revise our views of animals are the claims of contemporary science (especially evolution and animal studies) and the shift in interpretations of the theological themes found in the first chapters of Genesis—most importantly, the dominion mandate, the fall, and humanity as the *imago Dei*. The chapter argues that the goal of God's creative act is to establish a covenant with all creation, not just humankind. I suggest this while also supporting a tempered claim for human uniqueness, what I call a broken, covenantal anthropocentrism.

Chapter 3 argues that we have sound theological reasons for believing that the generosity and power of God displayed in Christ's life and death—the divine *magis*, as I refer to it—is also directed to redeeming nonhuman animals. I open by exploring some of the basic Catholic commitments regarding human nature and Christ's redemption of it (e.g., God preserves human nature even as it is elevated in Christ). I briefly examine biblical, patristic, and contemporary theologies to highlight support for nonhuman redemption, and I begin to make a case for it by appealing to the theology of creation found in the thought of Hans Urs von Balthasar. Balthasar believed that all creation will be redeemed, but to my knowledge he never explored how such a redemption occurs. Nonetheless, his view that every

covenant with ALL creation

Post - Noah's Ark, covenant w/ ALL creation
Gen ch. 9 God's covenant w/ non-human creatures

creaturely existence has been endowed with a dialogical inclination provides a ground for such a creaturely inclusive redemption. All creatures can be embraced within a covenantal relationship with the Father because they are all able to *respond*; even the trees and mountains give God praise. These earthly natures are, in Catholic idiom, preserved and elevated in Christ.

I employ Balthasar's concept of "theo-drama" to propose a way of understanding nonhuman redemption. For Balthasar, the salvific narrative leading up to the paschal mystery is *the* drama that explains and gives meaning to every other drama in creation. Every creature's life unfolds dramatically, and these dramas must ultimately be interpreted in light of the salvific drama revealed in Christ. In Christ, God has made it so that there is no longer a fundamental antagonism between the life of the Godhead and that of creaturely existence. Because of this alignment between God and creation, each creature can be embraced by the triune God without losing its innate, relative meaning or threatening God's absolute unity.

In chapter 4, I develop the redemptive inclusion of animals (what I call their "sanctification") by incorporating the work of the Holy Spirit. The first part of the chapter depends significantly on Balthasar's trinitarian theology. Within the processions of the triune Persons, the Spirit is both co-subject of the love between the Father and the Son and the objective expression of the bond between them. Building on this, we can suggest that in God's labor for the world, the Spirit acts as both co-subject with the animal creature and objective bond between it and the divine life. The Spirit is thus able to enfold into the drama of the triune life not only human existence but also the creaturely drama of animals. I pursue this trinitarian inclusion of the animal in two directions. First, I look at how the Spirit incorporates the life and drama of the individual animal, using the particularly difficult case of animal predation as an example. Second, I explore historical and contemporary teachings that base their soteriologies on the view that all creatures are bound together in a fundamental solidarity. The work of redeeming humanity, then, is always also the work of redeeming all creation. Through the gift of the Spirit, this work is ritualized and effected in the Eucharist.

Finally, chapter 5 examines the ethical implications of the framework developed in the preceding chapters. This framework is based on a number of theological claims—including the views that the suffering that marks the lives of animals in the present age is not desired by God; that animals have a purpose beyond serving humanity; that God delights in animals and cares for their well-being; and that God intends to enter into covenantal relationships with animals, in ways appropriate to each, and draw them together in Christ.

These *theological* commitments give rise to *ethical* ones. The eschatological destiny of animals should inform how we treat them. However, like other eschatological ideals (e.g., pacifism, hospitality toward the stranger, and communal sharing of one's goods), the ideals associated with animal life—as depicted, for example, in the peaceable kingdom of Isaiah 11:6–9—must be tempered by an eschatological reserve that acknowledges the brokenness of the world around us and the impossibility of simultaneously realizing all the important values at stake in our treatment of animals. Because the kingdom's fullness is still to come, this eschatological framework permits, at times, practices that are at odds with the values of the kingdom but are needed to protect other important values (e.g., we will sometimes need to kill animals to preserve human life and health). In the world to come, no violence will be done to animals, but in this world such acts will be necessary.

Christian care for nonhuman creatures is an ecclesial and personal responsibility. God has given the Christian community the task of witnessing to the kingdom inaugurated in Christ, and this task includes care for animal life. The Church should work against instrumentalizing attitudes toward animals by fostering a worldview that sees them as sentient subjects and fellow creatures of the covenant, living in relationship with us and with God. As creatures of the covenant, they should receive the Church's prayers for their flourishing and its hope for their restoration. All Christians are called to follow universal norms regarding care for animals, but some will be called to a personal vocation that goes beyond what is strictly required. In such a calling, the person strives to regularly embody, sometimes with significant hardship, relationships with animals that reflect the ideals of the kingdom.

Even while advocating for a keener sense of our significant responsibilities toward animals, I also recognize that the needs of the human community are massive and grave. Given the injustice and oppression in our world, some might suggest that we have enough pressing issues to address without adding concerns for animals. In response, I offer two observations. First, the sufferings of the human community and those of animals are sometimes linked, so addressing one can help us in addressing the other. Thus, for example, a reduction of meat consumption will not only lessen the amount of animal suffering but will also reduce greenhouse gas emissions and help us avoid the disastrous climate disruptions that disproportionately affect the world's poor. Also, reducing meat consumption should lead to shifts in food production that will better serve the world's hungry and malnourished. An "integral ecology," to use Pope Francis's term, requires that we pursue an integrated approach in addressing environmental issues and social justice.[2]

However, second and more important, I believe that any adequate discernment of how to care for animals, in light of the many other demands we face, must begin with a basic recognition that animals are genuine objects of moral concern; this itself is a moral achievement. After first gaining this moral awareness, we can then move to the complicated task of discerning how to respond given the weighty problems faced by so many in our world. It would be a false strategy to preemptively reduce these enormous demands by dismissing any serious responsibility for animal well-being or closing our hearts to their claims on us. The consequence of recognizing honestly and openly that animals make claims on us will be a moral messiness, but we cannot avoid it. Even acknowledging, as I do, that human need has an ethical priority over that of animals does not eliminate this untidiness.

The attempt to develop a comprehensive theology of animals and a corresponding ethics of animal care requires that we cover a wide range of issues and discussions expeditiously. The risk in doing so is a brevity that overlooks significant complexities, distinctions, and voices in the debates. I hope to have avoided these offenses or at the very least to have mitigated their severity.

In closing, I offer a few miscellaneous notes for the reader. I use "covenant" to express the relationship that, I argue, God desires to have with all God's creatures. I understand this relationship in terms of qualities like companionship, care, communion, and interchange. My use of the term is grounded in a reading of the various covenant offerings recounted in the Old and New Testaments, but it is not intended as a technical development of any one of those accounts. In addition, because the new covenant established in Christ is eschatological, its fulfillment, as I understand it, is intertwined with the realization of God's kingdom.

On the term "animals": As I noted above, I use the term to mean more than mammals. Generally, it refers to any non-plant life, with a particular emphasis on those creatures that we can most easily imagine being recipients of God's gift of restoration. "Creatures," however, refers to all that is created—that is, all that is not God. This, of course, includes the human person. Often, I refer to all-except-human-creatures as "nonhuman creatures." I am aware that such phrasing is problematic because it seems to imply an absolute binary of "human" and "not-human," something this

[Margin handwritten notes:]

If animals live as God's representations of covenant, then will that make them have a place in heaven?

representing (God's relationship, representing covenant

are animals representative of the covenant?

book challenges. Unfortunately, alternative phrasings are awkward (e.g., other-than-human-creatures), and do not entirely escape an implicit binary. I use the phrase for clarity and stylistic simplicity.

I use "ecotheologians" as an inclusive term of convenience to refer to theologians working in areas such as the environment, ecology, evolution, animal lives, and nonhuman lives. I do not mean to suggest that any scholar so designated is primarily working in one of these areas or identifies as an ecotheologian.

All Scripture citations use the *New American Bible, Revised Edition* (2011); the text is available on the website of the United States Conference of Catholic Bishops.[3]

NOTES

Epigraph: Ratzinger, *Spirit of the Liturgy*, 27.
   1. Cahill, *Love Your Enemies.*
   2. See Francis, *Laudato Si'*, nos. 137–62.
   3. See http://www.usccb.org/bible/.

humanity → a macrocosm ; "microcosmos"

non-human world "saved" thru humanity

human - animal relationship representative of covenant

interchange → reciprocal relationship

MAIN ARGUMENT OF THIS BOOK
↳ ① Jesus' message → talks about the kingdom of God ; what did he do when he started it? starts world w/ everything good in it, fulfilled in age to come

↳ ② Role of church in regard to the kingdom of God to continue Jesus' work through Christian community, try to overcome injustice, suffering, working for the kingdom of God

↳ ③ If Goal is to work for kingdom of God, whos fullness will be realized in the world to come, what does this have to do w/ animals? If we do want to say animals are involved? or have anything to do with it, we must first say they are part of the kingdom. This book → animals are included in work of Jesus and in work of God. If this is true, Christian community must treat animals in a way

CHAPTER I

TRADITION

Learning to See Animals

Indeed, an objective of our prayer is to change the way we perceive
the world in order to change the way we relate to the world.

—Joint Statement of Pope Francis and Patriarch Bartholomew

Evolutionary biology has shown us how many and varied are
the organic connections that bind humans to the animal kingdom—common
physiological structures, ecosystem codependencies, and shared
primitive passions. Theology has become increasingly committed to its
own set of disciplinary beliefs regarding the interconnections between
humans and animals; we are all creatures fashioned with care by the same
Creator, joined together in praising God, and drawn to the same eschatological end—that is, to be summed up in Christ. Animals are part of our
human world because we are both part of God's world. Theology and
science tell us these things, but what is it that we *see* when we look at
animals?

I suggest in this chapter that many of our culture's instincts about creation and the animals within it are not dependable guides for the Christian. At this important juncture in environmental history, the Christian
community needs to disengage from these instincts and explore anew the
question of God's plan for creation. The evangelical imperative demands
not only our action but also the prior and more fundamental task of cali-
brating our moral imagination so that we render faithfully, for each generation, the world as illuminated by the Gospel. We only choose within a
world that we allow ourselves to see; seeing the world of animals well,
gaining an authentic vision of them, is itself a moral achievement.[1]

The endeavor to cultivate an authentic perception is hindered by a number of factors. In addition to the inertial drag of past assumptions about animals that continues to afflict contemporary culture, Catholic Christianity faces its own peculiar challenge: the legacy of its teaching about the immortality of the human soul and the lack thereof in animals. Historically, animals were assumed to be excluded from the life to come, not so much because of a divine decision but because their souls were inadequate to support a transition beyond death. Thus, when a comment by Pope Francis was misinterpreted by the media as offering support for the resurrection of pets, the ensuing debate in the Catholic blogosphere centered on the question of animal souls' mortality.[2] Similarly, when the Catholic bishops of England and Wales received a proposal for liturgical prayers for animals, they rejected it because "animals may well have souls, but they are not immortal souls."[3] These reactions reflect the singular rhetorical role that the distinction between animal and human souls has had in the Catholic world's understanding of animals. These beliefs feed each other—immortally ensouled and divinely valued humanity, ephemerally ensouled and thus instrumentally valued animals—leading to a vicious cycle of human privilege and animal disregard. The result has been a distorted understanding of how God values animals and, correspondingly, how *we* are to value them.

[handwritten marginal note, left: immortal soul; we can think abstractly; some part of mental operations that don't depend on physical things]

[handwritten marginal note, right: not actually in the bible but philosophers argue that there's some part of us that lives on even when our body dies. "By the light of human reason..."]

AQUINAS AND THE IMMORTAL SOUL

Thomas Aquinas (d. 1274) provided Christian thought with a comprehensive theological system that gained for him a rightly deserved standing as the preeminent theologian of the Catholic tradition. His ethical theory is grounded in profound and fundamental insights into the human condition and has fittingly retained its influence even today, over seven centuries after his death. His theological judgments have been cited with an authority second only to Scripture and magisterial teachings; his *Summa Theologica* even joined Scripture and the decrees of the popes upon the altar at the Council of Trent, so as to provide "counsel, reason, and inspiration" for the council fathers.[4]

The influence of Aquinas on Catholic thought about animals is likewise significant, though a bit more complex than sometimes perceived. Stripped of all nuance, Aquinas does suggest, in line with what is popularly assumed to be Catholic belief, that animals will not participate in the eschaton because their souls are not immortal. However, his view of animals depends on a constellation of philosophical and scientific beliefs to make it cohere with the rest of his theology—for example, the temporal (not eternal) goodness of creaturely diversity, the role of the heavenly bodies in governing animal activities, the cognitive capacities of animals, and Aristotelian metaphysics. Many of these theories now face questions and doubts, and a few of them outright dismissals, creating the opportunity and need for reconsidering his conclusions.

Aquinas's writings were pivotal in introducing Aristotle's hylomorphic theory of the body–soul composite into mainstream Catholic thought. In *De Anima*, Aristotle argued that the soul is an essential element of every creature's embodied existence—a vegetative soul for plants, a sensitive soul for animals, and a rational soul for humans. The soul and body together compose the one human person, with the soul as its formal principle. In contrast to the body/soul dualism of Plato's theory, the soul for Aristotle is incomplete apart from the body. Aquinas incorporates Aristotle's theory but allows more explicitly than Aristotle for the soul to subsist on its own, even though it is incomplete by itself.[5] His reasoning for the soul's subsistence follows arguments found in Platonic thought and in Augustine's *The Immortality of the Soul*. The soul is the "principle of intellectual operation,"[6] and because the intellect has the ability to know something according to its nature—that is, not as a concrete object but as the universal nature expressed in that particular object—the operation of the soul is not, entirely at least, dependent on our bodily operations. Simply put, we can know abstract universals, and such knowledge exists apart from sensory activities like sight, hearing, and smell. Thus, "the intellectual principle which we call the mind or the intellect has an operation per se apart from the body," and can, therefore, subsist apart from the body.[7]

The fact that the soul is subsistent and immaterial is not sufficient for proving its immortality. Aquinas adds another argument: The soul is incorruptible. His argument here is a bit difficult to follow for those not familiar with Aristotelian metaphysics. He argues that "no thing is corrupted [i.e., destroyed] with respect to that wherein its perfection consists." In other words, that which brings us to our perfection cannot be the same thing that destroys us. However, "the soul [which Aquinas has already defined as an 'intellectual substance'] is perfected by knowledge," all the more so as "it considers immaterial things." The soul is not "corrupted by being separated from the body," because "in leaving the body, [it] is perfected operationally"; that is, its perfection is not lost because it consists in knowledge of *immaterial* things that do not depend on the body per se.[8] It is not, of course, better that the soul be separated from the body. Aquinas's claim is only that the perfection of the soul's intellectual operation does not depend on the body and thus survives its demise.

Another version of the argument based on the nature of the soul appears in the *Summa Theologica*. Aquinas first argues that the soul cannot be corrupted "accidentally," that is, by something external to it. Although other substances are composites—unions of form and matter in which each depends on the other and cannot subsist apart from it—the soul, as Aquinas has shown, can subsist without the body and thus is not affected by the body's corruption. The soul, being subsistent, has "existence per se" and thus can only be corrupted per se. However, this

> is impossible, not only as regards the human soul, but also as regards anything subsistent that is a form alone. For it is clear that what belongs to a thing by virtue of itself is inseparable from it; but existence belongs to a form, which is an act, by virtue of itself. . . . It is impossible for a form to be separated from itself; and therefore it is impossible for a subsistent form to cease to exist.[9]

Aquinas's argument here depends on the idea that the subsistent form has "being" in virtue of what it is, not as an accident to it. It can thus be corrupted only through its own operation, but that is incoherent because it is the essence of the form to exist. Nonetheless, though the human soul may be immortal, the person is not. Abraham's soul, Aquinas tells us, "is not Abraham himself, but a part of him. . . . Hence life in Abraham's soul does not suffice to make Abraham a living being, or to make the God of Abraham the God of a living man."[10] The integral human person does not gain immortality except through a divine gift, namely, the resurrection of the body, because immortality is not an innate capacity of the composite human person.

The overall logical flow of Aquinas's argument for the soul's immortality depends on its starting point: The human person has a capacity for abstract, incorporeal reasoning. From there, his argument moves to the claim that the human soul is immaterial and subsistent form, and then to the argument that the soul is incorruptible based on the peculiarity of the soul as subsistent form. Correlatively, the argument against the immortality of animal souls, and thus animals themselves, is based on the contrary position: They lack the capacity to perform such intellectual activities, and thus their souls are not subsistent and cannot survive the decay of bodily life. As evidence of this intellectual deficiency ("they neither understand nor reason"), Aquinas observes "that all animals of the same species operate in the same way,"[11] and, like plants, they do not act by reason but rather are "moved, as it were by another, by a kind of natural impulse."[12] He adds that their inability to move themselves through reason is a "sign" that "they are naturally enslaved and accommodated to the uses of others," and thus we are justified in using them for our own good.[13]

The lack of understanding in animals and the mortality of their souls are not Aquinas's only reasons for denying the presence of animals in the world to come. He also argues that animals were created for the benefit of humans, and because they will no longer be needed in the age of humanity's glorified existence, they will not be part of God's new creation.[14] But lest one think that God is cruel to deny animals a resurrected life, Aquinas also argues that, unlike humans, animals do not have a desire for perpetuity as individual creatures because they do not have the intellectual abilities to comprehend such a future existence.[15] Instead, they desire only the continuation of their species. Furthermore, once the heavenly spheres cease their movements in the eschaton, animals will no longer even desire to continue living.[16]

Going through Aquinas's writings, one can be left with the impression that the principal reason for animals' existence is to serve humanity's needs and interests. Although this rationale regularly appears in his discussions of animals, it is not Aquinas's only account of why God created them. Offering a non-anthropocentric basis for valuing animals, Aquinas argues that they exist because God's goodness can be better communicated by a multitude of diverse creatures.[17] On the basis of this argument, it would seem that animals should also be included in the life to come, as their absence would impoverish the goodness and beauty to be found there. Aquinas, however, posits that animals will not be needed for this purpose in the eschaton.[18] In *De potentia* (from which was taken some of the material for the posthumous "Supplement" to the *Summa Theologica*), Aquinas explains that animals and plants "contain nothing" that is not already found "in the principal parts of the world (namely, the heavenly bodies and the elements [air, fire, earth, and water])." These living creatures are not essential for the perfection of the universe but rather are expressions of what *is* essential (i.e., the elements and the heavenly spheres whose movements govern nonhuman creaturely lives).[19] Aquinas also distinguishes between the perfection characteristic of the present order, which is one of change and mobility, and that to be attained in the final state, which is characterized by unmoving, unchanging goodness. There is movement in the present age because the universe is now progressing toward its divinely ordained state of perfection, and the lives of animals, as caused by the movements of the heavenly spheres, will continue to be part of the universe's perfection until the celestial bodies cease their movement in the eschaton. Because there will be no more "begetting" of new lives in the eschaton, "the movement of the heaven and the variations of the elements," which assist in bringing about human and animal reproduction, will no longer be needed.[20] In the perfection of that age, the elements and the stationary heavenly spheres will suffice for the corporeality of the new creation.

We can pause a moment to reflect on Aquinas's claims here, as more is at stake than his belief that Jupiter and the moon will make the eschatological cut, while elephants and dolphins will not. Aquinas portrays the eschatological life of the saints as a beatific vision in which the divine essence is known and loved.[21] Though it will be a spiritual knowing (i.e., not through our bodily senses), we will be able to see God indirectly with our bodily eyes because the glory of God will appear "in the glorified bodies [of the saints] and most of all in the body of Christ."[22] The other senses will also be available for our use, though Aquinas is understandably unsure as to their eschatological function. The saints will engage in heavenly praise, so our hearing will still have a purpose.[23] The sensation of touch will be triggered by "spiritual alteration,"[24] as will our sense of smell.[25] Taste will be unnecessary because we will no longer partake of food or drink; but "perhaps," nonetheless, taste will be "cognizant of flavors."[26] The beatific state visualized by Aquinas is one without material distractions; the clutter of our present world will be removed, and God, its goal and fulfillment, will be placed at the center of human experience and agency. The encounter with God is primarily a spiritual one, with our bodily senses providing secondary testimony to the joys therein.

Though Aquinas's eschatological vision affirms the goodness of bodily existence, human corporeality seems little more than an experiential veneer. The body is necessary for earthly happiness but not for the perfect happiness of the eschaton, as is evidenced by the fact that, for Aquinas, the "souls of the saints" will have already attained their eschatological joy even before the resurrection of their bodies.[27] The body's most significant contribution in the eschaton is that of adding a secondary "charm" to our new life with God; otherwise, its task is simply to avoid being a "hindrance" to the intellect's operation.[28]

Aquinas is right to make our relationship with God central to the eschaton, but Karl Rahner is also right to underscore the "eternal significance" of Christ's humanity for that relationship. In Aquinas's intellectualized life of the saints, the human body does not have a central role,[29] and neither, it would seem, does the corporeality of the God-Man. Its service is essential for earthly redemption but supplemental in the life to come.[30] In contrast, Rahner argues that Jesus Christ, precisely in his "created human nature," is eternally the Mediator of the God–creature relationship, "the indispensable and permanent gateway through which everything created must pass."[31] Underscoring the enduring, pivotal role of Christ's corporeality for our eschatological relationship with God is helpful for us in developing a theology of animals because it reminds us that God has, in Christ, decided to relate to the creaturely realm for all eternity as an embodied being. The corporeality of God's bond with creation encourages us to imagine that the modes of divine–creature relating in the eschaton are not limited to that of a spiritual, intellectual knowing. With this possibility in mind, I will argue in chapter 4 that animals can, through the work of the Spirit, become Christ-like participants in the triune life.

A chastening agnosticism about the next life must restrain our theological imaginings. Though it is appropriate to allow images and theory to feed our imagination about the life to come, we appeal to them not with the goal of adequately depicting that future existence but as a way of providing substance for humanity's hope and of heartening it during its earthly pilgrimage. It is an indication that we have transgressed an epistemic boundary, however, when eschatological speculation about one issue is allowed to preemptively decide a different one. The question of whether or how God's plan for nonhuman creatures includes their final redemption merits its own examination based on scriptural testimony and theological fundamentals. Its resolution cannot come as a secondary corollary of metaphysical speculation—that is, a particular construal of the beatific vision deemed incompatible with animal existence.

There are alternate ways to imagine the age to come that do not predetermine the question of animal redemption. In contrast to Aquinas's portrayal, and in line with Rahner's appeal to Christ's corporeality, many contemporary scholars interpret humanity's glorified existence in greater continuity with present experience.[32] Their approach finds support in scriptural images that draw on earthly experience (e.g., a banquet of food and drink). The images are, to be sure, not meant literally; but they encourage us to conceive the eschaton in terms of a "transformed continuity," one in which the embodied lives and creaturely relationships of the old aeon are glorified and extended into the new.[33] My development of an animal eschatology in the subsequent chapters of this book depends on this transformed continuity approach. In theorizing about animal life in that future age, I intend only to try to make some sense of our hope for it, not to construct with any precision the nature of their eschatological existence.

CATHOLIC ATTITUDES IN THE MODERN PERIOD

We can wonder what wisdom Aquinas might have bequeathed to the Church had he allowed the diverse goodness displayed in the creatures of this age to inform his ethics of animal care.[34] God desired that animals exist in part because their particular forms of goodness help the world more perfectly reflect the goodness of its Creator, and thus they have a value that is not indexed to human need. Such a good that is innate to animals could provide the basis for their distinct moral claim on the human agent. Aquinas does not pursue this possibility, and his debarring of animals from the eschaton (along with the stress he places on animal servitude to human needs) does little to recommend that animals be seen as legitimate objects of moral concern. Indeed, Aquinas tells us that God will not hold us accountable for our treatment of animals: "It matters not how man behaves to animals," as long as we are moved by reason, "because God has subjected all things to man's power." Cruelty to animals is forbidden, not because of any moral claim that animals make on us but rather "in order to inculcate pity" in us so that we become "more disposed to take pity" on our human neighbor.[35]

This disregard for animals is also reinforced by Aquinas's response to the question of whether "irrational creatures" should "be loved out of charity." Because animals do not share rationality with us or "the fellowship of everlasting happiness," we *cannot* love them out of charity.[36] This is a significant conclusion for Thomistic ethics, for two reasons. First, it means that, insofar as charity is the end and form of the other virtues (and thus the moral life itself), there can be no genuinely *animal* ethics, in which animals are the direct objects of Christian love, within the domain of Thomistic morality.[37] Their goodness by itself establishes no claim on us and does not provide us with virtuous principles to guide our moral passions toward them.[38] Second, it means that for Aquinas, there is a connection between the eschatological status of creatures and the determination of whether we have any moral duties to them. We owe charity only to those creatures who will share with us in "the fellowship of happiness," or at least potentially so—for example, angels and humans but not demons or dogs.[39]

With these views, Aquinas endows the tradition with what I call the "Thomistic framework" for animal ethics. It comprises three commitments:

Thematic Framework   *we can't love them in way we love other humans and God*

A friend

(1) We have no duties toward animals (i.e., they are not objects of charity); (2) animals have been created to serve human needs and will no longer be *traditional catholic thought* needed in the life to come; and (3) it is immoral to treat animals cruelly, not because it does them an injustice but because doing so violates our character, undermining our rational nature and coarsening our empathy for *human* suffering. Theologians who looked to Aquinas as an unquestionably trustworthy guide woodenly imposed this framework upon modern Catholic thought, compromising its resolve to foster animal care and fight its abuse. Beginning in the late eighteenth century, this weakness was increasingly exposed in heated debates over animal experimentation.

Initial efforts on behalf of animals centered on sports (bullfights, bull-baiting, cockfighting, hunting, horse racing, etc.), but the most spirited protests increasingly turned to vivisection, developing into an international crusade against the practice by the nineteenth century.[40] Experiments on live animals had been almost unknown during the Middle Ages. Opposition to them began to grow toward the end of the seventeenth century, when the practice became more common, especially when some particularly horrific cases raised public outcry.[41] Much of the movement's early Christian leadership came from the Puritan, Quaker, and evangelical (e.g., Methodist) traditions. The Puritans had long been known for their abhorrence of animal sports. "What Christian heart," wrote Philip Stubbes in 1583, "can take pleasure to see one poor beast to rent, tear, and kill another, and all for his foolish pleasure?"[42] Among the Quakers, George Fox (d. 1691) was noteworthy for his animal advocacy.[43] The founder of the Methodists, John Wesley (d. 1791), argued that animals will share in the earth's renewal, a message that he hoped would "enlarge our hearts" toward them.[44] There were significant Anglican voices as well, and, in the nineteenth century, a few Catholic ones, as we will see below. The eighteenth-century Anglican priest Humphrey Primatt (d. 1776), an early leader in the animal welfare movement, wrote an influential book, *The Duty of Mercy and the Sin of Cruelty to Brute Animals,* in which he made the impassioned plea, "Pain is pain, whether it be inflicted on man or on beast; and the creature that suffers it, whether man or beast . . . suffers *evil*" (emphasis in the original).[45] The advocacy for animals was not, however, always welcomed by Christians in the pew. In the postscript to the published edition of his 1772 homily, "An Apology for Brute Creation," the Reverend James Granger observes that his homily "gave almost universal disgust to two considerable congregations. The mention of dogs and horses . . . was considered proof of the Author's growing insanity."[46]

"Pain is pain."

Catholics sometimes shared in the aversion of Granger's congregants. When the Royal Chapter of the Society for the Prevention of Cruelty to Animals (SPCA) asked permission in 1863 to set up a chapter in Rome, Pope Pius IX (d. 1878) denied the request, stating that humanity had no duties toward animals. His rejection was motivated in part, it seems, by a concern that the mere "presence of such an organization would foster the theologically erroneous belief" that there existed such a duty.[47] Frances Power Cobbe, one of the most powerful voices against vivisection in the nineteenth century, was exasperated upon hearing the pope's response. In the October 1895 issue of *Contemporary Review*, she condemned the pope's statement for leaving "the minds of millions in Catholic countries closed against the rising tide of pity and sympathy which has swelled the hearts of Protestants, Theists and Agnostics all over the civilized world."[48]

Early animal rights activists made known their frustrations about Catholic views, but unfortunately they did little to change attitudes in the neo-scholastic tradition of the modern period. Catholic moral thought between the seventeenth and early twentieth centuries was typically presented in what came to be known as "manuals," textbooks of moral theology used by priests and as instructional resources for the laity. They were characterized by a clear structure that moved from fundamental principles (e.g., the end of the human person, law, and conscience) to a carefully delineated catalogue of sins. Regarding animals, they almost uniformly reflected what I am calling the Thomistic framework. For example, the *Handbook of Moral Theology*—written by the Dominican moral theologian Dominic Prümmer and translated into multiple languages, including five English editions—states simply, "Since animals have no rights they cannot suffer injury in the strict sense of the word," though "cruelty to animals (without grave cause) is sinful insofar as it is contrary to right reason."[49] The 1935 *Moral and Pastoral Theology* (a four-volume series used by many US Catholic seminaries up through the early 1950s), by a Jesuit, Henry Davis, says the same thing, with a bit more force: "Animals have no rights," and "we have no duties of justice or charity toward them." Their suffering in experimental vivisections is permitted because of the "increase in knowledge" they afford. We should not, however, be "wantonly cruel" to them, since that might "increase one's tendency to cruelty."[50] Another standard text, this one by the Capuchin moral theologian Heribert Jone, maintains that animals, "being ordained" for serving humanity, "may be used for any ethical purpose," including vivisection. This 1945 manual—which went through seventeen German editions and was translated into English, French, Italian, Polish, Dutch, Portuguese, and Spanish—goes on to say that it is sinful to cause animals "unnecessary pain," though not because the rights of animals prohibit it, but, as with Prümmer, because such acts oppose "reason which forbids the needless causing of pain and death."[51]

A seminary text on moral philosophy by the English Jesuit philosopher Joseph Rickaby is particularly severe, even for its time. First published in 1888, it went through at least four editions. The fourth edition (1918) repeats the standard view of the time: "Brute beasts, not having understanding and therefore not being persons, cannot have any rights."[52] We have no more "duties of charity" to them as we have "to stocks and stones."[53] The text seems to go out of its way to relieve the conscience of good Catholics by expanding as much as possible the domain of licit actions that cause animal suffering:

> But there is no shadow of evil resting on the practice of causing pain to brutes *in sport*, where the pain is not the sport itself, but an incidental concomitant of it. Much more in all that conduces to the sustenance of man may we give pain to brutes, as also in the pursuit of science. Nor are we bound to any anxious care to make this pain as little as may be. Brutes are as *things* in our regard: so far as they are useful to us, they exist for us, not for themselves; and we do right in using them unsparingly for our need and convenience, though not for our wantonness. If then any special case of pain to a brute creature be a fact of considerable value for observation in biological science or the medical art, no reasoned considerations of morality can stand in the way of man making the experiment, yet so that even in the quest of science he be mindful of mercy (emphasis in the original).[54]

In his 1897 book *Moral Principles and Medical Practice*, Charles Coppens, a Belgian Jesuit then teaching at Creighton Medical College in Omaha, was similarly expansive in accommodating human use of animals. The human person is "the master of the visible universe" and "can use all inferior things to his benefit."[55] "When a brute animal has served man's purpose, it has reached its destiny."[56] Medical teachers and students can perform vivisection not only "for the sake of science" but also for "mental improvement" and "intelligent observation" (i.e., for training and pedagogical purposes).[57]

Given arguments like those of Davis, Rickaby, and Coppens, it is no wonder that Cobbe "had many spirited bouts with the Jesuits" and believed that they "went out of their way . . . to point out that man had no *duty* to spare pain to animals" (emphasis in the original).[58] She considered views like Rickaby's a "dogmatic reassertion of definitions drawn in the

Dark Ages."[59] She was not alone in criticizing Jesuits; one contemporary sardonically described the view "commonly ascribed to Jesuits" as one in which "cruelty per se to animals is allowable and sinless."[60]

The authority of the tripartite Thomistic framework—there are no duties to animals, animals are created to serve humanity, and cruelty to animals is sinful not because it violates animals but because it violates the agent's character—was played out in a debate over vivisection that took place in 1894 in the pages of *The Tablet*, a Catholic weekly based in London. The debate began with a seemingly innocuous letter from Lady Margaret Domville (a Catholic convert). Domville presents her translation of two paragraphs on animal care taken from a Catholic catechism that had been recently approved by German bishops. The excerpt appeals to the fifth commandment (in the Catholic ordering, "You shall not kill"), and it notes that God cares for all creatures. The bishops urge Catholics to be "merciful" to animals, Domville writes. Like us, animals "feel pain," and thus when they are killed, it should be "as speedily as possible" with "no unnecessary pain caused." Examples of sins against the fifth commandment include "tortured calves and swine, the ill-used horses, [and] the fish cooked alive." Anyone guilty of such atrocities "does not deserve to be called a man."[61] In reaction to this letter, a heated discussion unfolded between opponents and advocates of vivisection. Among those who sent letters to the editor were two cousins, Father John Vaughan (eventually Bishop Vaughan) and Charles Weld-Blundell. Both were Catholics from prominent recusant families but were fervently committed to opposing sides of the debate. Vaughan, defending vivisection, referred to Weld-Blundell as "my not very amiable and not very consequent cousin."[62] Weld-Blundell responded in kind, describing Vaughan's arguments as "alternately fluttering like an impaled butterfly upon the horns of my dilemmas . . . in the hope of effecting a dignified escape under a sheltering mist of words."[63] In the May 12 issue, *The Tablet*'s editors said that they had "received more letters than [they] could ever hope to publish," and in the following week's issue, they closed the debate.[64]

What is particularly interesting for us is that two different frameworks were used to defend the respective positions. Vaughan—along with contributors writing under the signatures "Mens sibi conscia recti," "A Bubble Picker," and "F.O.S."—appealed to the Thomistic framework, coupled with a priority of logical reasoning over sentiment and to what they considered to be unchanging and authoritative teachings—the Church's and their own. Weld-Blundell—along with Lady Domville, Dr. Edward Berdoe (an English physician and, like Domville, a convert to

Catholicism), and Ernest Bell—appealed to biblical themes, Christian ideals and sentiment, and the need to develop Catholic teaching in line with the emerging moral consensus about animals.

In the opening salvo defending the use of animals, the contributor writing as Mens sibi conscia recti cites three points from John Vaughan's writings: (1) Cruelty is always wrong, (2) animals have no rights, and (3) animals are made for the rational use and benefit of man.[65] The contributor writing as A Bubble Pricker first condescendingly notes that it "is hard perhaps for untrained theologians, especially of the impressionable and emotional school, to grasp the full import of technical terms," and then argues that if such persons were able to understand the terms, they would realize that "beasts neither have, nor can have 'rights' in any proper or true sense." "The driveling nonsense about beasts," he concludes, "is unworthy of any intelligent person."[66] In a subsequent letter, he suggests the idea that a dog has rights is as "embarrassing" as believing a chimney pot has rights. We are limited in what we do to animals because we "must act reasonably. To act cruelly is to violate [our] own nature."[67]

Father John Vaughan weighs in, asserting his belief that he has "the entire school of Catholic Theology at [his] back." What makes an act cruel is its intent and purpose, not whether it causes pain. He suggests that we use "a little simple logic": Either we "must be able to inflict pain upon beasts for [our] convenience and advantage" or not. If it were always wrong to inflict pain upon beasts, we could not engage in commonly accepted activities like fox hunting. He dismisses the arguments of women leaders in the anti-vivisectionist movement: "Each of these amateur theologians wears the Tiara in turn and (without any tincture of a theological training), proceeds to give us an ex cathedra lecture."[68] In contrast to "the mere personal opinions of Weld Blundell," Vaughan's thinking is led by "those bright calm passionless stars shining in the theological firmament of the Church, guiding the way to truth and justice."[69]

In the last letter published by *The Tablet* in this cycle of the debate, Vaughan quotes a homily from Cardinal Newman (out of context, I believe), in which Newman states,[70] "*We have no duties toward brute creation.* . . . We may use them, we may destroy them at our pleasure, not our wanton pleasure, but still for our own ends . . . provided that we can give a rational account for what we do" (emphasis added by Vaughn).[71] The contributor writing as F.O.S. is more blunt. The "sole *raison d'être*" of animals is to serve humanity, and "that is the total extent of their being." Their lives "are entirely at man's unfettered disposal." There is "no duty in man" or correlative "right in brute animals, limiting man's free actions

[margin handwritten note: psychology: ppl are good at rationalizing | but do not always behave rationally ↑]

toward them." "The end of the existence of brute animals is entirely sub-ordinate to the end of man's existence." Even "wanton disemboweling of beasts alive and without anaesthetics is *in se* an indifferent action."[72]

On the other side of the debate, Margaret Domville appeals to Scrip-ture (Prv 12:10) and God's concern for animals. Edward Berdoe welcomes Domville's letter, he tells us, because of the "impression in the minds of many" that animals are not treated well in Catholic countries and because of the false "idea that Christians owe no duties to animals." He expresses the desire that "our clergy would, either in sermons or by other appropri-ate means, insist on kindness to animals . . . as a religious duty."[73] In another letter, he observes that history has shown that we have not always realized "what the Gospel of Christ demands of us" (he lists the examples of slav-ery, treatment of the insane, and inhuman legal punishments).[74] He believes "that mercy to animals and the humaner notions of our relations to the beautiful dumb creatures of God" are included "in the command to 'preach the Gospel to every creature.'" Moreover, vivisection is contrary to "the sacred art of healing" that was practiced "by our blessed Lord."[75] In Ernest Bell's letter, he maintains that the "principle that animals have rights is practically admitted by all civilized nations."[76]

Weld-Blundell also contributed a couple of letters. In one, he notes his experiences of the kindness given to animals by Muslims and Hindus, and regrets that Catholics do not have a "religious sanction" that we "respect God's creatures" as found in those other religious traditions. Experiment-ing on dogs is "an act of desecration of one of God's noblest creatures."[77] He describes God as "the gentle master" who cares for each fallen sparrow (referencing Lk 12:6). In a later letter, Weld-Blundell (after offering to allow his young children to operate on his cousin Father Vaughan) pre-dicts that he is part of a moral movement "which sooner or later will most surely be formulated in the words I have used or others closely similar." He goes on to suggest how unfortunate it is "that the Church should seem to lag behind a spontaneous moral movement which is at any rate more in accordance with the Gospel of Christ than its opposite."[78]

I am not so much interested in the success of these arguments as in their rhetorical strategies. The themes found in the appeals made by ani-mal care advocates suggest an argumentative framework in which com-passionate care, Gospel ideals, and the need to develop new moral insights are prioritized in a way that is not permitted in the Thomistic-cum-Church-authority approach used by Vaughan and his allies. That is, they did not find it possible for the goods and values advocated by them—for example, that creatures are objects of moral concern and divine care—to

history is evolving constantly ...

be defended and advanced in the Thomistic framework, at least as rigidly interpreted by Vaughan and his companions.

Vaughan was correct in assuming that there is no necessary, logical connection between the Thomistic tradition and the denigration and abuse of animals. Indeed, as we will see below, <u>belief in the mortality of animal souls can reasonably generate the opposite response: Because animals have no share in the resurrection, we must treat them with kindness and charity, given that this life is their only chance for happiness.</u> However, aspects of the Church's teachings, especially the idea of an immortal soul, were perceived as contributing to the rationalization of animal abuse; and in espousing these beliefs, Catholicism itself became an object of criticism. The late nineteenth-century animal rights activist Henry Salt attributed some of society's indifference toward animal welfare to "the so-called 'religious' notion, which awards immortality to man, but to man alone, thereby furnishing (especially in Catholic countries) a quibbling justification for acts of cruelty to animals, on the plea that they 'have no souls.'"[79] The historian William Edward Hartpole Lecky, also writing in the late nineteenth century, found a contradiction between Catholic legends that had "glorified" animals as "companions of the saints" and Catholicism's failure to do much of anything "to inculcate humanity to animals."[80] The countries "in which Catholicism has most deeply implanted its roots" are "those in which inhumanity to animals is most wanton and unrebuked."[81] The activist Anna Kingsford (again, writing in the late nineteenth century) criticized the Catholic leadership for its failure to address animal suffering: "Everywhere in Catholic Christendom the poor, patient, dumb creatures endure every species of torment without a single word being uttered on their behalf by the teachers of religion."[82] Keith Thomas, a present-day scholar of early modern history, notes how prevalent these criticisms of Catholicism had become. It was an "entrenched conviction" by Victorian times "that the unhappiest animals were those of the Latin countries of southern Europe, because it was there that the old Catholic doctrine that animals had no souls was still maintained."[83] The claim might be excessive but not entirely wrong. Though there were significant Catholic voices raised against cruel treatment of animals, they were not prominent within the growing chorus advocating reform; nor were they commonly understood as espousing authentic Catholic teaching.[84] Moreover, at least until the time of Pope Leo XIII (d. 1903), Catholic leaders gave little support for endeavors like that of the SPCA. Thus, by the end of the nineteenth century, Catholicism was viewed as a recalcitrant force vis-à-vis animal care.

THEORY → AQUINAS
immortal soul → humans have some kind of intellectual operation that doesn't depend on physical matter / reality in front of us
TRADITION   23
non-immortal soul → everything depends on material reality
(animals)

The perception, right or wrong, that Catholics were on one side of the issue and Protestants and anti-Catholics were on the other likely contributed to Catholic resistance. If the Protestants were in favor of it, surely it was the fruit of sinful minds. Thus, in Pius IX's rejection of the SPCA, he noted that "though such societies might exist in Protestant countries, they could not be allowed to be established in Rome."[85] In an 1898 letter to the editor of *The Spectator*, J. W. Stillman quotes at length a Vatican article criticizing Protestants for supporting animal rights. The "most furious advocates of the wellbeing of the beasts," the article states, "are the Protestants and Freemasons," whose "sentimentalism for the beasts" requires a public rebuke by the Church.[86] The 1948 *Catholic Encyclopedia* similarly cautioned that some (i.e., non-Catholic) endeavors to protect animals "base their activities . . . on false principles (attributing rights to animals . . . or alleging a duty of charity, which in the Christian sense of that phrase cannot obtain)."[87] The Catholic ethicist James Gaffney sums up the state of Catholic attitudes toward animals at the time as "typically defensive" and "not in the vanguard."[88]

⎰ Catholics attacked Protestants for supporting animal rights

ANIMAL-FRIENDLY WITNESSES AMONG CATHOLICS IN THE POST-AQUINAS TRADITION

Even if the history of the animal rights movement offers too many examples of the failure by Catholic leadership and laity to offer a prophetic voice against animal abuse, the medieval and modern periods have produced, nonetheless, significant witnesses for the compatibility of compassionate devotion to animals with Catholic thought and practice.[89] The admiration and deep affection among Catholics for Francis of Assisi and his treatment of animals indicates how, in some quarters at least, the tenderness he showed toward animals has been viewed as an evangelical ideal.[90] Similarly, the *Acta Sanctorum* is filled with delightful stories of saints' devotion and even ministry to animals.[91] For example, Anthony of Padua (d. 1231) told fish that they owed the "Creator a vast debt of gratitude," because, among other things, God left them "unmolested" by the waters of the flood and were given the privilege of "furnishing the tribute money for the Word Incarnate" (i.e., the Roman tax).[92] Robert Bellarmine (d. 1621) was reported to have allowed "vermin" to take up residence in his beard and bite him. "We shall have heaven to reward us for our suffering," he explained, "but these poor creatures have nothing but the enjoyment of this present life."[93] These accounts are likely partly or entirely apocryphal, but the fact that so many stories like these were successfully circulated and preserved, along with their sheer number, indicates the admiration with which the Catholic populace received them. It is not so much the witness of these saints that makes them interesting for our discussion but rather the fact that stories of their tender care for animals were recorded, shared, and acclaimed by the collective piety of Catholics as worthy examples of devotion.

Among Church leaders who can be commended for their concern for animals is Pope Pius V (d. 1572). In 1567, he issued the papal bull *De Salute Gregis Dominici* that in no uncertain terms condemned bullfighting and those who participated in it.[94] Some see the document as an example of early Christian support for animal protection. A more extended advocacy for animals by the Church hierarchy, however, can be found in the words and writings of the nineteenth-century cardinals John Henry Newman and Henry Edward Manning. In a homily, Newman compares the suffering of Christ on the cross with "the wanton deed of barbarous and angry owners who ill-treat their cattle, or beasts of burden" and "the cold-blooded and calculating act of men of science, who make experiments on brute animals, perhaps merely from a sort of curiosity." Tormenting God's creatures in such ways, he says, is "satanic."[95] The homily is not so much an exhortation to treat animals charitably; rather, it assumes that such kindness is morally obligatory. Newman also composed a novena to Philip Neri (who is the one other saint, along with Francis of Assisi, commended by the *Catechism of the Catholic Church* as a model for animal care). In it, Newman seeks the grace of charity toward all God's creatures: "Philip, my glorious Advocate, teach me to look at all I see around me after thy pattern as creatures of God. Let me never forget that the same God who made me, made the whole world, and all men and animals that are in it. Gain me the grace to love all God's works for God's sake."[96]

Though Newman also supported legislative protection for animals,[97] the Catholic voice most associated with the cause is that of Cardinal Manning, who regularly gave speeches in support of stricter rules for experiments on animals. He bristled at Pius IX's rejection of the SPCA: "It was true that man owed no duty *directly* to the brutes, but he owed it to God, whose creatures they are, to treat them mercifully" (emphasis in the original).[98] In March 1887, Manning stated that vivisection was not "the way that the All-wise and All-good Maker of us all has ordained for the discovery of the healing arts."[99] Apparently, Manning also spoke privately with Pius IX's successor, Pope Leo XIII, after his election as pope in 1878, and raised concerns with him about experiments on animals.[100] Though papal teaching did not undergo any radical change, subsequent popes did embrace the cause of animal protection. Leo's successor, Pope Pius X (d. 1914), sent his blessing on "all who protect from abuse and cruelty the dumb servants given to us by God";[101] and Pope Benedict XV (d. 1922) personally donated 1,000 lire to Rome's Society for the Protection of Animals.[102]

I noted above examples of the moral manuals that dominated Catholic seminary education up through the first half of the twentieth century. Their teaching on animals was typically brief and structured around some version of the Thomistic framework. There were, however, exceptions. About the same time as the publication of Henry Davis's *Moral and Pastoral Theology* (1934), the Catholic publishing house Herder Book Company published *Foundations of Morality: God; Man; Lower Creatures* (1936), a translation of *Die allgemeinen Grundlagen des sittlichen Handelns* by the German moral theologian and diocesan priest Ludwig Ruland. The translator's foreword tells us that "the work is intended as a help for priests to find their way from the knowledge of theoretic principles to the concrete realities of life."[103] (Hereafter, quotations and citations from this book are cited in the text by page number.) The book's last section, on animals (the "lower creatures"), is more extensive than is typical for these manuals. The author feels the need to address the issue of animal care because of the increasing attention given to the matter and because critics were accusing "the Church of having neglected an important aspect of moral progress" (360).

The basic starting points of Ruland's approach are consistent with official views at the time: There is an essential difference between human persons and animals (361); animal experiments "appear still to be necessary for the progress of medicine" (365); and animals "have no immortal soul, no rational powers, and no moral conceptions" (372). Although he relays the traditional concern that cruelty toward animals "has a pernicious effect on the character of men," he also states, with an emphasis uncharacteristic of the time, that such an act "is itself wrong" (373). In contrast to other manualists, he states that we *do* have duties toward animals, ones that cannot be summed up "by a short Latin definition and a few legal principles" (373).

However, what is astonishing in Ruland's reflection, again given its time period, is that it eschews a static understanding of Christian morality and instead looks with hope for progress in humanity's relationship with animals. Although Ruland does not, of course, explicitly situate his ethics in the context of the eschaton or Jesus's proclamation of the kingdom (the

[handwritten margin note: Seems as though peer pressure caused the Church to take a stance]

[handwritten margin note: ANIMAL EXPERIMENTS]

"kingdom of God" was not a significant theological theme at the time), he does appeal to evangelical ideals as norms for this ethical progress. Like other domains of Christian practice, he writes, "the Christian ideals" of animal care "have not yet been realized" (369). He believes that "the beautiful harmony" displayed "between the saints and the animals" is a desirable end for the Christian world. The reason that this end has not yet been attained is not because it is unrealistic but because other pressures have "consumed much time and energy of the Church" (371).

Like many contemporary ecotheologians, Ruland appeals to chapter 8 of Paul's letter to the Romans, in which all creation is described as "groaning" for its liberation (Rom 8:22). Paul's "glorious and mystical words" show us "exactly the Christian's attitude toward the creatures about him" (370). The passage explains that the brokenness and suffering of creaturely life is due to the fact that humanity and animals share in the curse of original sin. He makes the additional claim, following Paul's argument but atypical of the time, that our present predicament is not the final state for either human _or_ animal: "As the curse of sin affects the whole creation, so all creatures are to experience the blessing of redemption" (369). He goes on to connect animals' eschatological status and our moral responses to them. Because "all creation has been redeemed in Christ," the Christian "cannot be merciless toward the lower creatures." Rejecting "arbitrariness and tyranny," our treatment of animals must instead reflect the "likeness of God's rule," dealing with the "beings of nature in love and kindness" (370). Humanity has been given a lofty and serious vocation—to act as "mediator between God and the other material creatures" (373). The saints, he notes with admiration, "did not consider animals too low to preach to them the word of God" (371). "The Christian must listen to the groaning of the creatures; and where he hears it, transmit the blessing of redemption" (371). Progress in the love of God will enable the person to "see in the eye of the suffering animal the plea for mercy and love in the name of God" (373).

Ruland also offers practical norms for animal care, which regrettably are still unrealized eighty years later. Stables for cattle and the vehicles that transport them should have sufficient ventilation. Slaughtering animals for food must not happen without "first painlessly benumbing them." With prescience, he warns that absent "very strict supervision of the work in public slaughter-houses," the abuse of animals will inevitably occur. With regard to animal experiments, he hopes that progress will result in "a gradual restriction" in their frequency. They should be performed only

[handwritten marginalia: "does it?", "symbolical covenant", "loving animals = progress in love of God", "ANIMAL EXPERIM."]

when necessary; and once we have learned their lesson, there is no need to repeat the experiments or use them to educate students (375–76).

Finally, one other "voice" for animal care should be mentioned in this context: the Catholic sacramental tradition that sees creation as an expression of the divine. As Aquinas's contemporary Bonaventure exclaimed, "Whoever, therefore, is not enlightened by such splendor of created things is blind; whoever is not awakened by such outcries is deaf."[104] The sacramental tradition, as associated with creation generally and the creatures within it, endured neglect but was never completely marginalized in Catholic thought. Even if the passion commended by Bonaventure might have been stifled in the theological treatises of the modern period, it continued to inspire Catholic literature and poetry, as is strikingly evident in the works of the nineteenth-century Jesuit poet Gerard Manley Hopkins and famously expressed in his pronouncement that "the world is charged with the grandeur of God."[105] Appeals to this sacralized worldview regularly appear in contemporary Catholic statements in defense of the value and goodness of creation.

CONTEMPORARY DEVELOPMENTS IN THE TRADITION

Though these voices (Catholic devotion to animal-friendly saints, Church leaders supporting laws to protect animals, a relatively prophetic seminary manual, and the sacramental tradition) were not always heard, they witness, nonetheless, to an important strand in Catholicism's ethical instincts about animals. My belief is that the dominant Catholic approach to animals had been markedly influenced by a static interpretation of Thomas's teachings, in particular his arguments for the immortality of the human soul and the nonhuman creature's lack thereof. Before Vatican II, most Catholic thinkers, including the animal-friendly Ruland, appealed to the person's immortal soul as a point of reference for human uniqueness. It seems plausible that the perceived lack of an immortal soul in animals (and the commitments intertwined with it) contributed to the failure of the Catholic imagination to see their innate goodness and their significance within the divine economy. If God did not care enough for animals to include them in the eschaton, then it is hard to imagine how they could be theologically or ethically important in the here and now. God's only goal for the earthly realm is to ensure humanity's attainment of its own eschatological life. All other life forms were created as provisions for our temporal—and temporary—needs. It is not surprising, then, that the earliest opponents of animal cruelty in the vivisection debates were Christians who *also* believed that animals had an eschatological destiny (e.g., Methodists who followed John Wesley's belief in animal redemption).[106]

Its negative influence on animal eschatology is only part of the challenge confronting the traditional Catholic view of the soul. As a consequence of repeated criticisms, there has been a growing consensus in theological circles against the terminology of the soul's "immortality." Though official Catholic teaching has resisted this trend and continues to attribute an immortal soul to each human person, contemporary formulations of the teaching evidence notable shifts that have implications for a theology of animals.

Principally, theologians have argued that the idea of an immortal soul finds no justification in biblical texts and that its status in early Christian teaching is controverted at best. Scriptural support for a type of body/soul dualism can be found in passages like Matthew 10:28, "And do not be afraid of those who kill the body but cannot kill the soul"; 1 Corinthians 15:50, "Flesh and blood cannot inherit the kingdom of God"; and 2 Corinthians 5:1, "For we know that if our earthly dwelling, a tent, should be destroyed, we have a building from God, a dwelling not made with hands, eternal in heaven." However, many scholars argue that these passages, when interpreted in the broader context of New Testament teaching (including Paul's anthropology), cannot be used as support for a dualism whereby some aspect of the person (i.e., the soul) naturally survives bodily death. "Body and soul are united in an organic union," the New Testament scholar Murray Harris argues, "not associated in an external conjunction."[107] Immortality is not an innate characteristic of any aspect of the human person, soul, or body; God "alone is immortal" (1 Tm 6:16). Immortality is a biblical theme, but it is an attribute associated with the *resurrected* person, given as a gift through the Spirit; as a new creation, our bodies will no longer be vulnerable to decay. N. T. Wright argues that the contrast set up by Paul between a physical body and a spiritual body (e.g., in 1 Cor 15:44) "is between the present body, corruptible, decaying, and doomed to die, and the future body, incorruptible, undecaying, never to die again," and not between "a physical body and a nonphysical one."[108] "The idea that every human possesses an immortal soul, which is the 'real' part of them, finds little support in the Bible."[109]

Sorting out the views on the resurrection that developed in the early church, the patristic scholar Brian Daley distinguishes four approaches. It suffices here to briefly note three of them; the fourth, reflecting Gnostic views, can be left aside due to its suspect status in the tradition.

The first type identified by Daley is associated with the "Apologists," who were late second-century Greek writers. Their view "assumes that the human person himself is in some sense incomplete" until the resurrection. They believed "that the survival of the soul after death, in any sense worthy of the term 'life,' is not guaranteed by the soul's nature and that the fulfillment of our natural desire for continued existence can come only as a gift of God," to whom alone belongs "incorruptible life."[110]

A different approach appearing in the second century imagines the "resurrection as the reassembly of the scattered material fragments ('atoms' in the ancient sense) into which the body has been reduced by death and decomposition, and the rejoining of those fragments with the surviving soul to constitute a single person—the same one who now exists." In this approach, "each of us *is* both our inner consciousness and our material body," and thus "to be truly raised, there must be both material and spiritual identity between the persons we now are and the glorious figures we shall be." The matter that makes up our lives now "must all be reclaimed as ours" (emphasis in the original).[111] → *perhaps it's the "matter recreated but not the soul*

Third and finally, Daley sketches the approach to the resurrection developed by the third-century theologian Origen (d. 253/54). Indebted as it is to Neoplatonic thought, his theory is vulnerable to the problematic elements of Christian body/soul dualism (i.e., the suggestion that the separated, spiritual soul is the genuine seat of full personhood and a corresponding denigration of the materiality of human life). Daley defends Origen against the worst of these charges. Only the Trinity is without a body, Origen recognized; every other intelligent creature "needs to make use of a body as an instrument of activity, in Origen's view, even though its own nature is incorporeal."[112] In a move that finds similar expression in contemporary Catholic views, as we will see below, Origen, having argued for "the essential changeability of creatures,"[113] sees the soul "as the principle of *substantial continuity* within [the human person's] changing, organic body" (emphasis added).[114]

Biblical testimony and the witness of the early Church provide no support for the idea of a self-sufficient soul, flourishing and complete apart from the body. Nonetheless, it remains an open question whether some form of an integral, body/soul dualism can be defended in line with early Christian interpretations of the resurrection. For post-conciliar church teaching, the answer has been not only that it can be but also that it *must* be defended to make sense of two fundamental doctrines: (1) the belief that the resurrection of the dead does *not* follow immediately upon individual bodily death (and thus there is an interim period between individual death and the resurrection); and (2) the need for an identifiable continuity of personhood between the temporal and the resurrected lives of each individual.

In 1992, the Vatican-appointed International Theological Commission (ITC) addressed these issues in "Some Current Questions in Eschatology." The resurrection of the dead is a future transformation that occurs concurrently with the event of Christ's second coming, the commission contends. Because it is tied to an event at the end of time, it cannot be understood as "the encounter of an individual with the Lord" at the moment of the individual's own death.[115] Such a view does violence to the texts of the New Testament and replaces the "community aspect of the final resurrection" with a purely individual one.[116] Similarly, an atemporalist explanation—where, at death, each individual is brought immediately to the Parousia (Christ's second coming) to be united with all others who have died—violates biblical teaching because it "implies recourse to a philosophy of time quite foreign to biblical thought" and "does not seem to take sufficiently into account the truly corporeal nature of the resurrection; for a true body cannot be said to exist devoid of all notion of temporality."[117]

Given the Church's commitment to an intermediate state between individual bodily death and the resurrection, the concept of an immortal soul is crucial in protecting the continuity of personhood across the three states—temporal life, the intermediate state, and the resurrection. The 1979 document by the Congregation for the Doctrine of the Faith (CDF), "Letter on Certain Questions Concerning Eschatology," similarly maintained "that a spiritual element survives and subsists after death, an element endowed with consciousness and will, so that the 'human self' subsists. To *designate* this element, the Church uses the word 'soul'" (emphasis added).[118] Continued use of this word (or some similar term) "is absolutely indispensable in order to support the faith of Christians."[119] Without the ongoing survival of some dimension of the human person, there would be "no existential continuity" between the person who died and the one who is resurrected.[120]

However, ascribing the role of preserver of continuity to the immortal soul represents a slight shift away from its neo-scholastic function. The contrast made in these recent documents is not between the soul as incorruptible form and the body as corruptible matter, but rather between the soul as enduring personhood and the bodily dissolution of that identity.

rejection of Aquinas → soul = designator of personal continuity

The Church holds that <u>each person's unique personhood survives</u> the <u>transition from bodily death to resurrected life, and the "soul" is simply</u> a <u>way of *designating* this enduring identity, not a precisely defined, meta-physical reality.</u> As the ITC document recognized, understanding the soul in this way, as a designator of personal continuity, is at odds with Aquinas's thought, <u>which rejected the identification of the soul with personhood.</u>[121]

Also seemingly in tension with Aquinas is the meaning that the document attaches to "immortality." For Aquinas, in keeping with Plato's argument, the soul's immortality is an *innate* quality (even if ultimately grounded in God), something that flows from the intellectual nature of the person as a rational being. To my knowledge, no post-conciliar Vatican document defends the soul's immortality in precisely this way.[122] Rather, in line with biblical teaching, human immortality is understood first and foremost as a gift from God. Thus, the CDF document on eschatology attributes our "fundamental continuity" between this life and the next "to the power of the Holy Spirit," not to an innate quality of our human nature.[123] Pope John Paul II (d. 2005) likewise argued that the ultimate basis for surviving bodily death is the divine gift from the Father, who, in response to the Son, gives "his own paternal gift, that is to say the grant of new immortal life in the resurrection."[124] Collectively, these and other statements reflect a shift in the ground of human endurance beyond death from the innate integrity of the rational creature to a divine decision and the salvific accomplishment of Christ.[125]

This shift eliminates one problem with regard to animals while raising others. Humanity has not gained inclusion in the eschaton due to its intellectual abilities but because of the new relationship with God it has been given in and through the paschal mystery.[126] As for humans, so also for animals, one can argue: It is the divine prerogative to determine who or what will be included in the life to come, not some innate property of a creature's nature. God's choice is not bound by Platonic logic. At the same time, two new challenges surface. First, if the soul is to represent—or "designate," to use the CDF's language—the continuity of personhood across this life and the next, in what sense can individual animals be said to have the capacity for such a continuity? That is, what does it mean to attribute a sense of enduring personhood beyond death to, say, an elephant or to an earthworm? And second, if immortality is now to be seen as the fruit of the Spirit and the new relationship with God made possible in Christ, how do animals participate in such a spiritual gift?

Regarding the first challenge, I acknowledge that some creatures, based on present understanding, do not seem to have the requisites for continuity of life across bodily death and eschatological life. For example, for those creatures with no sense of past or future and no sense of self, it is hard to imagine that a substantive continuity could exist between their lives in the present order and their resurrected selves. For such creatures, their restoration in the age to come would be more a matter of re-creation than resurrection. However, I also believe that, generally speaking, higher-order animals like dogs and dolphins *do* have a capacity for a continuity of personhood. These creatures display sophisticated intellectual capacities (e.g., problem solving, communication, memory, anticipation of the future, sense of self), and they individually manifest distinctive personalities that go beyond a generic species identity.[127] God, we can imagine, could choose to raise such creatures to a new life in a manner that is in continuity with their concrete histories, distinctive personalities, and particular abilities. Thus, one possible response to the challenge is to allow that God could grant a renewal to diverse creatures in ways that are appropriate to each creature's natural capacities. The redemption of, say, an individual gnat might be part of an eschatological renewal of gnats in general rather than a resurrection of that particular gnat, whereas the redemption of an individual chimpanzee might take a form closer to that of personal resurrection. I will return to this question in the chapters ahead.

The second challenge—animal participation in the divine gift—is not easily addressed in a Christian tradition that understands the divine-human relationship as unique. According to the ITC document, because we can recognize in ourselves a "spiritual and immortal soul," we perceive ourselves as "superior to all other earthly creatures and indeed capable by knowledge and love of possessing God."[128] Similarly, Pope Benedict created a stir among animal lovers when he contrasted the life of grace, which enables the human person "to enter into a personal relationship with the Creator forever, for the whole of eternity," with the destiny of other creatures, for whom "death means solely the end of existence on earth."[129] In the chapters ahead, I will contest the exclusion of all animals from a covenantal relationship with God. At this point, however, I note that in a 1990 "General Audience," John Paul II was interpreted as suggesting that animals have spiritual souls.[130] In this address, the pope observes that even though the second creation story of Genesis, which states that God created the human person by breathing into his nostrils "the breath of life," does not depict animals as recipients of the divine breath (he earlier states that the word "breath" is synonymous with "spirit"), other texts do. The pope maintains that Psalm 104 refers to *all* creatures, human and nonhuman, when it says "Take away their breath, they perish and return to the dust. Send forth your spirit, they are created and you renew the face of the earth" (Ps 104:29–30).

John Paul II

John Paul II's statements are significant in themselves because they indicate that animals, like humanity, have been given a spiritual endowment. But his comments become all the more interesting when interpreted in light of the connection made in the *Catechism of the Catholic Church* between God's breath and the human soul: "The human person, created in the image of God, is a being at once corporeal and spiritual. *The biblical account expresses this reality* in symbolic language when it affirms that 'then the LORD God formed man of dust from the ground, and breathed into his nostrils the breath of life; and man became a living being'" (emphasis added).[131] It is no surprise, then, that John Paul II's comments were seen as an affirmation that animals have spiritual souls, an interpretation that the American media have taken to be fact, judging from the confirmations given by the *New York Times* and other outlets. Additional and exaggerated interpretations of the pope's address followed, with numerous reports attributing to him the statements that animals are "as near to God as men are" and that we "must love and feel solidarity with our smaller brethren" (neither of which, as far as I can tell, is supported by the text), leading People for the Ethical Treatment of Animals to declare John Paul II "a saint to animals."[132]

Thomistic Framework

Aquinas's eschatology of nonhuman life represents a dead end in his ethical thinking about animals, a terminus to which he was compelled more by the Greek logic of the immortal soul than the testimony of Scripture and the early Christian tradition. His body/soul dualism is Aristotelian in its hylomorphism, but his determination of what survives death is fundamentally Platonic. The Thomistic framework for understanding our responsibilities toward animals by itself did little to inspire compassionate regard for animals and was at times co-opted to justify animal disregard and abuse.

There are, however, telling examples within the Catholic tradition of voices that commend kindness toward all God's creatures, and even consider them as proper objects of the Gospel proclamation. These animal-friendly witnesses illuminate a promising direction for Catholic thought as its soteriology becomes freed of Platonic fetters. Aquinas, who was theologically innovative and keenly receptive to the latest scientific and philosophical thought, would be the first to encourage a critical openness to contemporary developments. Fortunately, the tripartite commitments of the Thomistic framework—we have no duties to animals, animals are created to serve humanity, and cruelty to animals is evil principally because of how it affects our character—were modified if not outright rejected in Pope Francis's *Laudato Si'*.[133] The question remains, however, whether Francis's innovations are innovative enough. I argue for further developments or clarifications of at least two aspects: (1) the hope we can have that individual creatures will share in our resurrected life, in ways appropriate to each animal; and (2) the recognition that this theological hope transforms the moral responsibilities we have to our fellow creatures.

Before moving to this constructive argument, however, let us consider what other lessons might be learned from this history of Catholic teaching on animals. Specifically, we can wonder whether the historical reticence about animal care was the product of bad theology or something more troubling. This is not a question that can be answered with any certitude. Still, Christian history attests to our proclivity for self-serving interpretations of the Gospel; and an honest scrutiny of past attitudes toward animals evidences, I believe, more than a theological error. It shows signs of a sinful failing of the Christian community. If so, responding to the story of our past requires more than a theological course correction; it also entails a contrite conversion and a prophetic counter-witness to that history.

SEEING ANIMALS: SEEING OUR SIN

This chapter's opening epigraph expresses Pope Francis and Patriarch Bartholomew's belief that through prayer, we "change the way we perceive the world in order to change the way we relate to the world." Changing our perception is a difficult moral task when doing so also obliges us to change ourselves. Our preferences, our joys and hopes, our strategies for protecting ourselves from pain and suffering, and our sense of self are all entangled in how we see the world, what we believe is permissible in it, and the possibilities we believe are legitimate for our distinctive flourishing within it. Seeing the world anew is a threat to this self-understanding. What Aquinas called the first practical precept, that "good is to be done and pursued, and evil is to be avoided," is experienced by us as a persistent imperative that not only compels us to carry out good acts but also, in turn, to judge ourselves as good—to preserve as part of our core identity the conviction that we are good.[134]

Oddly then, this moral imperative's pressing demand makes it difficult for us to acknowledge sin, because doing so is an existential risk. The path forward for the Christian is to admit our sin with humility before a

forgiving God, but the alternative path is tempting: self-deception. We
choose to remain ignorant of some aspect of our ethical responsibilities so
that, as Aquinas notes, we "may sin more freely."[135] The conflict between
the desire to do good (and be good) and the desire to do what is conve-
nient for us, even if sinful, means ironically that the "greater the integrity
of the person, . . . the greater is the temptation to self-deception."[136]
Because of the strength of the existential drive to deem oneself good, the
eighteenth-century Anglican bishop Joseph Butler could plausibly suggest
that "a great part of the wickedness in the world is, one way or other,
owing to [our] self-partiality, self-flattery, and self-deceit."[137] We are particularly vulnerable, he believed, in those domains of action in which moral
designations as good or evil are uncertain enough to allow interpretive
license.[138] In such cases, moral reflection is often done not to discern an
action's rightness but "to find out reasons to justify or palliate it."[139] Multiple studies support Butler's claims; neither in morality nor in any other
sphere are we the rational creatures we generally believe ourselves to be.[140]
The antidote is to allow the Gospel narrative to help us know ourselves as
sinners and thus place "limits on our claims to righteousness." Its "hard
and painful discipline" is necessary for growing beyond complacent surety
in our moral goodness.[141]

The stratagems of self-deception and the collective authority of group
bias are mutually empowering, and thus self-justification often finds ref-
uge in the conventional wisdom of an age. Our social circles are composed
of good people, and such individuals, we instinctively believe, just cannot
be wrong. In turn, the individual buttresses those same conventions by
affirming their truth within like-minded groups, thus rendering any challenging or alternative views epistemically unavailable. The incontrovert-
ible assumptions of the group simply do not allow such claims to appear
worthy of serious consideration. The history of US and European involvement in slavery provides ample testimony of this pernicious dynamic. "I
appeal to facts," stated the American statesman and slave holder John
Calhoun. "Never before has the black race of Central Africa, from the
dawn of history to the present day, attained a condition so civilized and so
improved, not only physically, but morally and intellectually."[142] Other
"facts" were also marshaled to defend slavery. The slaves were coarser
beings of lesser intelligence, and so were less able to experience the harsh-
ness of their circumstance and more able to withstand the suffering it
entailed. The effective working of societies depended on the institution of
slavery. Scripture showed it to be divinely ordained. Africans benefited
from enslavement because they were exposed to the civilizing effects of

slavery

Christianity. These "facts" found a ready audience whose confirming support conferred upon their absurd beliefs an aura of credibility and protected them from the assailment of objective reality.

As history reminds us, Christianity has not been immune to sinful and socially entrenched ignorance. For most of its history, the Catholic Church supported the institution of slavery, even if constraining it by what the Church understood to be just and rational norms (e.g., licit capture, enslavement as punishment for crime, exclusive targeting of non-Christians). The colonization period of the sixteenth century raised new questions not about slavery per se but about the enslavement of those who were seen as potential converts to Catholicism. Aspects of slavery—but not the institution itself—were criticized by popes Paul III (1537), Gregory XVI (1591), Urban VIII (1639), and Benedict XIV (1741). As late as 1866, the Vatican's Holy Office stated that "slavery per se was not repugnant to natural law or to divine law."[143]

Early Christian voices against slavery were mainly Protestant, often Quakers (Religious Society of Friends) in the United States and Methodists in England. Not only was the Catholic Church late in gaining its prophetic voice, but when it finally did, it reinterpreted history to absolve itself of sin. In 1890 Pope Leo XIII stated, "From the beginning, almost nothing was more venerated in the Catholic Church which embraces all men with motherly love, than the fact that she looked to see a slavery eased and abolished which was oppressing so many people."[144] John Noonan wryly observes, "Leo XIII did not see the need to establish the truth of what he so triumphantly and so inaccurately claimed."[145] The pope's revisionist history exemplifies what a former professor described as the "No, no, no, no, yes, like we've always taught before" development of Catholic doctrine.[146] Although John Paul II is rightly praised for his efforts at naming the Church's sins and asking for pardon, he succumbed to a similar whitewashing when in a 1990 address in Africa, he stated implausibly that it has been "a constant teaching of the ecclesial Magisterium" that "never can there be enslavement of one person by another."[147]

Cardinal Manning offered a more accurate and brutally candid assessment of Catholicism as he experienced it in nineteenth-century London. At the end of his life, in a diary entry dated August 1, 1890, the convert to Catholicism mourned its repeated failure to act prophetically. "All of the great works of charity in England," he laments, started outside of the Catholic Church. He lists as examples the end of slavery, the prevention of animal abuse, the defense of children against cruelty, and the protection of women and children who are "driven by starvation wages upon the streets."

[handwritten: ✱ ✱ great works of charity started outside the church]

None of these works "were started by us." He attributes this failure of Catholicism, in part, to the fact that Catholics "*do not take pains to know*" the hardships of others and thus they remain "unconscious that Lazarus lies at their gate full of sores" (emphasis added).[148] Such historical moments are at odds with the prophetic tradition on issues such as poverty, immigration, and human life that has emerged in Catholic social teaching since *Rerum Novarum.* A Church that is called to be the subject of prophetic witness has too often been its object.

My intent is not to posit a moral equivalency between the scourge of the African slave trade and animal abuse but only to suggest that a sort of parallel exists in the attitudes and rationales of those who supported slavery and those who currently facilitate animal abuse. *[handwritten: ✱ agree]* Our vantage point allows us to see what people in that earlier age could not see or refused to see: that the arguments used to defend slavery were generally a posteriori justifications for an already-desired and decided-on course of action. Christian responses to slavery tried to camouflage its evil under the cover of some sort of goodness—scriptural warrant, human and social necessity, the benevolence of the master, and the limited capacity of its victims to suffer. It is troubling to recognize the similarity of these arguments to those used to justify the unprincipled treatment of animals. *[handwritten: slavery/animal abuse connection]* An eighteenth-century defender of animal domestication argued that it was good for animals because "it civilized them."[149] Butchering animals for meat is not cruel, stated the Reverend Thomas Robinson in 1709, but rather "a kindness," because it spared them "the sufferings of old age."[150] The Anglican priest William Wollaston (d. 1724) argued that the suffering of animals was not great because they had no sense of past or future, and therefore to "kill a brute is to deprive him of a life . . . that is equal to little more than nothing."[151]

Similarly, in an 1888 article in *The Dublin Review*, Father John Vaughan (whom we met above as a contributor to the debate appearing in *The Tablet*) asserts that "there can be no doubt . . . that the most acute sufferings even among the higher orders of irrational animals are slight, as compared with what man would suffer in the same or similar circumstances." This is due not only to our higher "intellectual power" but also "*to the vastly superior nature of [our] human soul*" (emphasis added).[152] Of course, few arguments had more persuasive force than the near–universally accepted belief among Christians that Scripture had given humanity divine warrant to use animals for self-serving ends. Even a seventeenth-century beekeeper, when forced to defend his killing of bees (in order to take their honey), was able to do so by noting that God has "given all creatures unto us for our benefit."[153]

René Descartes [handwritten]

Another set of implausible justifications for disregarding animal suffering appears in the contorted arguments that surfaced in the wake of René Descartes's (d. 1650) theory of animals. In light of the increasing recognition within the scientific community, even before Darwin, that humans were physiologically more similar to animals than had previously been recognized, there was a growing awareness among Christian thinkers that the radical discontinuity between humans and all other creatures was being undermined. If animals and humans shared anatomical features, one might be tempted to believe that they also shared spiritual ones (e.g., an immortal soul). The solution by the devout Catholic philosopher Descartes was to attribute to the soul all that is commonly associated with subjective experience—for example, thought, sensation, and feeling—and then to exclude these same attributes from animals. Humans had souls; animals did not. They were not only soulless but also devoid of consciousness and passion—basically machines, even if complicated ones. This not only preserved the human/animal distinction but also had the benefit of alleviating any distress one might feel over the apparent suffering caused by animal experiments. Descartes was aware of this implication and explicitly endorsed it; his theory is, he wrote, "indulgent to human beings . . . since it absolves them from the suspicion of crime when they eat or kill animals."[154] Cartesians like the French priest Nicolas Malebranche and the Catholic philosopher Antoine Arnauld (a Jansenist) were said to demonstrate their absolute confidence in Cartesian beliefs by beating dogs in front of skeptics and announcing to dismayed spectators that the animals could feel no pain.[155] The claim by Cartesians, prima facie absurd, was that animals only *appeared* to have intelligence, senses, and feelings.

The most successful argument against animal suffering, however, centered on theodicy concerns: Animals, whether in the laboratory or in their natural habitat, cannot suffer because such suffering would challenge divine goodness. Nicholas Poisson, for example, stated in 1670 that it would violate God's justice to "produce a creature subject to pain and capable of suffering which had not deserved it."[156] This argument "quickly became a staple" among seventeenth- and early eighteenth-century Cartesians. In addition to the works of the priests Nicolas Malebranche and Antoine Dilly, versions of it can be found in the writings of seventeenth-century thinkers like André Martin, John Norris, and Isaac Jaquelot.[157] For Melchior Cardinal de Polignac, the suffering of innocent animals posed a threat not only to God's justice but also to our own. Animals could have no immortal soul; for if they did, we would daily be guilty of cruelty and

[handwritten margin note, left side:] "I think therefore I am" interesting because how can we know anything really?

[handwritten margin note, lower left:] CAN ANIMALS SUFFER, AT ALL?

murder.[158] Though Vaughan (again, whom we met above) was not a Cartesian, he also appealed to a theodicy argument in the nineteenth century to contest the possibility of significant animal pain. It would be contrary to "our knowledge of the goodness of God" to believe that animals "which perish from slow and violent deaths should be as sensitive to pain as man is."[159] *argument that animals don't suffer as much...*

Regardless of how doubtful one might find Descartes's understanding of animals (and by the early eighteenth century, few in the philosophical community supported his theory), Christian philosophers recognized that the Cartesians' appeal to theodicy had drawn attention to a significant vulnerability in Christian belief. If animals could genuinely suffer, how was the Christian to defend the goodness of God? The only way to address the issue would be to modify basic Christian doctrine (e.g., about God, animals, and/or redemption). Instead, they resolved the dilemma by changing the facts or introducing new ones. Thus, in another argument straining credibility, the French philosopher David Boullier maintained in 1728 that though animals have souls, their suffering would only impugn divine justice if it were so grave that it would have been better off had they never existed, a condition that God prevents from occurring.[160] Also *I don't get this really* embracing a form of divine micromanaging, Jean-Pierre de Crousaz claimed in 1773 that animals do not suffer much "because God has so constructed them as to ensure that whatever disagreeable sensations they do experience are nothing in comparison to the pleasures they get from agreeable ones."[161] In the most outrageous explanation, the Jesuit Guillaume-Hyacinthe Bougeant mused in 1739, perhaps in jest, that God punished demons by forcing them to animate animal bodies; animals have souls, but not their own.[162] The demon supplied the immaterial needs for the animal's life, while its body provided everything else. Any suffering was experienced only by the demon, who, as Bougeant noted, deserved it. We can be thankful that "although Bougeant's work was well known, and much discussed, few took it seriously."[163]

An alternative way to address animal theodicy would be to include animals in God's salvific plans so that their suffering in this world might somehow be redeemed. The view that God would restore creatures, however, was generally dismissed as offensive to Christian sensibility and "an absurdity to Catholic thinkers."[164] Nonetheless, contemporary theology cannot deny the possibility of animal redemption without also contradicting the plain sense meaning of the biblical testimony. As we will see in chapter 3, early Christian theologians argued for the presence of creatures in the eschaton precisely because the biblical text indicated as much. Later

Christian thought, however, was able to discount the testimony of the early church and that of Scripture by a combination of eisegesis and the "common practice," as Gaffney puts it, for Christians "to resort to allegorism" whenever they are "confronted with biblical passages whose plain import conflicted with their own notions."[165] Thus, Hosea's prophecy of "that day" when God would restore Israel and make a covenant "with the wild animals, with the birds of the air, and with the things that crawl on the ground" (Hos 2:20) was dismissed by at least one seventeenth-century scholar because such creatures were not suitable covenant partners;[166] and the clear animal-friendly exhortation of Deuteronomy 22 against taking for oneself a nurturing mother bird was contorted into an allegorical statement about Jewish converts to Christianity.[167]

The penchant to "correct" the plain sense meaning of Scripture so that it conforms to contemporary assumptions is well exemplified in Aquinas's strained interpretation of Romans 8. He allows that Paul's use of the word "creation" (e.g., "creation itself would be set free from slavery to corruption," Rom 8:21) *could* refer to nonhuman creation, but he offers it as the third of three possibilities, with the first two interpretations holding that creation means, respectively, the righteous human person and human nature.[168] His third interpretation of Paul's reference to "creation" is biotically barren. He implies that the creation to be set free here refers to the "sensible creation," by which he means the four elements—air, fire, earth, and water—and, with qualification, the heavenly spheres, but not living creatures like plants and animals.[169] In keeping with his view that the purpose of nonhuman creation is to serve human need, Aquinas states that in the age to come, the elements will "contribute" to humanity's glorification by providing the material for their renewed "dwelling place."[170]

The reason why the heavenly spheres, the four elements, and the human soul are able, in contrast to all other creatures, to make the transition from this life to the eschaton is that they are in some sense incorruptible,[171] a claim that is supported by classical Greek metaphysics but is difficult to reconcile with what we now know about the cosmos at both the macro and atomic levels. Thus, if we were to continue to follow Aquinas and make incorruptibility the criterion for determining which created realities of the present age will be restored in the age to come, we would be left with a matter-free eschaton or, at least, one composed of matter that is completely different from that which composes it now. The immaterial human soul would remain as the only link of continuity between the old and new creations.

[handwritten: → doing things "just because" it's good, not because you think you should because someone tells you it's right...]

Later interpreters also resisted interpretations of the passage in Romans that would give animals a place in God's redemptive plans. Though some commentators allowed, as Aquinas did not, that the passage implies a future creation that includes nonhuman life, they were not inclined to go so far as to populate that future creation with creatures of the present order. Monsignor Patrick Boylan in 1934, for example, restricts Paul's assertion that creation will "share in the glorious freedom of God" by making a distinction between creation's "release from the primeval curse," which he affirms, and the "positive glorification of nature," which he doubts.[172] Many Protestant interpreters during the late nineteenth and early twentieth centuries rely on similar exegetical qualifications to exclude the animals of the present age—which are, as Paul rightly observes, groaning for their salvation—from a real sharing in the redemption offered in Christ.[173] Characteristic of interpretations of the time was a resistance to attribute anything more radical to creation's future than a restoration of its original goodness. We can contrast that redemptive miserliness with the interpretation given in a contemporary commentary by the noted New Testament scholar Joseph Fitzmyer: Paul "affirms a solidarity of the human and the subhuman world in the redemption of Christ"; creation shares "in the destiny of humanity." "Material creation is thus not to be a mere spectator of humanity's triumphant glory and freedom, but is to share in it."[174] *[handwritten: true, why would some creation just be disposable?]*

Historical interpretations of Romans reflect a pattern that has appeared in other lamentable rationalizations by Christians of unjust practices: a skewed or outright erroneous interpretation of reality—whether textual, human, or animal—motivated by an unrecognized bias in favor of conventional Christian beliefs and/or the interests of Christians themselves. I will return to this Romans passage and other biblical testimony on animals in chapter 3 as part of my discussion of animal redemption. There, we will explore interpretations of Scripture that are more faithful to the text and, consequentially, more affirming of animal redemption.

CAUTIONARY WARNINGS:
DISSONANCE IN CONTEMPORARY CULTURE

[handwritten: constantly changing attitudes ....]

Christian attitudes toward animals and the rest of creation have changed significantly over the last several decades. The statements of recent popes reflect this shift, manifesting as they do a deep regard for creation and a readiness to denounce abuse and commend duties. Humanity has been given "a specific responsibility toward the environment," John Paul II tells us in *Evangelium Vitae*, and we must pursue a solution that "respects the great good of life, of every life"—that is, as the context makes clear, the well-being of both human *and* nonhuman lives.[175] Yet before we indulge in self-congratulations for our epistemic progress, we should note a couple of yellow flags appearing in our cultural context. Christians are embedded within and influenced by this context and are obliged to scrutinize its assumptions and biases.

One cautionary warning is our culture's inconsistency in how it directs its moral passions for animals based on arbitrary distinctions (e.g., non-food animals vs. meat-supplying ones). On the one hand, our culture is increasingly devoted to pets, as demonstrated by the $67 billion Americans spent on them in 2016.[176] Pet owners often regard their pets as members of the family, with two-thirds buying them Christmas presents.[177] They typically see themselves as devoted not only to pets but also to all animals, and thus committed to their kind treatment and horrified at their abuse. On the other hand, this passionate devotion, unfortunately, turns to indifference for meat-producing animals, whose lives are often distressed and deaths likely torturous. As Hal Herzog explains, "Cheap meat comes at a cost. A broiler chicken's bones cannot keep up with the explosive growth of its body. Unnaturally large breasts torque a chicken's legs, causing lameness, ruptured tendons, and twisted leg syndrome. According to Donald Broome, professor of animal welfare at Cambridge University, severe leg pain in chickens is the world's largest animal welfare problem. Arthritis, heart disease, sudden death syndrome, and a host of metabolic disorders are prevalent among industrial broilers."[178] The living conditions of factory-farmed chickens are "Dante-esque"; they spend most of their days "lying down, often in litter contaminated with excrement. As a result, many will develop breast blisters, hock burns, and sores on their feet." The air they breathe is "laced with ammonia produced by the action of microbes on the accumulated urine and the excrement of tens of thousands of birds," burning the lungs and the eyes.[179]

A willingness to permit these abuses is inconsistent with the prevalent outrage directed toward animal sports. The cruelty of cockfighting, for example, has led every state to make it illegal. We might suppose that only individuals who are immoral and uncaring—people unlike ourselves—could participate in such sports. We would be wrong, as Herzog shows in *Some We Love, Some We Hate, Some We Eat: Why It's So Hard to Think Straight about Animals*.[180] Cockfighting enthusiasts are often genuine animal lovers themselves. Their justification for what most deem cruel is disturbingly familiar: Chickens are too dumb to feel pain, it is natural, and the chickens enjoy it.[181] Given the revulsion that most chicken eaters feel about cockfighting, one might wonder how such censure can be harmonized with the "inconvenient fact that the life of a fighting cock is fifteen times longer and infinitely more pleasurable than the life of a broiler chicken."[182]

For Aquinas's virtue ethics, good actions encourage virtuous character; such actions train our affections and dispositions so that we more promptly and easily act in morally sound ways. The effect that an action has on one's character provides an initial indication of its moral status as good or evil. Within this ethical framework, serious questions should be raised about the factory-farming industry, if only for the morally corrosive effect it has on its laborers. One "sticker," the worker responsible for cutting the animal's carotid arteries and jugular vein in the neck, recounts the heavy toll that slaughterhouse work takes on the workers' character. He was fortunate; Alcoholics Anonymous had given him an outlet, where he "could go to people and talk to them." Many of his coworkers, however, "just drink and drug their problems away" and "end up abusing their spouses because they can't get rid of the feelings."[183] He left his job, he maintained, because the management refused to do anything about "people being mutilated and animals treated cruelly."[184] Another factory-farm worker describes abusing animals out of the frustration that comes with working at a slaughterhouse. Using a knife, he "sliced off the end of a hog's nose, just like a piece of bologna." After the "hog went crazy," he rubbed salt into its wound, causing the hog further distress. Using a glove, the worker then "stuck salt right up the hog's ass." The hog, he tells us, "didn't know whether to shit or go blind."[185] Given the effects that animal slaughterhouses have on their workers, it is not surprising that one study has shown that "the location of a slaughterhouse in a county was associated with increases in the total arrest rate, arrests for violent crime, arrests for rape, and arrests for other sex offenses in comparison with other industries."[186] Unlike other industrial work, which can benefit communities by having "suppressant effects" on violence and crime, "slaughterhouses have a unique and insidious effect on the surrounding communities."[187]

Most of the meat we eat is produced in similar slaughterhouses, places of misery for animal and worker alike, with ripples of baneful consequences for the surrounding community. As members of a culture that tacitly supports such systems simply by purchasing meat, we have to ask how they can be reconciled with the devotion we otherwise feel for animals and whether the existence of such systems is a symptom of an enduring animal myopia still impairing our cultural and even religious imaginations.

These two problems—the disconnect between the devotion our culture has for some animals and the disregard it has for others, and the dehumanizing effect that slaughterhouses have on workers—are not the only cautionary flags in our cultural context, but they might be the most vivid ones. Western Christianity is embedded in this cultural milieu and is vulnerable to its reigning assumptions. To resist their pull requires an intentional and explicitly counter-cultural response.

Our culture might plead ignorance to absolve itself, though cultivated obliviousness is a key weapon in sin's arsenal. Evil wants to remain hidden, and the food industry is happy to do its part to help us maintain our exculpating ignorance. Their factories are located in remote areas, and they refuse access to journalists. "*We don't see them because we're not supposed to*" (emphasis in the original).[188] The indifference our society has toward the horror of factory farming suggests a more fundamental problem: a failure of vision caused by a refusal to genuinely see animals as the creatures they are. The most effective way to assuage our conscience in the face of animal suffering is to transform these "nonhuman subjects into nonhuman objects."[189] We erase their subjectivity—the fact that they are individual creatures with interests, desires, and, sadly, a keen capacity to suffer. It is no surprise, then, that recent studies of the "psychology of eating animals . . . show that people who eat animals maintain an elaborate system of moral disengagement to protect them from feeling self-condemnation over the effects of their actions on animals."[190]

Refusing to see the face of the animal as part of our ethical horizon, and thus failing to recognize it as a conscious subject of joyful and painful experiences, occludes the power that the animal would otherwise have to disrupt our worldview and claim our ethical response.[191] In order to re-attune our ethical vision to the truth of our world and the moral claims it makes on us, Jay McDaniel recommends a discipline of "contemplative seeing"; we attend to animals "in their particularity, as subjects in and for themselves."[192] A practiced attentiveness to the full reality of the animal other would act as a spiritual discipline, in line with what Ignatius of Loyola calls *agere contra*, "to go against" our sinful tendencies. Doing so involves the virtuous but hard moral choice of bringing into focus what is more comforting to ignore. The saint is, as Iris Murdoch recognized, the one who sees "what is most real."[193]

In light of the cross, Christianity ascribes to the suffering of the other an essential heuristic role for understanding our moral responsibilities. It is an indispensable and formative object of a genuine Christian moral vision. The Gospel invites the Christian to enter into solidarity with the world's suffering, and this solidarity does not end with the human. To suggest as much does not deny the distinctive moral claim that human life makes. Innumerable possibilities of moral theorizing exist between the extremes of "humans alone make moral claims" and "the moral claims of humans and animals are equally binding." Excluding the former does not require the latter. The particular act of attending to *animal* suffering is necessary because of the immense power that humans exercise over animals. Having this power does not by itself create self-serving biases, but it makes it easier to act on them. The most effective counterbalance to exclusive power is a willingness to carefully regard the suffering of the disempowered "other." Margaret Farley's counsel that "it is inconceivable that moral norms can be formulated without consulting the experience of those whose lives are at stake" requires that we learn about animals' needs and, in particular, attend to their suffering.[194] The animal has no other ally to protect it from abuse than the human.

animals have no one else to protect their abuse than humans.

It is not hard to find hopeful signs that Christian teaching is increasingly animal friendly, and yet one can wonder whether a theological and ethical inertia still affects the Church, both its leadership and the Catholic community at large. Karl Rahner once observed that the development of Catholic doctrine over the last hundred years cannot be explained, *pace* the claims of many, as simply making explicit what had been implicit or "the simple addition of new supplemental insights." Sometimes, changes in Church teaching have entailed "the transition from error to true insight," accompanied by "struggle, pain, and bitter personal sacrifice."[195] In our shifting views of the theological status of animals and of our ethical obligations toward them, we have an example of both: a "transition from error to true insight," combined with new insights into that which can never be fully grasped or epistemically exhausted—the divine love revealed in Christ. Newness is an essential and enduring attribute of revelation, not a passing quality experienced exclusively by the first hearers of the Good News. The task of each generation of the Church is to preserve this newness by disposing itself to the Spirit's promptings.[196] We fail at this task when we substitute the vibrant freshness of the Gospel as it addresses us today with the safety of theological conventionality. Early in the twentieth century, Father Ruland remarked that "in many things, formerly taken so much for granted, . . . revolutions have occurred, . . . [among these] slavery, the degraded position of woman, contempt for manual work, and discrimination against the colored races."[197] It is unlikely that our present age is uniquely invulnerable to errors in what we take "so much for granted."

In 1915 Cardinal Gasparri, then the Vatican secretary of state, sent a note of praise to the Italian Society for the Protection of Animals on behalf of Pope Benedict XV. He wrote that the society's goals were in "perfect accord with the doctrine which the Catholic Church has always taught." He bemoans the fact that "the teaching of the Church and the example of the Saints has not always been followed by the people."[198] The cardinal's commendation of animal care is praiseworthy; but his claim that such care accords "with the doctrine which the Church has always taught" seems another instance of the "No, no, no, no, yes, like we've always taught before" model of doctrinal development. Confessing the sinful indifference of past Catholic voices is an important first step in moving beyond that past and gaining a prophetic, and humbled, voice in the present. Marc Bekoff, a renowned evolutionary biologist, muses in a recent book, "I often wonder if future humans will sit around and scratch their heads and wonder how we missed what is so obvious about the lives of other animals."[199] We can hope that the future will look back upon today's Christian community and judge it kindly, finding that it had escaped some of its cultural blinders and labored prophetically to get right what is "so obvious about the lives of other animals."

NOTES

Epigraph: Pope Francis and Ecumenical Patriarch Bartholomew, "Joint Message."

1. "I can only choose within the world I can *see*, in the moral sense of 'see,' which implies that clear vision is a result of moral imagination and moral effort." Murdoch, *Sovereignty*, 37; emphasis in the original.

2. "No other earthly creature has an immortal spirit for a soul. Their souls are not immortal, but mortal; it's their nature to come to an end when they die." Thigpen, "Do Animals Go to Heaven?"

3. Recounted by Linzey, *Creatures*, 93.

4. Pope Leo XIII, "*Aeterni Patris*," no. 22.

5. See Aquinas, *Summa Theologica*, I.74.4; and Aquinas, *Summa Theologica* I.89.1. Henceforth, *Summa Theologica* is abbreviated "*ST*," followed by a standard citation format.

6. *ST* I.75.2.

7. *ST* I.75.2.

8. Aquinas, *Summa Contra Gentiles* II.79.3–4. Henceforth, *Summa Contra Gentiles* is abbreviated "*SCG*," followed by a standard citation format.

9. *ST* I.75.6.

10. *ST* Supplement-III.75.1 *ad.* 2. Note: the "Supplement" to Aquinas's *Summa Theologica* was composed posthumously, incorporating Aquinas's writings from other texts (e.g., *De potentia*). It is sometimes referred to simply as the "Supplement" and other times as the "Supplement to the Third Part." In citing this posthumous section, I refer to it as "Supplement-III."

11. *SCG* II.82.2.

12. *ST* II-II.64.1 *ad.* 2.

13. *ST* II-II.64.1 *ad.* 2.

14. Now animals and plants were made for the upkeep of human life. . . . Therefore when man's animal life ceases, animals and plants should cease." *ST* Supplement-III.91.5.

15. "It is impossible that natural appetite be in vain. But man naturally desires to live forever. . . . Man by his intellect apprehends being not merely in the present, as brute animals do, but unqualifiedly." *SGC* II.79.6.

16. *ST* Supplement-III.91.5 *ad.* 5.

17. Because God's "goodness could not be adequately represented by one creature alone, He produced many and diverse creatures, that what was wanting to one in the representation of the divine goodness might be supplied by another." *ST* I.47.1.

18. *ST* Supplement-III.91.5 *ad.* 3.

19. Aquinas, *On the Power of God* [question 5, article 9], 141.

20. *ST* Supplement-III.91.2.

21. *ST* Supplement-III.92.1.

22. *ST* Supplement-III.92.2.

23. *ST* Supplement-III.82.4 *ad.* 4.

24. *ST* Supplement-III.82.4 *ad.* 1.

25. *ST* Supplement-III 82.4 *ad.* 3.

26. *ST* Supplement-III.82.4 *ad.* 2.

27. The souls of the saints, though "separated from their bodies," are able to see the "Essence of God" and thus experience "true Happiness." *ST* I-II.4.5.

28. *ST* I-II.4.6 *ad.* 1, *ad.* 2.

29. "The body has not part in that operation of the intellect whereby the Essence of God is seen." *ST* I-II.4.6 *ad.* 2.

30. In the eschaton, Christ is one glorified body among many (even if foremost among them), in which the saints indirectly perceive God with bodily senses. *ST* Supplement-III.92.2. Aquinas recognizes that the bodily, risen Christ continues to have some form of a mediational role. For example, he argues that Christ pleads for us in the resurrected life by "the very showing of Himself in human nature." *ST* III.57.6. However, the emphasis in neo-scholastic interpretations was not on the glorified Christ as the one who mediates the beatific vision itself—thus Rahner's complaint that everything becomes "swallowed up by the *visio beatifica*, the beatific vision." Although this "relationship to the very essence of God" was effected "historically by a past event—namely the event of Christ," it will not, at least as depicted by

the neo-scholastics, continue to be "mediated by Jesus Christ." Rahner, "Eternal Significance," 37–38.

31. Rahner, 43.

32. E.g., the New Testament scholar N. T. Wright balances the central, vertical dimension of our eschatological life—the experience of God and the triune life—with its horizontal dimension: "The redeemed people of God in the new world will be the agents of his love going out in new ways, to accomplish new creative tasks, to celebrate and extend the glory of his love." Wright, *Surprised*, 105–6. Matthew Levering, a defender of Aquinas's understanding of the spiritual soul and humanity's eschatological life, finds this view unattractive, threatening "to bog us down in endless work." Levering, *Jesus*, 110. He defends Aquinas against the critique that his eschatological vision is "fundamentally otherworldly rather than a place of transformed bodiliness." Levering, 114–25.

33. Any valid, Christian depiction of the eschaton will entail both continuities and discontinuities with life as we know it today. The decision about which continuities to include and which to exclude will inevitably reflect the biases of the theologian proposing them. In this book, I endeavor to make the case that our embeddedness in a biotically rich world is a continuity that will extend into the eschaton.

34. My critique of Aquinas on this point pertains to his theology insofar as it has been interpreted by the Catholic tradition, especially during the modern period, and has shaped its views of animals—expressed in terms of what I call the "Thomistic framework." The question of whether neo-scholastic interpretations adequately reflect Aquinas's views on nonhuman creatures or what resources Aquinas might offer for addressing contemporary environmental concerns is not within the scope of this book. Given its richness, Aquinas's thought undoubtedly offers fruitful ecological resources, but my suspicion is that greener theological pastures can be discovered elsewhere. In support of Aquinas's potential as an ecological resource, William C. French appeals to Aquinas's "expansive view of the community of being" as a way of drawing our attention to the relationships that bind together human and nonhuman creatures. French, "Beast Machines," 37–38. Willis Jenkins identifies a different resource to be found in Aquinas's sacramental theology. His view that all creatures participate in God's goodness and thus resemble and represent it means that a loss of biodiversity reduces the variety of ways we can encounter and know God. "The more kinds of created things we see, the more modes of God's availability for us, the more actively can our reason seek its desire. Ecological diversity is a sort of adumbration of God (God's own phenomenological self-description, given for us), and its preservation promises the continual issue of surprising new descriptions." Jenkins, "Biodiversity," 412. Francisco Benzoni believes, however, that Jenkins's appeal to Aquinas is unsuccessful in establishing a "noninstrumental environmental ethic" that values nonhuman creatures as something more than instruments of an anthropocentric good. Benzoni, "Thomas Aquinas," 473. Ryan Patrick McLaughlin similarly concludes that Aquinas is not "particularly helpful" for environmental theology. McLaughlin, *Christian Theology*, 20.

35. *ST* I-II.102.6 *ad.* 8.

36. *ST* II-II.25.3.

37. "Charity is said to be the end of other virtues, because it directs all other virtues to its own end." *ST* II-II.23.8 *ad.* 3.

38. Gaffney, "Relevance," 152–53.

39. Thus, we love sinners "so long as there is hope of their mending their ways." *ST* II-II.25.6 *ad.* 2. Angels, unlike animals, are a proper object of charity because they are also "partakers of everlasting happiness." *ST* II-II.25.10 *ad.* 2. Demons, conversely, cannot be loved with charity because they will not share in everlasting life with us. *ST* II-II.25.11 *ad.* 1.

40. Patrizia Guarnieri describes some of the debates that took place in Italy. Guarnieri, "Moritz Schiff." Other essays in the book by Nicolaas Rupke, *Vivisection*, describe nineteenth-century discussions in Germany, Switzerland, and Sweden. See Tröhler and Maehle, "Anti-Vivisection"; and Bromander, "Vivisection Debate."

41. Nicholas Fountaine (d. 1709): "They nailed poor animals up on boards by their four paws to vivisect them." Cited by Singer, *Animal Liberation*, loc. 3876–77 of 6425, Kindle.

42. Cited by Turner, *All Heaven*, 35.

43. Ryder, *Animal Revolution*, 55.

44. John Wesley, *Sermons*, 131–32, cited by Clough, *On Animals: Volume One*, 135.

45. Primatt, *Duty*, 21.

46. Granger, *Apology*, 23.

47. Gaffney, "Relevance," 149.

48. Cited by Turner, *All Heaven*, 166.

49. Prümmer, *Handbook*, 109.

50. Davis, *Moral and Pastoral Theology*, 258.

51. Jone, *Moral Theology*, 144–45.

52. Rickaby, *Moral Philosophy*, 248.

53. Rickaby, 249. The phrase "stocks and stones" was used in the nineteenth century as a collective term for all the natural objects that compose a terrain, with "stocks" referring to the stalks of plants and the trunks of trees.

54. Rickaby, 250.

55. Coppens, *Moral Principles*, 38.

56. Coppens, 42.

57. Coppens, 40.

58. Turner, *All Heaven*, 212.

59. Turner, 163, citing Cobbe's 1895 essay in *Contemporary Review*. As medieval scholars remind us, such references to the "Dark Ages" should be taken metaphorically, not as an adequate evaluation of an historical era.

60. Charles Weld-Blundell, in a letter to the editor published in *The Tablet*, May 12, 1894, 737. The complaint is hyperbole, even if statements by Jesuits like Rickaby can be rightly criticized for their lack of compassion for animals. In fairness, the

"Jesuit" view—as expressed in the writings of Davis, Rickaby, and Coppens, along with that found in Jone and Prümmer—was basically the exposition of what was widely held to be authentic Catholic teaching, i.e., the neo-scholastic interpretation of Aquinas.

61. *Tablet*, March 24, 1894, 458–59.

62. *Tablet*, May 5, 1894, 696.

63. *Tablet*, May 12, 1894, 737.

64. *Tablet*, May 19, 1894, 777.

65. *Tablet*, April 7, 1894, 536.

66. *Tablet*, April 21, 1894, 618.

67. *Tablet*, May 19, 1894, 777.

68. *Tablet*, May 5, 1894, 696.

69. *Tablet*, May 5, 1894, 696.

70. In this homily, delivered on the First Sunday after the Epiphany, Newman was attempting to show how wondrous it was that the "Omnipotent God" decided to become a creature and place God's own Self at the mercy of humanity. Newman appeals to an analogy between God's obligations to humanity (there are none) and humanity's obligation to animals. The thrust of the analogy is to lead us first to imagine how incredible it would be for us to hand ourselves over to the mercy of animals, and then to stir in us awe and wonder that God has done something analogous with us. Newman was not attempting to address debates about protection for animals. Newman, *Sermons*, 106–7.

71. *Tablet*, May 19, 1894, 777.

72. *Tablet*, May 19, 1894, 777.

73. *Tablet*, March 31, 1894, 498.

74. *Tablet*, April 14, 1894, 576–77.

75. *Tablet*, April 14, 1894, 577.

76. *Tablet*, May 5, 1894, 696.

77. *Tablet*, April 21, 1894, 617.

78. *Tablet*, May 12, 1894, 738.

79. Salt, *Animals' Rights*, 8. Technically, animals did have souls in Thomistic thought, though not spiritual ones. However, after Descartes, whom we will visit below, the issue was increasingly framed by the premise that humans have souls and animals do not.

80. Lecky, *History*, 173.

81. Lecky, 177.

82. Kingsford and Maitland, *Credo*, 239.

83. Thomas, *Man*, 144.

84. Guarnieri notes that the influential *Civilta Cattolica* never criticized the practice. Guarnieri, "Moritz Schiff," 115.

85. Cited by Cobbe, *Life*, vol. 2, 171.

86. Stillman, "Jesuits," *The Spectator*, February 12, 1898, 235. The author says that *Voce della Veritate* was a Jesuit organ, hence the title of the letter to *The Spectator*. However, I believe it was clerical, not specifically Jesuit.

87. Rathe, "Animale," in *Enciclopedia Cattolica*, cited and translated by Gaffney, "Relevance," 160–61.

88. Gaffney, 160.

89. A helpful examination of animal-friendly voices in the Catholic tradition can be found in Jones's *School of Compassion*.

90. Cobbe did not believe that the nineteenth-century sons of Saint Francis shared their founder saint's love for animals. She expressed her "impatience" that Francis's name is "perpetually flaunted whenever the lack of common humanity to animals visible in Catholic countries happens to be mentioned." "No modern Franciscan that ever I have heard of, has stirred a finger on behalf of animals anywhere." Cobbe, *Life*, vol. 2, 174.

91. The *Acta Sanctorum* is a sixty-eight-volume encyclopedia of the lives of Catholic saints published between 1643 and 1940. An English translation of some of the entries can be found in *Church and Kindness to Animals*, whose author is anonymous.

92. *Church and Kindness to Animals*, 50.

93. Lecky, *History*, 172n3.

94. For a brief discussion of the bull and its significance for animal ethics, see Widener, "Papal Bull."

95. Newman, *Parochial and Plain Sermons*, 136–37.

96. Newman, *Meditations*, 105.

97. Brody, *Ethics*, 14.

98. Cited by Cobbe, *Life*, vol. 2, 171–72.

99. Cited in *Zoophilist*, February 1, 1892, 231a. The quotation appears after Manning's death in 1892 as part of a commemorative summary of his participation in the anti-vivisection group, the Victorian Street Society, of which Manning was vice president. See *Zoophilist*, February 1, 1892, 230–31. For a brief discussion of Manning's involvement in the anti-vivisection movement, see McClelland, *Cardinal Manning*, 209.

100. Cobbe, *Life*, vol. 2, 173.

101. *Tablet*, July 28, 1906, 134.

102. *Tablet*, September 6, 1919, 297.

103. Ruland, *Foundation*, v.

104. Bonaventure, *Journey* [1.15], 10.

105. Hopkins: *A Selection*, 114.

106. Preece, *Brute Souls*, 164.

107. Harris, *Raised Immortal*, 203. See also Green, *Body*; and Murphy, *Bodies and Souls*.

108. Wright, *Surprised*, 155.

109. Wright, 28.

110. Daley, "Hope," loc. 1780–93 of 4757, Kindle.

111. Daley, loc. 1875–81 of 4757, Kindle.

112. Daley, loc. 1941–42 of 4757, Kindle.

113. Daley, loc. 1951 of 4757, Kindle.

114. Daley, loc. 1968 of 4757, Kindle.

115. International Theological Commission, "Current Questions in Eschatology," no. 2.1.

116. International Theological Commission, no. 2.2.

117. International Theological Commission, no. 2.2. N. T. Wright also argues that the idea of an "intermediate state, in fact, is more or less a constant feature of resurrection belief both Jewish and Christian." Wright, *Surprised*, 162.

118. Congregation for the Doctrine of the Faith, "Letter," no. 3.

119. Congregation for the Doctrine of the Faith, no. 3.

120. International Theological Commission, "Current Questions in Eschatology," no. 4.3. This approach to understanding the soul—seen more as a symbol of the enduring reality of human personhood than a substance—finds support among contemporary theologians. See, e.g., Godzieba, "Bodies," 220–23. Similarly, Anderson defines the soul "as that which represents the whole person as a physical, personal, and spiritual being, especially the inner core of an individual's life as created and upheld by God." Anderson, "On Being Human," 193.

121. International Theological Commission, "Current Questions in Eschatology," no. 5.4. Cf., *ST* Supplement-III.75.1 *ad*. 2.

122. For example, though the International Theological Commission notes the argument that has been raised against "the natural immortality of [human] souls," it does not defend the soul's immortality as an innate quality. Rather, it simply argues that there *is* some reality that endures between bodily death and resurrection and that this reality can be properly indicated by use of the traditional language of "soul." International Theological Commission, "Current Questions in Eschatology," no. 4.3.

123. Congregation for the Doctrine of the Faith, "Letter," no. 7.

124. Pope John Paul II, *Redemptor Hominis*, no. 20. Also: "Every life and every living movement proceed from this Life which transcends all life and every principle of life. It is to this that souls owe their incorruptibility." Pope John Paul II, *Evangelium Vitae*, no. 84. I also note that Levering's book, which defends a Thomistic account of the spiritual soul, does not, as far as I can tell, try to defend Aquinas's idea of the soul's innate immortality. Levering, *Jesus*.

125. See *Catechism of the Catholic Church*, nos. 362–68, for a discussion of soul/body unity.

126. John Berkman argues that even if we do appeal to rationality as a basis for who or what can be resurrected, there is good reason to believe that some animals, judged by criteria appropriate to them, display forms of reasoning that meet Thomas's understanding of the rational creature. Berkman, "Towards a Thomistic Theology."

127. Carere and Maestripieri, *Animal Personalities*.

128. International Theological Commission, "Current Questions in Eschatology," no. 5.1.

129. Benedict XVI, "Homily: Baptism of the Lord." I am not convinced that Benedict's statement here is meant to address the question of animal resurrection. The primary focus of the passage seems to be a contrast between humans, who face

condemnation due to their sin, and animals, which do not. The contrast is not between the eternal destiny of humans and the lack thereof for animals but between the moral judgment that humans face and the absence of such judgment for animals.

130. The address is provided on the Vatican website in Italian and Spanish. Pope John Paul II, "General Audience (January 10, 1990)."

131. Catholic Church, *Catechism*, no. 362, citing Gn 2:7.

132. The *New York Times* reference is to Gladstone, "Dogs." The article, which was written in the wake of a widely misinterpreted statement by Pope Francis, states that "Pope John Paul II appeared to reverse Pius in 1990 when he proclaimed that animals do have souls and are 'as near to God as men are.' But the Vatican did not widely publicize his assertion, perhaps because it so directly contradicted Pius, who was the first to declare the doctrine of papal infallibility in 1854." And see People for the Ethical Treatment of Animals, "John Paul II." The Catholic television network EWTN assumed the animal-affirming quotations to be accurate and proceeded to address them; see EWTN, "JPII Said Animals Do Have Souls." The source of these mistaken claims about John Paul II's address seems to be an interview with the Italian priest Monsignor Canciani. It includes numerous quotations from both John Paul II and the monsignor without adequately identifying each quotation's original source, so these quotations (e.g., animals are "as near to God as men are") were likely from the monsignor but were later misattributed to John Paul II. See Pacifici, "Pope Has Said: 'Animals Too Have Souls.'"

133. I discuss this document in chapter 4.

134. *ST* I-II.94.2.

135. *ST* I-II.76.4.

136. Fingarette, *Self-Deception*, 140, cited by Burrell and Hauerwas, "Self-Deception," 104.

137. Butler, *Whole Works*, xviii.

138. Butler, *Fifteen Sermons* [sermon X], 248.

139. Butler, 243.

140. The social psychologists Mahzarin Banaji and Anthony Greenwald offer a fascinating and comprehensive exploration of the biases operating in otherwise good people; Banaji and Greenwald, *Blindspot*. A study by Dan Ariely suggests that our inability to rationally perceive our actions is hardwired into our brains; Ariely, *Predictably Irrational*. Another recent study suggests that the brain has psychological defenses to protect a person's sense of self that are analogous to our body's defense system. Kaplan, Gimbel, and Harris, "Neural Correlates."

141. Burrell and Hauerwas, "Self-Deception," 114.

142. Calhoun, *Speeches*, 630.

143. Noonan, *Church*, 115.

144. Maxwell, *Slavery*, 117. Maxwell cites *Letter Catholicae Ecclesiae*, November 20, 1890; *Leonis Papae Allocutiones*, 1898, IV, 112.

145. Noonan, *Church*, 114.

146. This is from a private conversation with Father Stephen Duffy of Loyola University New Orleans.

147. Cited by Accattoli, *When a Pope Asks*, 244.

148. Cited by McClelland, *Cardinal Manning*, 20–21.

149. Thomas, *Man*, 20.

150. Cited by Thomas, 20–21.

151. Wollaston, *Religion*, 58.

152. Vaughan, "Ethics," 167.

153. Cited by Thomas, *Man*, 22.

154. Descartes, *Philosophical Writings*, 366, cited by Clough, *On Animals: Volume One*, 139.

155. Tröhler and Maehle, "Animal Experimentation," 26–27.

156. Poisson, *Commentaire*, 157, translated and cited by Strickland, "God's Creatures?" 293. Strickland's essay provides a great overview of the debate between Cartesians and their critics.

157. Strickland, "God's Creatures?" 294.

158. Rosenfield, *From Beast-Machine*, 52.

159. Vaughan, "Ethics," 168.

160. Strickland, "God's Creatures?" 294.

161. Strickland, 295.

162. Bougeant, *Philosophical Amusement*. His proposal is made in the context of recounting a dinner conversation; hence, my suggestion that it might not have been made seriously.

163. Strickland, "God's Creatures?" 295.

164. Smith, *Teaching*, 1116.

165. Gaffney, "Can Catholic Morality Make Room?" 102.

166. Thomas, *Man*, 24.

167. Gaffney, "Can Catholic Morality Make Room?" 102–3.

168. Aquinas, *Commentary on Romans*, 221.

169. Aquinas, 221.

170. Aquinas, 223.

171. "Therefore *it will be impossible for anything to be the subject of that renewal, unless it be a subject of incorruption.* Now such are the heavenly bodies, the elements, and man. For the heavenly bodies are by their very nature incorruptible both as to their whole and as to their part: the elements are corruptible as to their parts but incorruptible as a whole: while men are corruptible both in whole and in part, but this is on the part of their matter not on the part of their form." *ST* Supplement-III.91.5; emphasis added.

172. Boylan, *St. Paul's Epistle*, 144.

173. We find examples of such constricting interpretations, where the stress is not on the liberation of present creatures but on the advent of a new creation, in the works by the French Reformed theologian Frédéric Godet (d. 1900), *Commentary on St. Paul's Epistle*, 92; by the Lutheran theologian Friedrich Adolph Philippi (d. 1882), *Commentary on St. Paul's Epistle*, 10–11; and by the American Presbyterian theologian William S. Plumer (d. 1880), *Commentary*, 408–10.

174. Fitzmyer, "Letter" [nos. 86–87], 854a.

175. John Paul II, *Evangelium Vitae*, no. 42.

176. This statistic and others related to it can be found on the website of the American Pet Products Association, www.americanpetproducts.org/press_industrytrends .asp.

177. Herzog, *Some We Love*, 75.

178. Herzog, 167.

179. Herzog, 168.

180. Herzog, 149–72.

181. Herzog, 160–65.

182. Herzog, 170.

183. Eisnitz, *Slaughterhouse*, 88.

184. Eisnitz, 87.

185. Eisnitz, 93.

186. Fitzgerald, Kalof, and Dietz, "Slaughterhouses," 158.

187. Fitzgerald, Kalof, and Dietz, 175.

188. Joy, *Why We Love Dogs*, 40.

189. Adams, "a very rare and difficult thing," 594.

190. Timm, "Moral Intuition," 226.

191. See Davy, "An Other Face."

192. McDaniel, "Practicing the Presence," 133.

193. Murdoch, *Metaphysics*, 400.

194. Farley, "Moral Discourse," 79.

195. Rahner, "Historicity," 78.

196. The Spirit "remains free to throw new light" on Christ's "fullness." Balthasar, *Theo-Logic*, vol. 3, 199.

197. Ruland, *Foundation*, 360.

198. "The Pope on Kindness to Animals," *Sacred Heart Review*, July 24, 1915, 87. Published between 1888 and 1918, the *Sacred Heart Review* was a weekly Catholic newspaper that focused on news items related to the Catholic Church in general and the Church in New England in particular. The article is available at https://newspapers .bc.edu/?a=cl&cl=CL1&sp=BOSTONSH.

199. Bekoff, *Why Dogs Hump*, 44.

CHAPTER 2

CREATION

The *Imago Dei* and a Covenantal Anthropocentrism

Does an evolutionary perspective bring any light to bear upon . . .
the meaning of the human person as the *imago Dei*?

—Pope John Paul II

THE MORAL claims that animals make on the Christian gain their meaning and traction within the Christian narrative; only there do we begin to see animals as God sees them. An animal ethics requires an animal theology. In addition to questions about historical Catholic attitudes toward animals examined in chapter 1, pressures to revise the traditional theology of animal life have been fueled by developments in two areas: the emerging insights of contemporary science (arising principally out of evolutionary theory and animal studies); and theological shifts in established interpretations of Genesis. On the latter, theological front, several themes—which are centrally important for Christian anthropology and, often by way of contrast, its views of animal life—have come under critical scrutiny: the notion of the fall, the assertion that humanity has been made in the image of God, and the belief that God has given humanity dominion over all nonhuman life. In this chapter, we consider the first two of these theological issues (some aspects of which intersect developments in scientific understanding) before turning to the challenges raised by contemporary animal studies. The third issue, the debate about humanity's dominion, is touched on below, but I postpone a more complete exploration of it until chapter 5, wherein I examine the ethical implications of our theory.

① THE FALL

In light of what we now know about the evolutionary development of life on earth, we must discard the idea that the suffering and hardships of our world are the result of a historical fall that disfigured a once-paradisiacal creation. Acknowledging this fact, however, I believe we can still defend the notion of an ahistorical or transhistorical fall. One reason for preserving some notion of the fall is that it underscores that this world as animals experience it is not what God had originally desired for them. Something is fundamentally warped about our world. The disfigurement caused by sin has affected all creation, and, we can hope, God's lavish labor to redeem will be similarly universal. *disfiguration = affected all creation*

We are more aware than ever of the degree to which our natural world fails to reflect the biblical ideal of the peaceable kingdom. The often-purposeless suffering endured by creaturely life across an extensive evolutionary history becomes even more disturbing when coupled with another brutal fact. We now recognize that animals are often cognitively sophisticated, and with this knowledge, we can rightly suspect that their capacity to experience the full depths of physical and emotional suffering approaches our own.[1] The intensity of animal suffering requires that we expand the theodicy question to include nonhuman creatures. The claim by Pierre Teilhard de Chardin that creaturely suffering, understood as an essential part of the evolutionary process, "ceases to be an incomprehensible element in the structure of the world and becomes a *natural feature*" may be true from a scientific perspective, but it is not theologically adequate as an explanation for why a gracious God would create a world with such features (emphasis in the original).[2]

The challenge that evolution poses to theological accounts of the violence and suffering of the natural world is that it would seem to exclude the explanation offered by the idea of a *cosmic* fall—that is, a fall in which *all* creation, not just humanity, is corrupted due to human sin.[3] Because natural violence existed long before the appearance of moral beings, we can no longer appeal to sin as a way of making sense of animal suffering. In contrast to a *cosmic* fall, the notion of a merely *human* fall is easier to adapt to an evolutionary worldview. One could argue, for example, that at some point early in human evolutionary history, sin entered into the social and cultural dynamics of human life and thus poisoned these dynamics in a way that affected all subsequent human history.[4] The idea of a *cosmic* fall, however, one that affects human *and* nonhuman life and is to blame for the

cosmic fall v. human fall

suffering of both, is more difficult to defend. The main argument against it is the simple fact that there is no correlation between the suffering of nonhuman creation and the appearance of human sin. The violent exchange of predation and prey can be traced back more than 2 billion years, long before creatures developed any significant cognitive capacities—long before, that is, there could be anything like sin. Rightly rejecting the idea of a historical fall, many scholars, especially those influenced by process theology,[5] view evolution as the means chosen by God to create, and appeal to it as an explanation for natural evils like animal suffering and death.[6] The presence of natural evils, which had been previously explained by human sin and the corruption it caused to the harmony of creation, are now attributed to God's decision to create a universe such as ours.[7]

We can tease out three arguments that regularly appear in these evolutionary theodicies: (1) The goods of the natural world are unavoidably tied to its evils; (2) the universe as we experience it is incomplete and developing toward something greater; and (3) it is appropriate, and even necessary, that a universe giving rise to human freedom should itself develop through its own autonomous processes.

Taking each of these in turn, first, and most important, the goods and evils of our world are unavoidably tied together. Holmes Rolston notes that what we perceive as natural evils are often the instruments that "systematically drive" the creation of new "value achievements." A world "with only herbivores and no omnivores or carnivores would be impoverished."[8] Evolution is "value-*enhancing*," says Lisa Sideris (emphasis in the original).[9] The natural evil of death, Arthur Peacocke maintains, is essential to evolution's "creativity . . . [and] its ability to produce the new."[10] "The statistical logic is inescapable," he concludes, that "*new forms of matter arise only through the dissolution of the old; new life only through the death of the old*" (emphasis in the original).[11] Christopher Southgate agrees, advocating what he calls the "only way" argument: If God desired a world of goodness and beauty such as ours, then struggles and suffering must inevitably be part of the mix.[12] The diverse forms of goodness and beauty in our world, therefore, must be seen as a "package" that is "interlocked" with the realities of violence, suffering, and death.[13] "Life arises in passionate endurance. Struggle is the dark side of creation."[14]

Second, creation is oriented toward something greater and more wonderful; in the natural unfolding of the universe, we can look forward with hope to ever greater possibilities yet to be achieved. This is not proposed as an evolutionary utopianism but rather is intended to highlight the incompleteness of our world and thus provide an explanation for its present imperfections. As many have noted, a version of this view appeared in the writings of Irenaeus of Lyon (d. 202). He argued that God created humanity in an immature form and ordered creation so that "at some future time," the human person might be "brought to maturity" and "attain perfection."[15] However, what was for Irenaeus a human-centered growth to maturity is now, in light of evolution, identified with a *cosmic* development. We live within a creation still dramatically unfolding. God's creation then should be judged not according to what it is now but what it will be. The suffering that surrounds us "is part of an unfinished universe, . . . [one that] is not yet fully intelligible or real."[16] In answer to the question of why God would "create a universe without finishing the job immediately, hence eliminating the prospect of suffering and death from the outset," John Haught speculates that "an instantaneously complete original creation would leave the world [without] a real future." It would be a world "less significant and certainly less interesting than the one we have."[17]

Finally, many evolutionary theodicies appeal to a "free process" defense, praising as good and valuable the fact that creation has been allowed to develop autonomously, uncontrolled by a dictatorial Godhead. God preserves creation's autonomy by allowing it to develop through its own evolutionary laws and principles. Through the work of the Spirit, God has brought into being "a universe endowed with the innate capacity to evolve by the operation of its own natural powers, making it a free partner in its own creation."[18] "Creation is an act of kenotic love; in creating, God limits self and allows a cosmos to emerge with its own autonomy."[19] Sometimes these arguments imply an additional claim: that the autonomy of humanity, its freedom, suggests or even requires that creation itself be, collectively, autonomous: "God accords cosmic processes the same value and reverence that God accords to human choices."[20] In God's kenotic act of creating, God "makes room for human freedom and autonomy to emerge and for a natural order to be characterized by open-endedness and flexibility."[21] God's faithfulness to creation requires that God not only allow human freedom but also, John Polkinghorne suggests, that God give "the divine gift of freedom to *all* of the creation, not just to human kind alone" (emphasis in the original).[22]

Because God allows creation its autonomy, God must also allow the possibility that it go astray and become marked by strife and struggle. This is the argument that Ryan Patrick McLaughlin advances with his notion of a "cosmic wandering." He argues that God cannot absolutely prevent the possibility of natural evil because of the "distance" between creation and God that follows upon God's decision to "consecrate" creation, that is, "to sanctify it, to make it holy, to set it apart."[23] "Empowering creation to be itself by divine withdrawal opens the possibility that creation's being and becoming itself will not cohere to the divine desire for creation."[24] To use McLaughlin's term, creation "wanders" away from God's original plan, a development that McLaughlin interprets as its fall.

There are, however, weaknesses in these arguments. First, I am not convinced that a tragic and pain-filled evolutionary process is the only way that God could have created a world such as ours, one blessed with dramatic possibilities and abundant forms of goodness. Claiming to know the limits of divine omnipotence seems excessively speculative given the complexities and counterfactual possibilities it involves (e.g., the idea that we can imagine all the possible alternatives by which God could create).[25] It is a different case for the traditional "free will" theodicy. The argument there is fairly straightforward with two clearly defined factors: true freedom and the possibility of evil, each requiring the other. The prospect of God creating a world with only one of these factors is a logical impossibility. That is, freedom without the possibility of freely chosen evil would paradoxically require that God both "give a creature free-will and at the same time withhold free-will from it."[26] The question of whether or how suffering must be allowed in order to create a diversely beautiful and good world is not as simple and is thus more impervious to our speculative attempts.[27]

Second, the tendency to align evolution's future endpoint with the fullness of the eschaton threatens to obscure both the innate goodness of life forms existing before that endpoint and the horror of their tragic suffering in evolutionary history. This stands in tension with the first creation account, where each form of life is valued and treasured by God for its own intrinsic goodness. Teilhard is particularly vulnerable on this count. His work remains valuable and fittingly esteemed for showing how an evolutionary worldview can be integrated within the Christian theological tradition. But it has also been rightly criticized for an anthropocentric focus that overlooks "the ambiguity of evolution itself" and pays "no attention to evolution's victims." "Evolution," Jürgen Moltmann writes, "is a kind of biological execution of the Last Judgment on the weak, the sick and 'the unfit.'"[28]

Third and finally, the appeal to creation's autonomy as a defense of its goodness becomes overextended at times. Specifically, the lauding of creation's autonomy is sometimes loosely and misleadingly associated with a questionable claim: that God has endowed the process of evolutionary development with a type of personal agency that makes this world more valuable, and thus more defensible as good, than a non-agential creation whose development is directly governed by God. When Elizabeth Johnson says that "it is as if at the Big Bang the Spirit gave the natural world a push saying, 'Go, have an adventure, see what you can become,'"[29] she anthropomorphizes inanimate creation. Johnson's statement is intentionally metaphorical, but the argument that these discussions seek to advance—that is, that granting the world's evolutionary development its own "agency" is a praiseworthy act by God, similar to that of allowing human freedom[30]—rests, I believe, on two dubious suppositions: that creation's collective agency is real and that the goodness of that agency helps redeem creation of the evolutionary suffering that its autonomy entails.

These authors are right to affirm that God has given the world a relative autonomy, one that can, rightly, be considered a relative good. As *Laudato Si'* states, "The mystery of Christ is at work in a hidden manner in the natural world as a whole, without thereby impinging on its autonomy."[31] My concern is primarily with a metaphorical overreach in the argument. The distinctive goodness that characterizes the freedom and agency of individual creatures is made to imbue creation as a whole, and, as such, it ostensibly helps redeem those developmental processes that are common to that whole—that is, the costly and tragic evolutionary dynamics of the present order. However, it is doubtful to me that the goodness of creation's autonomy is of the same order of goodness as that found in the remarkable gifts of freedom and agency shared by human and nonhuman creatures. If so, our theodicies should keep distinct the value we attribute to the two forms of autonomy—that of the world's evolutionary processes and that of creaturely agency—and not elide them into the same package of autonomous goodness gifted by God.[32]

In addition to these three weaknesses, a deeper problem with some theological appropriations of evolution is the inadequate separation made between God's economic labor and the evolutionary process. My concern here echoes that of Celia Deane-Drummond, who criticizes views in which "redemption seems to be reduced to what happens to creation, expressed entirely in evolutionary terms."[33] The source of the problem is the excessive heuristic weight given to evolutionary dynamics in theological reflections. Because evolution directly challenges aspects of the traditional understanding of creation and redemption, some theological realignment is necessary. In negotiating this new terrain, some theological beliefs must be summarily dismissed (e.g., the idea of a historical fall). However, other theological trajectories, even if suggested by an evolutionary worldview, are not conceptually or theologically required by it (e.g., the idea that the cosmos is evolving toward a collective spiritual perfection). I believe some ecotheologians allow evolutionary dynamics to govern trajectories in theological thinking and too quickly embrace this second set of possibilities (i.e., theological approaches that align with evolutionary theory but are not strictly required by it). Insufficiently cautious in this regard is Ilia Delio's suggestion that the "risen Christ is the inner power of this evolutionary universe"[34] and Haught's explanation that "what is *really* going on in evolution is that the whole of creation . . . is being transformed into the bodily abode of God" (emphasis in the original).[35]

Hopes for an evolution-driven eschaton are untenable. First, evolution is not capable of answering our redemptive needs. We "long for" a future that is more discontinuous and drastically different than that which can ever be achieved through evolutionary change. The "data" do not justify any "buoyant optimism" for an evolutionary deliverance.[36] Instead, we need a savior who can radically transform our evolutionary context: A "*Christus evolutor* without a *Christus redemptor* is nothing other than a cruel, unfeeling *Christus selector*, a historical world judge without compassion for the weak, and a breeder of life uninterested in the victims."[37]

Second, humanity's technical prowess will likely displace evolution as the engine of the world's transformation, for better or worse.[38] If humans do not cause their own destruction, they will be able soon—by cosmic standards—to control the adaptation and changes of all life far more quickly, intentionally, and efficiently than evolution.[39] Even now we are approaching the point of being able to radically engineer new animal life forms to fit our needs and desires.[40] I do not believe that human technology is any more the answer to our eschatological hopes than evolution. My point is only that of the two, human technology is much more likely to be the agent of significant biological change in the not-too-distant future.

Addressing the challenges posed by evolutionary theory is imperative for Christian theology, and the contributions by scholars like those mentioned above have been critical for advancing this engagement. But I believe we can and should retain a notion of a cosmic fall even in light of evolution, in part because of the explanatory importance it has had in Christian theologies of creation and redemption and because of its prominent place in liturgical prayer. The genuine insights provided by a theological appropriation of evolutionary theory can be supplemented by a revised notion of a cosmic fall. Such a supplement is important as part of a comprehensive defense of divine goodness. Andrew Linzey is right to caution that if we "reject the fallenness of creation," it will be difficult to avoid seeing the natural world—with all its strife, violence, disease, and suffering—as something God intended. There would be, he believes, no such thing as natural evil,[41] and the Creator of such a world would appear "morally capricious."[42]

Linzey does not attempt to provide a specific, conceptual solution but instead challenges theologians to recognize the need for a "complex" imagination in reflecting on the core mysteries of Christianity. Great art and literature have been valuable genres for Christian belief because they are best able to convey the multifaceted intuitions and non-systematizable truths that are at Christianity's heart. Confronting the contradiction between a good Creator and a suffering world requires a similarly expansive imagination. Linzey appeals to Rachel Trickett's work to advance the idea of a "complex truth." Applied to our discussion, such a truth requires us to recognize the Christian view "that God as the Creator of all things must have created a world which is morally good," in tandem with "the insight that parasitism and predation are unlovely, cruel, evil aspects of the world ultimately incapable of being reconciled with a God of love."[43]

Linzey is not alone in defending the idea of a cosmic fall.[44] David Clough also appeals to an imaginative reconsideration of the fall, but he approaches it Christologically. We know sin only in the encounter with God, and thus we "should avoid an account of the fall that is detached from the work of Christ." The world's "estrangement" is illuminated by God's grace "backwards and forwards through time," allowing us "to see how humans and other creatures have departed from God's ways and become trapped in patterns of sin."[45] Predator–prey relationships, for example, reflect this sinful pattern and "are not part of God's original creative purpose."[46] Clough's explanation functions better on an epistemological level (how we come to know that the world is fallen) than an ontological one (what is the cause of the world's fallenness). His answer to the latter seems to be tied to the belief that animals share in a capacity for sinfulness, and thus their disobedient acts, like those of humanity, contribute to the fall and its consequences.[47]

Even if we are willing to stretch the meaning of sin to include some acts by animals, I do not believe the idea of animal sin provides much service to us in addressing the mystery of creation's fallenness. An alternative approach is to imagine an ahistorical fall, in line with the account given first by Gregory of Nyssa (d. 394) and later adopted by Maximus the Confessor (d. 662) and John Scotus Erigena (d. 877).[48] God, Gregory writes, "looking upon the nature of man in its entirety and fullness by the exercise of His foreknowledge, . . . saw beforehand by His all-seeing power" the eventuality of human sin. In anticipation of this fall, God created the sexual drive and the differentiation of the sexes so as to ensure procreation by animalistic, instinctual drives, because rational motivation would not be sufficient.[49] Thus, God created expressly with foreknowledge of human sin and fashioned the world in anticipation of that reality.[50]

Taking a cue from the approach of these early Christian theologians, we can speculate that out of all the possible worlds that God could have brought into existence, God created ours with foreknowledge of any number of factors, one of which is the appearance of human sin. The rightness of this present world—the reason why God created this one and not another—is not due to any one consideration but a number of them: human autonomy, sin, God's desire to establish an arena for creaturely growth and creativity, the drama of creature-divine encounters, the opportunity for God to display the radicalness of divine love in creaturely form, and the like. Similarly, the world's apparent flaws and imperfections cannot be explained by any one factor but by a constellation of many.

I am suggesting, then, an approach that allows for the convergence of multiple influences in understanding the mystery of creation's entanglement in evil. This approach builds not only on Linzey's notion of a complex imagination but also on Hans Urs von Balthasar's idea of "aesthetic fittingness." Reflecting on the redemptive work of Christ, Balthasar suggests that it was not necessary that any one aspect of his work occur in the way that it did (e.g., the world that God chose to create, the covenantal relationship with Israel, Christ's birth at a particular time, and the manner of his life and death). However, we can appreciate how these same elements might be fitting, even necessary, once we consider them as part of the organic whole of salvation history.

Balthasar appeals to Mozart's *Magic Flute* as an analogy. The brilliance of the opera does not require that any one element be included. Mozart could have chosen to insert "new arias or delete existing ones . . . without thereby endangering the harmony of his work."[51] With regard to why God created this world with its suffering and loss and not another, we can suggest that no single one of the factors noted above was necessary for God to create in the manner God did. However, as we look at creation in light of these factors and other considerations—for example, God's foreknowledge of sin, God's creating through evolution, the good and beautiful diversity of creation, the suffering of nonhuman creation, the connection between sin and creation's woundedness, the glory of divine love appearing in creaturely garment, the graced invitation to the free human person to participate in the divine self-giving, and the eschatological transformation accomplished through divine intervention—we can perhaps more readily affirm that the complex story of creation and redemption with its transhistorical, cosmic fall is marked by a fittingness and rightness.

We might retain the notion of a cosmic fall, then, by understanding it as a transhistorical disfigurement that God allowed the world to undergo in light of human sin (among other factors). I offer this admittedly very speculative suggestion to avoid aligning God's creative intent and redemptive labor too closely with the evolutionary process. Preserving the notion of a cosmic fall serves another aspect of my argument: It highlights the fundamental solidarity of all creatures in bearing the consequences of human corruption. This solidarity provides an additional reason for believing, as I will argue in chapter 3, that all creatures will share in God's redemption of humanity, just as they have shared in the travails caused by its sin. The idea of a cosmic fall, of course, does not fully explain the "why" of creaturely suffering, human or nonhuman, or make sense of the world's wounded fallenness. Our theoretical musings only indicate, without explaining, what Pope John Paul II calls "that sin which in its original form is obscurely inscribed in the mystery of creation."[52]

THE *IMAGO DEI*

The teaching that the human person is made in the image of God, the *imago Dei*, has been and continues to be fundamental for a Catholic understanding of the human person. It has provided a clear rationale for the inviolable sacred dignity that Catholic thought attributes to every human person, irrespective of any conceivable measure (e.g., health, capabilities, moral character, and stage of life). The basis of the teaching is found in Genesis 1:26a: "Then God said: Let us make human beings in our image, after our likeness." Though the teaching is found almost nowhere else in Scripture (the exceptions being Gn 5:1–3; Gn 9:5–6; and, perhaps, Ps 8:6 ["you have made him little less than a god"]), it would be hard to overstate its impact on Christian theology. Scholars continue to engage it as a mandatory, scriptural touchstone for Christian anthropology. As Claus Westermann notes in his commentary on Genesis, "Scarcely any passage in the whole of the Old Testament has retained such interest as the verse which says that God created the person according to his image. The literature is limitless."[53]

The debate over what exactly it is about humanity that constitutes it as the *imago Dei* has gained no clear resolution, though scholarly thinking on the topic has shifted away from some views and toward others. Until recently, the Catholic answer centered on what was perceived to be the unique intellectual capacity of the human person.[54] Such "immaterial" approaches—that is, ones emphasizing nonmaterial qualities like "intellectual ability, self-determination, moral-consciousness"—dominated both Catholic and Protestant thought through the middle of the nineteenth century.[55] Contemporary scholars have moved away from appeals to these ostensibly uniquely human capabilities to other interpretations, two of which regularly appear in Catholic thought: the relational and the functional approaches. The relational approach understands the *imago Dei* as signifying the fact that the human person has been invited into a distinctive relationship with God that is not shared by any other creature. Biblical scholars find support for this interpretation in Genesis 5:1–3, where the editor creates a verbal parallel between God's creation of Adam "in the likeness of God" and Adam's fathering of Seth "in his likeness, after his image." Through this parallel, the passage "suggests that man as the image of God means that man has a relationship with God that is in some sense like the relationship that a son enjoys with his father."[56] The relational approach has gained considerable attention within Christian thought, in part due to the influence of the Reformed theologian Karl Barth and his argument that the human person is the image of God because he or she stands before God as a "thou."[57]

Those supporting the functional interpretation—that humanity's status as the *imago Dei* reflects the fact that it has been given a particular function to perform—build on an alternative interpretation of the Hebrew text. The human person is not "created *in* the image of God but rather *as* the image of God" (emphasis in the original).[58] As such, the person is expected to function as God's representative (or steward), advancing the goals and desires of God within the created order. Support for this view is found in the fact that it is consistent with the royal ideology of Near Eastern cultures of the time, which viewed the king as the local deity's representative or vice regent.[59] After cautioning that the "lack of unanimity among Old Testament scholars regarding the meaning of the biblical concept of the *imago Dei* set forth in Genesis 1:26–28 suggests that the divine image ought not to be viewed from too narrow a perspective," Stanley Grenz goes on, nonetheless, to propose that "the representational [i.e., functional] motif is likely to have formed the heart of the concept."[60]

The 2002 document on the *imago Dei* by the Vatican's International Theological Commission, approved by then–head of the Congregation for the Doctrine of the Faith, Joseph Cardinal Ratzinger, stakes out a position incorporating both of these interpretations, stating that "communion and stewardship are the two great strands out of which the fabric of the doctrine of the *imago Dei* is woven."[61] In discussing the first strand, the document underscores that relationality is part of the nature of the human person: "Created in the image of God, human beings are by nature . . . made for one another, persons oriented towards communion with God and with one another." The capacity for relating to the other is a natural endowment of the human person, not an additional gift bestowed through grace. The document breaks down this relational capacity in terms of three features that distinguish the human person from "other bodily beings": "intellect, love, and freedom."[62] In the document's examination of the stewardship strand, it states that human persons "participate in [God's] work" and "in the divine governance of creation." Such governance must conform to God's "project of love and salvation."[63]

In addition to these two themes, the document references a facet of the *imago Dei* that has played a foundational role in Catholic ethics: The *imago Dei* "is the basis of human dignity and of the inalienable rights of the human person."[64] Being created in the image of God bestows upon each human person, unique among all of God's creatures, an inviolable moral claim, and in turn a responsibility to respect the moral claims of others.

Variations of the first two themes—communion and stewardship—well serve the approach I develop in this book with regard to animal redemption. I argue in chapter 3 that the world reflects the triune life and thus the capacity to relate and be in communion is pervasive among the world's creatures. Then, in chapter 4, I argue that the responsibility of the human person to participate in God's plan for creation, to act as "stewards," includes not only the care and cultivation of creation but also a coparticipation with the Spirit in creation's redemption. I recognize that the language of "stewardship" has been criticized for a number of reasons, and thus address these concerns in chapter 5 in the context of my discussion of ethics. I note here, however, that the type of stewardship I defend is primarily ecclesial: The community of Christ has been given a distinctive task to labor for the kingdom and for the redemptive liberation of all creation. Christians are called to be "stewards [*oikonomos*] of the mysteries" (1 Cor 4:1).

The third theme—the unique dignity of each person—merits scrutiny for two reasons. First, as noted above, it is used to defend an absolute distinction between the type of loving concern that God has for the individual person and that which God has for all other creatures. The second reason refers to the distinction between humans, who are uniquely dignified by being made in the image of God, and other creatures, who bear only the divine *trace*, to use Aquinas's term.[65] This distinction has been interpreted, as we saw in chapter 1, to *exclude* any serious obligations to animals beyond those related to personal virtue and human well-being, our own and that of future generations. It is no surprise, then, that environmentalists see in Christian practice and its intellectual legacy a relentless anthropocentrism that, if not the cause of our present environmental crisis, at least contributed to the attitudes that gave rise to it, a view that gained widespread credence with Lynn White's infamous critique of Christian influence in the instrumentalization of nature.[66] We will return to these issues later in the chapter, where I make a case for softening, though not eliminating, the theological boundary erected between humanity and all other creatures. However, for this account to be adequate, we first need to explore what scientific basis there might be for such a boundary. The surprising findings of contemporary studies of animals and of our shared evolutionary history with them make it difficult to sustain the absoluteness of the distinction between humans and all other creatures that many believe to be signaled by the designation of humanity as the *imago Dei*.

CONTEMPORARY SCIENCE AND ANIMALS

The official Catholic teaching that there is a clear, ontological distinction between humans and all other creatures is being challenged by evolutionary science and animals studies. The abilities often associated with human distinctiveness appear in the animal world in ways that are often more a matter of degrees of difference than the absolute binary that has been traditionally assumed between the human and the "brute." I have chosen in this book to focus on "animals" (understood as any biological life—terrestrial or aquatic—with higher cognitive capacities like memory and subjective awareness), in part because their abilities and cognitive sophistication most challenge that binary. The functional differences between humans and higher animals like the bonobos, though still substantial in my mind, are not enough to sustain the neat ethical and soteriological borders assumed in Catholic thought. The fact that the human/all-else contrast effectively places creatures as diverse as Koko, the linguistically talented gorilla, and fleas on the same level had not until recently provoked any theological disquiet. Reigning assumptions about the lack of any significant differential capacities among God's creatures excluded such considerations; the gap between the human person and the rest of

[handwritten annotations: "→ biodiversity = good for human entertainment and for human use"]

[handwritten annotation: "→ humans above all else ; claim is moderate anthropocentrism"]

creation was of a different qualitative order than any difference existing between the various species of nonhuman life. We now know this to be wrong, at least on a biological level. What had been an easy theological question to answer—Why humans and not other animals?—is now so problematized that serious theological reflection on animals cannot be deferred agnostically to the inscrutable will of God.[67]

Recent decades have seen an explosion of evidence regarding the advanced capabilities of animals, including many associated with the "immaterial" measures that have been used to define human uniqueness—for example, reasoning, language, moral agency, self-awareness, and friendship. In contrast to the scientific assumptions that dominated well into the middle of the twentieth century, which "viewed animals as either stimulus–response machines out to obtain rewards and avoid punishment or as robots genetically endowed with useful instincts," ethologists (scientists studying animal behavior and psychology) have begun to understand that animal behavior is often guided by a cognitively rich and complex internal life. Such discoveries would have once been dismissed by the scientific community as "anthropomorphic, romantic, or unscientific."[68]

It has become fairly common knowledge that some species have surprisingly evolved levels of intelligence and cognate abilities (e.g., foresight, awareness of other minds, and memory of past achievements). For example, orangutans are known escape artists; they are able to stealthily and patiently dismantle their cage across several weeks, "keeping dislodged screws and bolts out of sight" in order to hide their escape plans from their keepers.[69] A number of chimpanzees and orangutans successfully completed an intelligence test that only 58 percent of eight-year-old humans were able to pass.[70] Sometimes, an aspect of animal intelligence is superior not only to young children but even adults; a study showed that young chimpanzees have a better capacity for memorizing a series of numbers than the typical human adult.[71]

We often fail to appreciate animals' abilities because their intelligence is different from ours, developing in ways appropriate to the evolutionary needs of their species. One experiment, for example, studied differences in the problem-solving skills of dogs and apes in uncovering the location of hidden food. Dogs, evolved as companions to humans, were particularly successful in discovering the food when they received subtle communications from humans. These clues did not help the apes, however. Their reasoning, characteristic of a species that evolved as foragers of food, depended more on logical inferences from small environmental changes.[72]

Tool use had been viewed not only as a sign of intelligence but also as an ability that set humanity apart from all other creatures. Again upending traditional views, a number of tool-using animals have been discovered in recent decades, demonstrating the thoughtful ingenuity of our fellow animal creatures. Chimpanzees hunting for honey in Gabon, for example, have developed an elaborate tool kit, made up of five pieces: "a pounder (a heavy stick to break open the hive's entrance), a perforator (a stick to perforate the ground to get to the honey chamber), an enlarger (to enlarge an opening through sideways action), a collector (a stick with a frayed end to dip into honey and slurp it off), and swabs (strips of bark to scoop up honey)." The cascaded complexity of the steps is such that this practice cannot be an accidental discovery. Developing these tools requires that animals have "foresight" and are able to plan in "sequential steps."[73] And tool use is not exclusive to primates. Bottlenose dolphins carefully choose sponges that fit on their noses, which they then wield to gently shift the sand on the ocean floor and flush out hidden fish burrowed below the surface.[74] This tool use is taught by mother dolphins to their female offspring. Even more striking, however, is that like humans who prefer to "associate with others who share in their subculture," tool-using dolphins prefer to be around other tool users, "suggesting that sponge tool use is a cultural behaviour."[75] Chimpanzees, likewise, teach their tool skills to their offspring, enabling them "to refine their tools over generations."[76]

These are only a few examples of the burgeoning discoveries being made with regard to animal cognition and a small glimpse of the shifts underway in our views of animals' abilities. Perhaps more important to note, however, is that the initial reaction within the scientific community to many of these feats was dismissive, showing just how ingrained views of animal limitation have been. Only after the evidence became overwhelming did scientists begin to stop disparaging the conclusions as anthropomorphic projections and concede their startling claims.

Given the growing appreciation of animals' cognitive skills, it is no surprise that attention has increasingly turned to the internal life of animals, raising questions like whether animals are conscious, experience pain as we do, or share with us the capacity for self-awareness.[77] It is a conversation that has been too long delayed. Against all commonsense experience of wounded animals, the idea that animals could genuinely suffer only began to be taken seriously in philosophical circles in the eighteenth century, and only became part of regular scientific study in the last several decades. Until the eighteenth century, many philosophers minimized the presence of animal sentience and downplayed the possibility of serious animal suffering, even though the idea of animal sentience was widely accepted in popular culture.[78] In the late eighteenth century, the utilitarian philosopher Jeremy Bentham raised awareness about the issue with his often-quoted statement, "The question is not, Can they *reason*? nor, Can they *talk*? but, Can they *suffer*?" (emphasis in the original).[79] In part because of the influence of behaviorism, whose analysis shunned consideration of animal internality (e.g., subjectivity, feelings, and consciousness), the focus of animal studies had been on external stimuli and the resulting behavior. Only in the latter part of the twentieth century did scientists begin to engage in serious investigations of animal pathos.

The question of the interior life of animals raises a black hole of methodological and interpretive problems. We cannot do justice to those discussions here; but broadly, studying animal consciousness faces two fundamental obstacles. First, scientists do not understand the nature or exact cause of *human* self-awareness and consciousness. Second, we have no direct experience of the subjectivity of animal life, and because animals cannot communicate their experiences to us, we face boundaries in pursuing indirect investigations.[80] Terminological debates about the meaning of basic terms like sentience, consciousness, and self-awareness make cursory summaries difficult.[81] However, for the sake of our discussion, two general observations suffice. First, consciousness presents itself within the animal world as a complex spectrum, incorporating one or more qualities like a basic capacity to experience painful and pleasurable stimuli, a basic subjective awareness of experience, a non-objectifiable sense of self-presence and of the animal itself as the one having the experience, and a self-awareness in which the animal has the ability to reflect on itself. Second, all animals are at least sentient and are thus capable of experiencing stimuli as negative if not painful. The basis for these claims lies in a combination of observational studies of animal behavior and evolutionary biology. The latter builds on the idea that those parts of our physiology shared with animals likely serve similar purposes and functionality. Thus, a recent statement by an international group of prominent scientists argued that because animals have the same "neuroanatomical, neurochemical, and neurophysiological substrates" that have been shown to be the basis of human consciousness, we can assume that animals are also conscious.[82]

Self-awareness is difficult to ascertain, but scientists have appealed to the "mirror test" to make the case that at least some animals are self-aware. The basis of the test is that animals with self-awareness will react differently to their reflected image compared with those who are not self-aware—examining their bodies in the former case and ignoring the reflection or treating it as another animal in the latter. The test sometimes involves the administration of a mark on the animal's body in a location outside its visual range. Self-aware animals know to use the mirror as a way of looking at the mark. Animals who have passed the test represent species as diverse as Asian elephants, great apes (bonobos, chimpanzees, orangutans, and gorillas), bottlenose dolphins, orca whales, and the Eurasian magpies. The test is not without criticism, especially with regard to its reliance on a visual response. This sets up the potential for false negatives for those species in which other, nonvisual senses dominate, with dogs and their amazing olfactory abilities being a prime example.[83]

One of the more uplifting discoveries made by ethologists—in that it counters the conventional, survival-of-the-fittest view of evolutionary dynamics—is the varied and highly developed sociality found among animals. Though we might be tempted to dismiss heartwarming stories of animal friendships as anthropomorphic projections, ethologists have increasingly recognized that there is some truth to the accounts. In her *Animal Friendships*, Anne Dagg, an ethologist known as the "Jane Goodall of giraffes," uncovers a treasury of complex social interactions that appear in the animal world, both within individual species and between different species. A number of factors encourage the formation of these special bonds, including food, protection, emotional support, child raising, and even the pleasure of enjoying another's company. Dagg considers "two animals to be special friends if they act as if they like each other, even if we do not know why they do so."[84] She excludes cases of reciprocal altruism, where the desire for companionship is likely to be a matter of self-interest, along with species-specific practices that have alternative explanations.[85] Among the examples she explores are female friendships (e.g., chimpanzees, horses, whales), the less common male friendships (e.g., spider monkeys, horses, lions, penguins), and elderly companions (baboons, elephants, buffaloes). The occurrence of unusual cross-species friendships (e.g., a badger and a coyote, a dog and an elephant, a wolf and two goats) suggests, she believes, that "companionship and close bonds" are of "central importance" to many species.[86] Perhaps because of their sociality, some species have developed a finely tuned ability to distinguish among the faces of their fellow creatures, another skill that had once been seen as unique to humans. In one study, sheep were able to learn and retain twenty-five different faces for up to two years. Reminding us once again of our shared evolutionary history, the sheep relied on "the same brain regions and neural circuits as humans" to accomplish this feat.[87]

Famous in their development and complexity are the social networks of elephants. Guided by their matriarch, elephants have fairly clear social roles within the herd. They know how to cooperate in achieving desired ends—for example, acting to assist handicapped members and protecting those who are wounded in assaults. Elephants regularly establish special bonds with other members of their herd, especially females who "can stay friends for sixty years."[88] The species has become a social media sensation as its grieving rituals, not yet fully understood, have come to light. These rituals include spending hours at the location of a deceased relative days after her death.[89] The bonds of affection and the grief that ensues upon the death of a herd-mate are intense for elephant families, akin, it would seem, to that of human families. Carl Safina recounts the story of a researcher who played a recording of a deceased elephant. "The family went wild calling, looking all around. The dead elephant's daughter called for days afterward." Safina dolefully adds, "The researchers never again did such a thing."[90]

Although the Christian tradition has often seen rationality as the distinguishing mark of humanity, a more appropriate candidate is morality, given the centrality of morally informed relationships in the Christian narrative (e.g., the divine–human covenant, love of neighbor, and Christ's call to discipleship). The verdict on this front is mixed. Studies show that animals have something like moral passions and drives (a development that some argue arose to help animals negotiate their social environments). The ethologist Marc Bekoff goes a step further and attributes moral agency to some animals.[91] Bekoff and his coauthor, Jessica Pierce, appeal to numerous ethological studies that show animals exhibiting moral behavior: vampire bats sharing their meal with bats needing food;[92] elephants tending to the sick;[93] and chimpanzees, wolves, and dogs displaying a sense of justice (and frustration when violated).[94]

The question facing such accounts is whether or to what degree these morally expressive actions are the result of a genuine moral choice—that is, one that involves some element of reflection—or are instead the direct products of moral passions and instinctual drives. Bekoff and Pierce make four points to address this issue. First, there is a difference between animal and human morality, but it is a difference in degree and not in kind.[95] Second, we cannot restrict morality to the form it takes in human activity. To do so would be to ignore the distinctive ecosystem needs that shaped each species' version of morality.[96] The question of whether animals are moral must be investigated in terms of species-relative norms. Third, the authors caution against theories of morality that exaggerate human autonomy and freedom.[97] Fourth and finally, given our shared evolutionary physiologies, it is unlikely that the moralities of animals and humans are radically different; those capacities that could be interpreted as uniquely human "are all grounded in a much deeper, broader, and evolutionarily more ancient layer of moral behaviors that we share with animals."[98]

A version of this last argument has found a sympathetic hearing among Catholic ethicists. Animals and humans, it is argued, share an evolution-formed matrix of moral passions and dispositions, and this deeply wired structure plays a greater role in decision-making than is allowed by traditional moral theory, with its emphasis on dispassionate reason. "The kinds of complex reasoning usually associated exclusively with the recently evolved neo-cortex of the higher brain," the Catholic ethicist Stephen Pope argues, do not "just 'ride on top of' the much older and more primitive lower brain associated with the emotions and physical states. Both parts of the brain are intimately involved in processes that involve reasoning and emotional experience."[99] A recent study of individuals with impaired access to emotions provides a confirmation of this dual, reason/emotion operation in human choice. Participants in the study were limited in their ability to make decisions, suggesting that our decisions are not just the end result of rational deliberations but also importantly depend on human emotions.[100]

Nonetheless, Pope is right to argue that our cognitive ability—including our moral imagination and our considerable capacity for deliberations about possible courses of actions—"empowers us for the kinds of agency that are impossible for other animals."[101] It is telling that Bekoff and Pierce acknowledge the distinctiveness of human moral agency, due in part to humanity's "highly developed capacities," such as "self-control, self-assessment, and foresight."[102] A second-order reflexivity can be added to this list. Unlike other animals, "we human animals turn our attention on to our perceptions and desires themselves, on to our own mental activities, and we are conscious *of* them . . . [and] we can think *about* them" (emphasis in the original). We can distance ourselves from our thoughts and moral possibilities and "call them into question," ultimately asking whether they are good or not.[103]

The sample given here of a few of the surprising findings by ethologists challenges the neatly bounded difference between humans and nonhumans assumed in common interpretations of the *imago Dei*. I believe we are still able to affirm a functional distinctiveness of humanity (for example, in its highly developed capacity for reflexive moral agency), but there is less of a disparity between humanity and animals than has often been assumed.

The difficulty of preserving humanity's singular status becomes even more acute once we consider our genetic history. Given the close hominoid relatives of humanity that have been part of our world's evolutionary history (including the Neanderthals, with whom some of our ancestors apparently interbred[104]), the clear, interspecies boundaries that are depicted in Genesis and upon which traditional interpretations of the *imago Dei* depend are hard to sustain.

We can sharpen this challenge even more by considering the case of the generation that directly preceded the bearers of the *imago Dei*. This was the generation that gave birth to those who, according to traditional teaching, were ensouled and offered an eternal destiny with God. The difference between one generation and the next is a genetic hair-splitting. We can further imagine a representative mother from that un-ensouled generation—call her "Lucille," a descendant of Lucy, the famous fossil discovery.[105] Lucille thought, felt, chose, cried, suffered, feared, rejoiced, communicated, and, we can imagine, sinned in ways not too different from her offspring. Lucille, as a highly developed and loving anthropoid mother, would have no doubt rejoiced had she known that her offspring would have a chance for eternal life, even as she mourned missing such an opportunity herself by an evolutionary nanosecond. To appreciate the challenge that evolution poses to human uniqueness, we need not rely on the intellectual sophistication of bonobos, dolphins, or elephants. Nor does its challenge to Christian doctrine depend on whether there were thousands of Lucilles or only a few. We need only suspect that one such entity existed for the Christian to be troubled by the neat boundaries that God (or the Christian tradition) seems to have drawn. It is, of course, likely that there were myriad Lucilles, but it is enough to focus on our one imaginary innocent whom evolution sacrificed so that the first generation of God's children might arise. The genetic complexities of evolutionary history have closed what had been the only rhetorical path available to avoid this disturbing scenario—that is, a functional binary separating all creatures into two cleanly delineated categories: the rational, self-aware human and the brutish, subsentient creature.

In the face of the challenge represented by this evolutionary gradualism, one might appeal to the immortal ensoulment of Lucille's offspring to justify the different eternal destinies of Lucille and her human descendants. This strategy, however, only defers the problem; it is still God making the decision whether to ensoul Lucille. It is a decision that seems capricious and contrary to the lavishness of the divine love revealed in Christ. As Haught rightly protests, the idea that our "common ancestry" with other creatures is irrelevant because our "human souls are what makes us special," is "evasive, artificial, and theologically shallow."[106] To be sure, there are no creatures like Lucille in our present age; but we must, nonetheless, make theological sense of their historical existence and the challenge they represent to our soteriology and ethics.

AN INITIAL THEOLOGICAL AND COVENANTAL FRAMEWORK FOR ANIMALS

In lowering a bit the high wall separating the human and nonhuman, these deliberations lead us to another challenge in developing a theological ethics for animals: The diversity and complexity displayed in the animal world is such that a uniform, one-size-fits-all code for animal care is not possible. As Aquinas recognized, any valid moral analysis is based on a complete and adequate description of the moral object, that is, the action we are discerning. In our case, the moral object—treatment of animal life—is unavoidably muddled, not because we have as yet to gain scientific or theoretical clarity about animals (though that certainly is the case) but rather because the animal world resists the kind of tidy categories upon which a clear theoretical system could be built. Moving beyond the absolute distinction between the human "us" and the animal "them" leads us right into the confounding reality that the "them" of the nonhuman world can hardly be evaluated along some one-dimensional axis, with humans at one end and rocks at the other. The virtually countless forms of nonhuman goodness are too diverse and complex.

The human/all-else ethical binary relies on an untenable clarity about the differential moral status of nonhuman creatures. Ironically, a contrasting ethical approach, directly opposed to the traditional binary of Christian ethics, also relies on a set of overly simplified categories. Ecocentric (or biocentric) approaches reject traditional anthropocentric hierarchies but do so by reducing value judgments about individual creatures, humans and nonhumans, to one set standard: the good of the environmental whole in which they participate.[107] Like the human/all-else binary, this approach fails to adequately appreciate the bewildering complexities of our moral horizon. Instead of relying on deceptively well-ordered theories that either absolutize the human or value it according to an ecological whole, we are required to undertake the more difficult task of discerning, with intellectual nuance and moral nimbleness, the sorts of theological and ethical discriminations that can help us form appropriate responses to our fellow creatures.

Incorporating this complexity does not require that we relativize human life vis-à-vis other life forms. To anticipate the discussion below, I believe that because of the distinctive role given to humanity within the salvific economy, all those bearing the human countenance share in an unquantifiable sacred dignity, not because of functional abilities or a uniquely human ensoulment but because God's covenantal choice, as revealed in Christ, is to redeem creation through the human. I recognize that this appears inconsistent—first rejecting an absolute distinction between humans and animals but then reintroducing a tempered version of it to protect the sacredness of each human life. However, though the argument against absolutizing the division between humans and animals is based in part on the biological gradations revealed by contemporary science, my argument in support of human distinctiveness is grounded in a divine choice about humanity's role in the salvific economy. My hope is that we can raise the estimation we give to the ethical claims made by nonhuman animals without reducing the privileged claim that each human person makes on us regardless of his or her developmental status or capabilities.

To begin developing an adaptive, ethical framework for animals, I return now to the *imago Dei* and the claim of human uniqueness it has been used to support. Because of the influence of the doctrine on our theology of the human person, it is appropriate to ask anew, in light of the discussions above, how the doctrine might also instruct our theology of animals, whether by drawing a contrast between animals and humanity and/or by shedding light on our shared commonality. To address this question in a more explicitly Christian context, I introduce a Christological perspective. As the International Theological Commission's document notes, the *imago Christi* is the "completed" *imago Dei*, the image of God revealed in its eschatological fulfillment.[108] Christology is key to understanding the work of both creation and redemption. First, it clarifies the end toward which God's economic labor is directed. Second, it reveals the ideal form of humanity. And third, it instructs us in how human persons are to "image" Christ in their actions. After developing these Christological insights, I will return to the *imago Dei* and suggest that its most important instruction as it relates to a theology of animals is found not in any contrasts it establishes between humans and animals but in its illumination of the forms of goodness cherished by God and present in the lives of animals.

First, we can describe the end of the divine economy as the establishment of the new covenant in Christ. God's covenantal overtures to the Israelite people are central to the Old Testament's theological reflection. The Hebrew word for "covenant" (*berith*) appears 286 times in the Old Testament,[109] including in 26 of its books.[110] Of particular interest to us is the fact that developments in the covenantal relationship are often associated with the changing conditions of creation; creation prospers when the divine–human relation is harmonious and withers when it is not.[111] On the basis of this and other ties between the two themes, it is possible to argue that creation and covenant together "represent the whole of the theological subject matter" of the Old Testament.[112] The New Testament builds on this covenantal history and proclaims its fulfillment in God's offer of a new covenant in Christ. The covenant is, then, an essential mark of continuity between the two testaments, acting as a leitmotif across salvation history and anchoring the New Testament firmly within the narrative of the Old.

The covenant takes different forms in the Old Testament (e.g., Noahic, Gn 9:8–17; Abrahamic, Gn 12:1–3; Mosaic, Ex 19:5; and Davidic, 2 Sm 7:10–13), but the Mosaic covenant has been particularly influential in Christian thought. In the Christian interpretation, the Mosaic covenant established a set of divine expectations that humanity failed to fulfill, creating the need for the divine intervention that appeared in Christ. In contrast to the Mosaic covenant, the Abrahamic and Davidic covenants set no expectations for human performance. God makes abiding commitments to future events (i.e., that Abraham would become the father of a great people and that David's descendants would rule forever) with no stipulations for Israel's corresponding duties. In the wake of Israel's defeat and captivity, the Abrahamic and Davidic covenants understandably became a source of encouragement, as those covenantal forms did not depend on Israel's righteousness but on a divine fidelity whose persistence even sin could not weaken.[113] In the aftermath of the exile, the apocalyptic dimension of the covenant's fulfillment becomes more prominent. The prophets increasingly tie Israel's covenantal expectations to a radical intervention by God. Isaiah, Jeremiah, and Ezekiel (along with the "minor" prophets like Joel, Amos, and Hosea) refer to this future apocalypse as the "day of the Lord," and imagine it as a transformation that not only restores Israel and realizes its covenantal hopes but, as we will see, also renews creation.

Christianity interprets Jesus as the realization of Israel's hope for a renewed covenant. Much attention in Christian theology has been given to the important role that the "kingdom" plays in Jesus's preaching. Though the covenant has less of an obvious presence in the Gospels or in the New Testament in general, it nevertheless forms the backdrop for much of its theology and is reflected in cognate themes like divine–human reconciliation, peaceful relations, and the establishment of a just order.[114] Examined in light of these themes, one can suggest that the unifying "rubric" of the scriptural canon, the Old and New Testaments, is the progressive history of God's covenantal relationship.[115] Thus, Hebrews 7:22 describes Jesus as "the guarantee of an [even] better covenant," and in Hebrews 8:7 the author states that "if that first covenant had been faultless, no place would have been sought for a second one."

More significantly, however, scholars have become aware of the importance of the covenant for Pauline theology. E. P. Sanders's 1977 study challenged the long-established view that Paul's rejection of "works righteousness" was a response to the Jewish legalism of the time.[116] The law was meant to be, Sanders argued, the means provided by God for Jews to maintain their covenantal relationship with God; it was "a privileged gift" and not "a way to merit salvation."[117] James Dunn's influential 1983 essay "The New Perspective on Paul" built on Sanders's work to address the question of what prompted Paul's defense of justification by faith.[118] He argues that Paul was reacting to what he saw as a lack of covenantal faithfulness in the Jewish culture of his time. The covenant that God made with the Israelites was meant to be a "light to the nations," breaking down walls between peoples, but it had become instead a trophy of ethnocentric pride. Thus, Paul's preaching against works righteousness was not intended to promote the faith-based, individualistic soteriology common in post-Reformation thought. Rather, it "focuses largely if not principally on the need to overcome the barrier which the law was seen to interpose between Jews and Gentiles." The works of the law were not meant to determine one's "standing within the covenant."[119] Paul's exhortations against legalism were ultimately meant to restore the relationship that the covenant established with God and make it available, as God intended, to all nations.[120] It is in the context of this renewal of God's covenantal intent that we should interpret the important passage of 1 Corinthians 11:25 that links the new covenant to Jesus's paschal mystery and the celebration of the Eucharist ("This cup is the new covenant in my blood").

With this background, we turn to examine the Noahic covenant of Genesis 9:8–17, an important resource for a Christian theology of creation. Like the Abrahamic and Davidic covenants, the relationship into which God enters is not conditioned on the response of God's covenant partners. Its fulfillment depends only on God. More consequential for our discussion is the fact that the Noahic covenant gives God's promise a universal scope; it is directed to both human and nonhuman creatures: "I am now establishing my covenant . . . with every living creature" (Gn 9:9–10). The reference to nonhuman creatures in the passage is no embellishment. The text's repeated emphasis on individual nonhuman creatures—in Genesis 9:10–16, the phrase "every living creature" is repeated four times—shows that the editor "wants to hammer home the goal of the narrative,"[121] that "God binds himself unilaterally and without reservation" to creation.[122] The Noahic covenant of Genesis 9, then, provides a biblical starting point for arguing that the economy of salvation is directed toward a creation-inclusive covenant.[123] It depicts creation as an ongoing work that is intertwined with God's covenantal history with humanity. Interpreted in light of the Noahic covenant and the postdiluvian restoration of the earth, the covenantal theme of the Old Testament becomes, as Patrick Miller puts it, a "structure" in the salvific narrative as it develops across the prophetic texts, bringing together divine and human labor "in the struggle against evil and for creation."[124] The ultimate fruit of this struggle will be a transformation that is both interior and exterior. Jeremiah describes God's future relationship with Israel in terms of a new covenant written on the heart (Jer 31:31–34), whereas Hosea depicts God as the guarantor of a future covenant that will draw humanity and animals together and eliminate violence among them (Hos 2:20). For Hosea, the "benefits" of God's reconciliation include "the sphere of all creation."[125]

The New Testament does not explicitly tie nonhuman creatures to the new covenant, but the deutero-Pauline notion of an eschatological union of all creatures with Christ implies such a connection. In Ephesians, we are told that the mystery of God's plan for creation has been revealed to us; it is "to sum up [*anakephalaiōsthai*, to gather into one, under one head] all things in Christ, in heaven and on earth" (Eph 1:10). Similarly, Colossians states that "all things were created through [Christ] and for him," and that in Christ "all things hold together" (Col 1:16–17). The allusion to an all-embracing covenant is even stronger in the important passage of Romans 8:18–23. Paul here presupposes the Jewish tradition that sees "the non-human created world as intimately bound up with the fate of human beings."[126] In Paul's "view of the created world," as the New Testament scholar Joseph Fitzmyer observes, it is "striving toward the very goal set for humanity itself." Paul "affirms a solidarity of the human and the subhuman world in the redemption of Christ" and "recalls Yahweh's promise to Noah of the covenant to be made" between God and "every living creature."[127] God's covenantal fidelity and the redemptive solidarity of all creatures are joined together in Paul's theology of creation.

The importance of these covenantal accounts is that they underscore how fundamental relationality is to God's plans for creation. God desired beings whom God could draw into a relationship, not just creaturely others whom God could watch and admire from afar. The fullness of this plan is found in Christ, the one who addresses God as Father and surrenders himself to the divine will. In Christ's life, we see that God's goal is achieved in a specific type of creature, one who could respond freely and self-givingly to God's offer and in so doing reflect, analogously, God's own triune life. God's hope that creation could receive the divine address and respond freely to it is realized in the human person.

However, the goal of creation as I am describing it here is not so much the human person per se but rather more broadly a creature who can receive and respond to the divine address. Its full form appears in an agent capable of a free and deliberative response to the covenantal offer, and in this sense I believe that God has created the human person with a distinct dignity. But in the Noahic covenant, we see that God's covenantal hopes are not exhausted by the human person, that they can and do take other forms. Here, we might recall Aquinas's adage that "whatever is received into something is received according to the condition of the recipient."[128] God, we can hope, will offer the gift of the covenant to all creatures, even while doing so in ways that conform to each creature's particular capacity. Given the diversity of relational possibilities found among nonhuman creatures, it would be oddly incongruous if God, whose hopes and labors for creation center on fostering a covenantal relationship with "all things," were ultimately to value only the covenantal capacity of humans and ignore the relational capacities (and their eschatological potentialities) found in the animal world.

The human capacity for a covenantal relationship brings us to our second Christological insight—that is, the ideal form of humanity as revealed in Christ. I take seriously the claim of Chalcedon that in Jesus, two natures are unified in one person; he is both consubstantial (co-essential) with the Father and with humanity. The two natures / one person definition—given at the Council of Chalcedon (451 CE) and developed through early Christianity's struggle with a number of Christological heresies—underscores the full mystery of the Incarnation: The Son truly became human without ceasing to be God.[129] The Chalcedonian definition requires that human nature share in a distinctive set of prerequisite qualities—for example, freedom, relationality, reason, self-awareness, self-identity, and moral agency—so that it is not just an external shell for God's presence in the world but rather the full, genuine abode of God within creation. For this reason, Karl Rahner describes the human person as that which comes to be when "God wants to be what is not God."[130] Human nature "was created and 'tailored' to be the human mode of existence and the human expression of the divine Logos."[131] In the Incarnation, the human person becomes the place where creation enters into a perfect covenantal relationship with God (i.e., in Christ's relationship with the Father).

My position here is in tension with what has become known as "deep incarnationalism."[132] This view proposes that in the very act of taking on flesh (Jn 1:14a: "And the Word became flesh"), Jesus embraced all creation and—through his life, death, and resurrection—redeemed it. I generally support this view, in the sense that all creation is bound together in solidarity, and thus the economic labor of Christ, from incarnation to resurrection, reverberates throughout all creation. But I also believe that a "deep incarnationalism" must be qualified by a "Chalcedonian incarnationalism"; that is, the fact that Jesus became *human*, and not some other creature or "flesh" in general, is theologically and anthropologically relevant. It tells us something about who God is and who the human creature is (e.g., a being capable of a free giving of self to the other). God could, perhaps, take on the external appearance of, say, a fish or a tree, but only in such a creature as the human could God achieve the full and paradoxical unity of two natures as taught by Chalcedon and, correspondingly, only in such a creature could the divine be fully united with the creaturely.[133]

Nonetheless, the human covenantal capacity, fully expressed in Jesus's relationship with the Father, need not be made into a threshold benchmark excluding the nonhuman. Instead, we can see it as the privileged expression of a divinely desired good that also appears in diverse forms within the domain of nonhuman creatures. God's redemptive plan for the covenant's fulfillment is directed toward all creation, and thus in Christ the covenantal potential of humanity and that found in nonhuman creatures is sacralized—that is, graced and elevated. Pope John Paul II captured the prevailing tradition when he described humanity's *imago Dei* as "the capacity of having a personal relationship with God, as 'I' and 'you,' and therefore the capacity of having a covenant."[134] The idea, however, that God can have a covenantal relationship only with humanity and no other creature needs reconsideration, not only in light of the Noahic covenant but also because of the evolutionary heritage we share with animals, the stunning variety of cognitive skills we find among them, and their spectacularly diverse forms of relationality (e.g., consider the social lives of elephants, the organized life of a bee colony, and the bond between humans and their dogs). The goodness displayed in these relationships is the kind of diversity within creation that Thomas Aquinas believed praiseworthy, even if only temporally so, because God's goodness cannot "be adequately represented by one creature alone."[135]

Given the centrality of the covenant for God's purpose in creation, God's emphatic commitment to "every living creature" in Genesis 9, and the fact that God's relational capacity is not exhausted by the divine–human covenant, we have good warrant to believe that God desires to enter into multiple forms of creaturely relationships and to do so in ways appropriate to the relational capacities found throughout creation. And if, as I am suggesting, humanity's new covenantal relationship with God effected in and by Christ is the always-intended culmination of humanity's status as the *imago Dei*, might it not be that our fellow creatures can also be said to bear the *imago Dei*, even if not in the same form found in humanity? Pope Benedict XVI implied that nonhuman creation has a covenantal capacity when he encouraged us "to reinforce the covenant between human beings and the environment" so that it might better "mirror the creative love of God."[136] Attending to the complex and varied ways that basic covenantal goods are present in nonhuman creatures—that is, relational building blocks such as expressiveness, responsiveness, friendship, altruism, a sense of fair play, and grief for lost companions—can help us recognize how God treasures these creatures and calls us to act in ways that strengthen the covenant with them.

This last ethical note brings us to the third Christological insight—that is, how humanity should "image" Christ. God's covenantal expression to the wounded world takes its most radical form in Christ's self-offering on the cross. Christians are called to be this *imago Christi* by holding on to the redemptive possibility of love in the face of forces aligned against it. Because the reign of God is not yet here in its fullness, Christian attempts to love will, like those of Christ, be marked by the wounds of a fallen world. They will too often be spurned, unsuccessful, and limited in their immediate fruit—and even met with hostility.

Because God desires, as I will argue in chapter 3, that nonhuman creatures share in the fruit of Christ's redemptive act, Christian endeavors to image the love of Christ should include expressions of care toward them. The brokenness of our world will, however, mark these endeavors. We and our fellow creatures live and die in a world groaning for its redemptive transformation; the kingdom proclaimed by Christ is not yet here in its fullness. Care for the animal neighbor, both at the personal and social levels, will often include perplexing and frustratingly inadequate practices—for example, ones that cause animal suffering and death. Such acts will disappointingly accord better with the manifest woundedness of our world than our hopeful aspirations for it. As I will discuss in chapter 5, animal ethics will need to reflect an eschatological reserve, anticipating the kingdom while recognizing that its fullness is yet to come.

My argument so far is that a Christologically informed interpretation of the *imago Dei* can serve us well in constructing a theological vision of animal life. Animals are covenant-worthy, and thus are sharers in the dignity associated with it, however refracted that dignity might be in the diverse forms of creaturely life. Because they will be invited into a covenantal relationship with God (again, in ways appropriate to the capacity of each creature), we can argue that animals share in two of the *imago Dei's* threefold marks discussed above, dignity and communion. We can suggest as much while also affirming the human person as the privileged reflection of the *imago Dei's* ideal form, the *imago Christi*.

Regarding stewardship, the third of the *imago Dei's* threefold marks, I will argue in the chapters ahead that God has given the Christian community a distinctive task that includes an ethical and soteriological stewardship of nonhuman creatures. I understand this stewardship as humanity's participation in God's redemptive plan to draw all creation together in Christ. However, it should not surprise us, given that we are all creatures of the same God, that even among nonhuman creatures, stewardship makes its appearance, though in ways often fractured by the brokenness of the world—examples of which were provided above by Bekoff and Pierce. Nonetheless, more common are behaviors in which a creature's efforts to preserve its own life, those of its offspring, and those of its animal group conflict with the well-being of other animals, significantly exemplified in the predator–prey relationship. Perhaps, we can speculate, even these behaviors reflect a form of stewardship, however twisted and deformed by the fall (e.g., that the prey "sacrifice" themselves for the well-being of others). We will explore this possibility further in chapter 4.

A BROKEN, COVENANTAL ANTHROPOCENTRISM

Building on these Christological reflections, I suggest that the image of God is exemplified in the human person's distinctive covenantal capacity.

This capacity incorporates and develops the themes of communion, stewardship, and creaturely dignity; we are embedded within relationships with God and other creatures, tasked with God's eschatological hopes, and graced with a unique dignity due to this calling. However, I additionally suggest that this covenantal capacity is also embodied in varied ways in the lives of animals, and as such is cherished by their Creator. In light of this capacity, we should strive to see animals as sharers in the covenant and to cultivate relationships with them that model the covenantal life of the kingdom. Nonetheless, the present reality of sin and brokenness will often thwart realization of these ideals. Our ethical and soteriological commitments become blurred in the face of the muddled complexity of the present world and of the brokenness in which we and our fellow creatures live.

My argument is that we preserve a form of anthropocentrism within this muddled complexity, in this sense: Ethical judgments that favor human desire and need over that of animals and other creatures are licit because humanity is distinctively the *imago Christi* and has been given a Christological role in the divine economy. I will unpack the nature of this role in the chapters ahead. To suggest a privileging of the human is not, of course, without controversy. For understandable reasons, critics argue that support for even a constrained form of anthropocentrism continues the self-serving, human-centric biases that have so endangered our world. Although scholars have thoroughly dissected the weaknesses of Lynn White's influential essay, the underlying concern remains, both within the Christian community and without, that Christianity has been and still is frustratingly myopic in its theological treatment of nonhuman creation.[137]

Because theological biases against animals are seen as so ingrained in Christian thought, it has become common in ecotheological circles to appeal to theocentrism as a safeguard against anthropocentrism's seemingly ineradicable toxicity.[138] A theocentric norm does indeed provide us with an important corrective and needed chastening—sobering us before the absoluteness of divine sovereignty and humbly reminding us of our shared creatureliness. However, by itself, theocentrism provides no normative content or help in ethical deliberations about which earthly distinctions and discriminations are morally defensible in our service to God's creation and to the creatures within it. Theocentric appeals have been used to justify any number of abhorrent behaviors—sexism, slavery, state totalitarianism, homophobia, and, of course, environmental abuse. My sense is that the contrast set up between theocentrism and anthropocentrism is often driven more by a valid desire to forestall sinful appropriations of anthropocentrism than a considered rejection of any form of the concept itself. Anthropocentrism does not, necessarily, include support for human domination over the nonhuman, and, as history has shown, theocentrism does not, necessarily, exclude such a possibility. A bare-bones anthropocentrism, claiming little more than some form of an ethical priority of human need, is consonant with the theocentric appeals of many ecotheologians. The version of anthropocentrism I want to defend is grounded in humanity's distinctive covenantal capacity and the role it has been given in God's redemptive plan. In this sense, anthropocentrism as used here is a theologically rather than anthropologically governed concept. I reject "anthropomonism," the idea that humanity is God's sole interest in creating and redeeming; but I also believe that the biblical narrative's focus on God's relationship with humanity is too significant to dismiss any and all forms of anthropocentrism.[139]

God's gifts always entail a corresponding calling. Whatever anthropocentric distinctiveness has been bestowed on humanity, it comes with a corresponding theocentric claim and responsibility. We might refer to this as a "servant anthropocentrism," but the unidirectionality implied in the term (humans giving and animals receiving) fails to acknowledge the giftedness of creation to humanity, not only in the basic goods it provides but also in its inspiring beauty and sacramental evocation. Thus, I prefer the term "covenantal anthropocentrism," to capture a combination of humanity's task within the divine covenantal calling *and* the mutuality and solidarity that should characterize our creaturely relationships.

Nevertheless, given the history of abuse fostered by distorted versions of Christian anthropocentrism, concerns for its continued use are warranted. In response, I suggest that a covenantal anthropocentrism must be seen as broken and humbled in three respects: sinfully, epistemologically, and theologically. Covenantal anthropocentrism is broken first by the recognition of our sinfulness—that is, of the "violence present in our hearts, wounded by sin," which has left the earth "burdened and laid waste . . . among the most abandoned and maltreated of our poor."[140] We have "covered God's good creation" with "a thick layer of dirt," making "it difficult if not impossible to perceive in it the Creator's reflection."[141] An anthropocentrism that is thus broken requires a profound ecological conversion that "can inspire us to greater creativity and enthusiasm in resolving the world's problems and in offering ourselves to God."[142]

Second, our knowledge of animal lives and their interrelations with each other and with us has been woefully inadequate throughout Christian history. This is changing; we live in a time of monumental developments that

give animals benefit of the doubt

have transformed our understanding of animal life. However, these trans-formations will continue for the conceivable future; our knowledge of animal life is incomplete and will remain so. In light of this epistemological *knowlege* limitation and our historical tendency toward anthropocentric distortions, we should presume more and not less with regard to the dignity, relational richness, and ecological value of animals. *presuming more, not less*

Third and finally, as the Church's teaching has shifted explicitly away from the idea that "the ultimate purpose of other creatures" is to be found in us,[143] we must acknowledge how limited is our knowledge of God's desires for nonhuman creatures. A covenantal anthropocentrism must be broken theologically, in that we cannot claim to understand all God's purposes and plans for God's creatures. The *Baltimore Catechism* expressed God's reason for creating humanity with characteristically simple clarity: "God made me to know Him, to love Him, and to serve Him in this world, and to be happy with Him for ever in heaven."[144] I would like to hope that if there were a *Baltimore Catechism* for our time, it could include an analogous statement about nonhuman creatures—not a detailed claim about all the purposes God has in mind for them but a simple affirmation that God created them to give God glory in this world and be happy with God in the next. At the very least, the Christian community must humbly recognize that with regard to the mystery of God's plans for creatures, it stands with Job in the awareness that it speaks of things "too marvelous" for it to understand (Jb 42:3).

NOTES

Epigraph: John Paul II, "Correspondence."

    1. Schloss, "From Evolution to Eschatology," loc. 1027 of 4757, Kindle.

    2. Teilhard de Chardin, *Christianity*, 82.

    3. Willis Jenkins provides a helpful overview of Aquinas's approach to natural evil; see "Natural Evils and Ecological Goods" in his *Ecologies of Grace*, 144–48. He argues that for Aquinas the existence of natural evil (at least insofar as it affects nonhuman creatures) is not caused by the fall but is rather the necessary condition for the created order that God desires: "God intends the sort of self-organizing, complex order that requires the corruption of individual creatures, but that corruption is only accidental to God's will for a rich display of goods immanently harmonized in a universal order." Jenkins, *Ecologies of Grace*, 145. The main effect of the fall on nonhuman creation is a deterioration in its obedience to humanity's rational governance. Humanity's sin introduces "a kind of unruliness to the natural order, but not so pervasively as to undermine the integrity of creation or produce a cataclysmic change in the natures

of other creatures. 'For the nature of animals was not changed by humanity's sin, as if those creatures which naturally devour the flesh of others, like the lion and falcon, would then have lived on herbs.'" Jenkins, 146–47. Willis cites *ST* I.96.1 *ad.* 2, using his own translation.

4. Raymund Schwager offers one version of this. He sees the origin of sin as the human inclination to "heed the voices of their familiar (animal) past," which in turn "led to a problematic self-formation of human consciousness." Schwager, *Banished*, 94. Paul Tillich, John Polkinghorne, and others see the fall as a symbol illuminating the human condition, not as a historical explanation of human suffering. The story of the fall is "the symbol of turning away from God into the self that occurred with the dawning of hominid self-consciousness, so that thereby humanity became curved-in upon itself, asserting autonomy and refusing to acknowledge heterono-mous dependence." Polkinghorne, *Exploring Reality*, 139. See also Tillich, *Systematic Theology*, vol. 2, 29–44.

5. Process theology argues that God not only participates in the world's pro-cesses but is affected by them and is thus, in some sense, changeable. The approach has been influential among those interested in developing an evolutionary theology. For a critique of process theology, see Burrell, "Does Process Theology Rest on a Mistake?" Philip Devenish offers a critical response to Burrell: Devenish, "Postliberal Process Theology."

6. For example, Jack Mahoney: "God could not do other than accept the intrin-sic characteristics of matter once he has decided to create it in the first place." Mahoney, *Christianity*, 104–05.

7. Until the modern period, Christian theodicies had not, generally, been con-cerned with how natural evils affected nonhuman lives. Even in paradise, Aquinas maintained, death and violence would have been the common lot of animals. *ST* I.96.1 *ad.* 2.

8. Rolston, "Does Nature Need to Be Redeemed?" 213.

9. Sideris, "Censuring Nature," 34.

10. Peacocke, *Theology*, 62.

11. Peacocke, 63.

12. Southgate, *Groaning*, 12–17, 47–53, at 53: "Suffering is a necessary driver of progressively richer and more intense experience."

13. Hughes, *Is God to Blame?* 47.

14. Rolston, *Science*, 135.

15. Irenaeus, *Against Heresies* [book IV, 37.7], 520–21.

16. Haught, *Resting*, 98.

17. Haught, 81.

18. Johnson, *Ask the Beasts*, 155.

19. Richard, *Christ*, 136.

20. Schaab, *Trinity in Relation*, 201. Cited by McLaughlin, *Preservation*, 330.

21. Richard, 136.

22. Polkinghorne, *Reason*, 84.

23. McLaughlin, *Preservation*, 327.

24. McLaughlin, 328.

25. Nathan O'Halloran raises another critique of the "only way" argument: It weakens the *contingency* of evil and thus seems to implicate God in the evil that has resulted from God's choice to create. O'Halloran, "Cosmic Alienation."

26. Lewis, *Problem of Pain*, 25.

27. Another issue, one that opens up a line of speculation beyond what can be addressed here, is the status of these "free process" constraints in the eschaton. Why is it, for example, that natural evils will no longer be needed for divine creativity and creaturely fruitfulness in the age to come given that they are so essential to the creativity and fruitfulness of the present age? The question is particularly problematic for eschatologies that, like my own, envisage the age to come less in terms of a static perfection and more as an eternal, covenantal drama, one composed of fruitful and endlessly new relationships between and among God and all God's creatures.

28. Moltmann, *Way*, 294. Regarding Rahner's thought, Moltmann similarly complains that "it too fails to draw attention to the victims which the process actually costs." Moltmann, 299.

29. Johnson, *Ask the Beasts*, 156.

30. The literature is filled with such lauding, personifying descriptions. The world unfolds "by responding to the divine allurement at its own pace and in its own particular way." Haught, *God after Darwin*, 57. God does not "limit the freedom of creation." Zyciński, *God*, 250. Creation has been gifted "with its own creativity and freedom to explore." Rolnick, *Origins*, 47. I recognize that this language reflects the influence of process theology, but I think the argument's weakness remains, even when placed in the context of process theology.

31. Francis, *Laudato Si'*, no. 80.

32. For a related critique, see Wahlberg, "Was Evolution the Only Possible Way?"

33. Deane-Drummond, *Christ*, 36.

34. Delio, *Christ*, 137.

35. Haught, *Making Sense*, 53. Similarly, Richard Bauckham complains that the ecotheology of Matthew Fox reflects a tendency "for the transcendence of God to be reduced to the cosmos and for the particularity of Jesus to be dissolved in the cosmos." Bauckham, *Living*, 198.

36. Schloss, "From Evolution to Eschatology," loc. 1040–42 of 4757, Kindle.

37. Moltmann, *Way*, 296.

38. The developments on this front are astounding and rapidly progressing; see Walsh, "New Natural Selection."

39. Scott, "Technology Factor"; Cole-Turner, "Toward a Theology."

40. Regalado, "Rewriting Life."

41. Linzey, "Unfinished Creation," 23.

42. Linzey, 25.

43. Linzey, 22. Linzey builds on the work of Trickett, "Imagination."

44. Among the scholars who support the idea of a cosmic fall are Clough, *On Animals: Volume One*; Messer, "Natural Evil"; and Lloyd, "Are Animals Fallen?"

45. Clough, *On Animals: Volume One*, 125.

46. Clough, 127.

47. Clough, 105–19, discusses the possibility of animal sin.

48. Balthasar references Gregory of Nyssa's account in his discussion of the fall. Balthasar, *Theological Anthropology*, 91.

49. Gregory of Nyssa, "Making" [chap. 17.4], 407. Scripture gives examples of God acting in anticipation of human sin—e.g., God foresees Pharaoh's refusal to let the Israelites leave (Ex 3:19).

50. Maximus's reflections on creation and God's foreknowledge of human sin can be found in his *Ambigua to John*, nos. 8 and 41. God could have "created matter in this way from the beginning, according to His foreknowledge, in view of the transgression He had already seen in advance." Maximus, "Ambiguum 8," *On Difficulties*, vol. I, 145. The "property of male and female" is not "linked to the original principle of the divine plan concerning human generation." "Ambiguum 41," *On Difficulties*, vol. II, 105. Erigena's version of the argument can be found in his *Periphyseon: On the Division of Nature*, Book IV, 807A–808A. A partial English translation and summary of *Periphyseon* is provided in the *Periphyseon* volume edited by Edouard Jeauneau. The referenced section is summarized at 264.

51. Balthasar, *Theo-Drama*, vol. 2, 269n40.

52. John Paul II, *Dominum*, no. 33.

53. Westermann, *Genesis 1–11*, 148.

54. "It is clear, therefore, that intellectual creatures alone, properly speaking, are made to God's image." Aquinas, *ST* I.93.2.

55. Curtis, "Man," 44.

56. Curtis, 350.

57. Barth, *Church Dogmatics*, vol. III.2, 203ff.

58. Curtis, "Man," 46.

59. See the overview provided by Middleton, *Liberating Image*, 93–146.

60. Grenz, *Social God*, 200.

61. International Theological Commission, "Communion," no. 25.

62. International Theological Commission, no. 56.

63. International Theological Commission, no. 57.

64. International Theological Commission, no. 22.

65. "While in all creatures there is some kind of likeness to God, in the rational creature alone we find a likeness of 'image' as we have explained above (Articles 1 and 2); whereas in other creatures we find a likeness by way of a 'trace.'" *ST* I.93.6.

66. White, "Historical Roots," 1203–7.

67. Eric Daryl Meyer challenges the neat divide between human and nonhuman creatures from a different direction. Instead of exploring how nonhuman animals share, in varying degrees, some of the capabilities traditionally seen as distinctively human (i.e., the emphasis of this section), he examines how humanity shares in the "animality"

of animals and argues that Christian theology has tried to ignore or denigrate that reality. See Meyer, *Inner Animalities*.

68. De Waal, *Are We Smart Enough*, 4.

69. De Waal, 81.

70. De Waal, 92. In the "floating peanut task," a desirable peanut is placed at the bottom of a tube. The animal (or eight-year-old child) cannot reach it but must instead figure out to add water to the tube until the peanut becomes reachable.

71. Inoue and Matsuzawa, "Working Memory."

72. Bräuer et al., "Making Inferences."

73. De Waal, *Are We Smart Enough*, 79.

74. Mann et al., "Tool-Using Dolphins."

75. Mann et al.

76. De Waal, *Are We Smart Enough*, 78. Ravens have the rare ability to distinguish among human faces and retain memories of particular humans who have hassled them years later. They teach their dislike for particular humans to their offspring, and these grudges then shape their social practices. Cornell, Marzluff, and Pecoraro, "Social Learning."

77. Every publishing cycle seems to bring a new installment of the "inner lives of animal x." Balcombe, *Inner Lives*; Hatkoff and Goodall, *Inner World*; Horowitz, *Inside*; Montgomery, *Soul*; Shanor and Kanwal, *Bats Sing*.

78. Duncan, "Changing Concept," 11–12.

79. Bentham, *Introduction*, cited by Duncan, "Changing Concept," 12.

80. This is a problem famously raised by Nagel, "What Is It Like?"

81. A helpful summary of the issues is given by Chalmers, *Conscious Mind*.

82. See "The Cambridge Declaration on Consciousness," a 2012 statement affirming that animals have consciousness; Francis Crick Memorial Conference, "Cambridge Declaration."

83. Horowitz, *Inside*, 218–19. Among other animals that have failed this particular test are African elephants and several species of monkeys.

84. Dagg, *Animal Friendships*, 13.

85. Dagg, 13–17.

86. Dagg, 196.

87. De Waal, *Are We Smart Enough*, 72.

88. Safina, *Beyond Words*, 38.

89. Safina, 69.

90. Safina, 67.

91. Donald Griffin builds on recent developments in the science of animal consciousness to argue that animals should be recognized as "subjects and actors." Griffin, "From Cognition to Consciousness," 502. In contrast, Marc Hauser argues that animals are not moral agents in that they lack a developed capacity for inhibition; that is, they are not able to resist acting on desires that are, by some measure, bad. Hauser, "Are Animals Moral Agents?"

92. Bekoff and Pierce, *Wild Justice*, 7.

93. Bekoff and Pierce, 102.

94. Bekoff and Pierce, 110–25.

95. Bekoff and Pierce, 139.

96. Bekoff and Pierce, 138, 147–49.

97. "Western philosophical accounts of morality are outdated, . . . ascribing too much volition and intentionality to moral behavior." Bekoff and Pierce, 149.

98. Bekoff and Pierce, 141.

99. Pope, "Darwinism," 196.

100. The study is recounted by Deane-Drummond, *Wisdom*, 60. See also Porter's discussion of Aquinas's views: "The passions and their corresponding emotions do indeed play a central and necessary role in shaping our perceptions, volitions, and choices; *ST* I-II q. 9, a. 2; q. 10, a. 3. They cannot provide an adequate basis for human morality, but nonetheless, our moral lives would literally be unthinkable without them." Porter, "Moral Passions," 95–96.

101. Pope, *Human Evolution*, 194.

102. Bekoff and Pierce, *Wild Justice*, 147.

103. Korsgaard and O'Neill, *Sources*, 93.

104. Williams, "Neanderthal DNA."

105. Hogenboom, "'Lucy' Rewrote the Story."

106. Haught, *Making Sense*, 46.

107. E.g.: "The primary norm of reality and of value is the universe community itself in its various forms of expression, especially as realized on the planet earth." Berry, "Dream," 205.

108. International Theological Commission, "Communion," no. 11.

109. Stackhouse, "Moral Meanings," 249.

110. Hiuser and Barton, "A Promise is a Promise," 344.

111. N. T. Wright notes "the scriptural sense," which holds that "the fate of the land is bound up with" Israel's "covenant behaviour." "When Christians are finally redeemed," he goes on to state, "the whole cosmos . . . will be redeemed." Wright, *Pauline Perspectives*, 163.

112. Miller, "Creation," 155.

113. Mendenhall, "Covenant Forms," 71–76.

114. The term used to distinguish the two parts of the Christian Bible—i.e., "testament," a translation of the Greek *diatheke*—refers to an arrangement or relationship.

115. Miller, "Creation," 156.

116. Sanders, *Paul*.

117. Stegman, "Run That You May Obtain,'" 4. I am indebted to this essay for understanding these shifts in Pauline theology and its literature.

118. This essay was first published in 1983 and appears in the collection by Dunn, *New Perspective*, 89–110. In a 2004 essay, he describes the process that led him to posing this question and the arguments that shaped his conclusions. Dunn, 1–88.

119. Dunn, 15.

120. "Jesus has taken the curse on himself, enabling God to fulfil the purpose of the covenant, which was that the blessing of Abraham might come upon the gentiles." Wright, *Pauline Perspectives*, 29.

121. Westermann, *Genesis 1–11*, 472.

122. Westermann, 473.

123. The Noahic covenant had been seen as less significant because, in part, it was believed to be a late addition to the canon. Contemporary biblical scholarship, however, has challenged that understanding. Katharine Dell, for example, uncovers textual connections that exist between the Noahic covenant and the Old Testament's theology of creation, indicating that a covenantal approach to creation was not "simply or necessarily a late idea." Dell, "Covenant," 130.

124. Miller, "Creation," 166.

125. Kelle, *Hosea 2*, 277.

126. Byrne, *Romans*, 256.

127. Fitzmyer, "Letter," 854a.

128. Aquinas, *ST* I.75.5.

129. These heresies include Apollinarianism, for which Jesus had a divine mind but a human body and emotions; Docetism, for which Jesus's body was merely an outward shell of his real spiritual reality; Monophysitism, for which Christ's divinity dominates his humanity; and Nestorianism, for which Jesus Christ is constituted by two persons, human and divine.

130. Rahner, *Foundations*, 225; at 224: Jesus is "the self-revelation of God [precisely] through who he is," and thus Christ's human nature is itself "the expression of God."

131. Dych, *Thy Kingdom Come*, 62.

132. See the essays on "deep Incarnation" collected by Gregersen, *Incarnation*.

133. Because of Chalcedon, I do not think the suggestion by some that Jesus's humanity has no more soteriological relevance than his ethnicity, nationality, religious identity, or gender can be sustained. See, e.g., Clough, *On Animals: Volume One*, 81–103. Clough considers the possibility of God becoming incarnate as an ostrich or an ant. He rejects it not because it would be impossible for God to do so in a way consonant with Chalcedon's claims but because, in part, such an act by God is unnecessary given the cosmic sweep of Christ's work. Clough, 82. Against such a view, I do not see how Chalcedon's radical affirmation that Jesus is fully human and fully divine could be realized in any other creature presently known than a human.

134. John Paul II, *Dominum*, no. 34.

135. Aquinas, *ST* I.47.1. See also Francis: "The universe as a whole, *in all its manifold relationships*, shows forth the inexhaustible riches of God" (emphasis added). Francis, *Laudato Si'*, no. 86.

136. Benedict XVI, "Message" no. 10.

137. For a helpful discussion of these issues, see the collection of essays edited by LeVasseur and Peterson, *Religion and Ecological Crisis*.

138. "Christianity should be distinguished by its theocentrism, rather than anthropocentrism"; Clough, *On Animals: Volume One*, xx. "In this common attribution of glory to the one Creator there is no hierarchy or anthropocentricity. Here all creatures, including ourselves, are simply fellow-creatures expressing the theocentricity of the created world, each in our own created way, differently but in complementarity. In the worship of God there can be no hierarchy among creatures." Bauckham, *Living*, 150. "Theologically, I think that what is needed is neither the extreme anthropocentrism that offers no respect for the dignity of other creatures, nor the biocentrism that would seem to reject the unique dignity of the human person, but a position more nuanced than either anthropocentrism or biocentrism—one that is explicitly theocentric." Edwards, *Partaking*, 167. "In shifting to a theocentric basis for animal concern, the temptation toward an inappropriate reading of the lives of other animals through that of human societies is reduced, though not avoided entirely." Deane-Drummond, *Wisdom*, 257. "In keeping with land ethics and a theocentric orientation, love recommends participating cautiously in natural processes." Sideris, *Environmental Ethics*, 254.

139. Lukas Vischer uses the term "anthropomonism" as a way of critiquing the view that humanity is the exclusive focus of God's economic labor. He contrasts anthropomonism with a form of anthropocentrism—which, he says, "must be maintained"—where God's redemptive plan includes nonhuman creatures, even though humanity retains a distinctive importance in that plan. Vischer, "Listening," 21–22. Vischer's use of the term is discussed by Hunt, Horrell, and Southgate, "Environmental Mantra?" 574–75.

140. Francis, *Laudato Si'*, no. 2.

141. Benedict XVI, "Homily: Solemnity of Pentecost."

142. Francis, *Laudato Si'*, no. 220.

143. Francis, no. 83.

144. Kelley, *Saint Joseph Baltimore Catechism*, 16.

CHAPTER 3

REDEMPTION

The Divine *Magis* and Animals

Our birth would have been no gain, had we not been redeemed.

—Exsultet

THE *EXSULTET* of the Easter vigil powerfully captures the extravagance of God's care for creation. Sin should have brought divine wrath and condemnation; but, at least in the traditional scholastic view, it instead moved God to offer a gift greater than originally intended: friendship with God. The first humans enjoyed a kind of perfection that is natural to the human condition—life without injury, disease, or death; harmony with nature; and peaceful coexistence with one another. Sin corrupted this world. In response, God decided to send Christ not only to save us from sin and heal our broken lives, thus restoring us to our original condition, but also to bestow on us an additional grace: a relationship with God that exceeds our natural ability—that is, a supernatural gift. The choice to sin, which led to our fallen condition, became the occasion for an even greater outpouring of divine love. In the beautifully paradoxical words of the *Exsultet*: "Oh happy fault [*felix culpa*], that earned so great, so glorious a Redeemer!"[1]

What is noteworthy about this Easter proclamation for our discussion here is not only its lauding of divine love's extravagance but also its celebratory description of the divine–earthly encounter: "Be glad, let earth be glad, as glory floods her, ablaze with light from her eternal King." The Easter liturgy celebrates the event whereby "things of heaven are wed to those of earth, and man is divine to the human!" The language intimates

the joyful *elevation* of creation, not its replacement. The light of the paschal candle shining in the darkness is a gift from creation itself, "the work
of bees . . . drawn out by mother bees to build a torch so precious." This
prayer at the opening of the Church's most solemn liturgy proclaims not
only God's regard for humanity but also the good news that the event of
Christ's death and resurrection resounds throughout all creation.

The *Exsultet* suggests that God's shocking generosity is contingent on
the advent of sin (a theological approach some refer to as "infralapsarian-
ism"): Christ was sent on account of human sin and would not have come
otherwise. I likewise want to underscore the extravagance of God's gift,
the *magis* of divine tenderness toward creation. However, along with many
contemporary theologians, I see this gift as something always intended by
God and at work in human history and not the result of a divine plan
occasioned by the fall. This gift, I will further argue, is directed toward all
God's creatures, not just humanity. Finally, in keeping with the contours of
the nature/grace interplay characteristic of the Catholic tradition, this
eschatological destiny is such that it preserves, not replaces, the natures of
these creatures.

NATURE AND GRACE

The Catholic understanding of the nature/grace distinction grew out of
scholastic interpretations of Thomas Aquinas (many would say distortions of him). On the one hand, human nature comprises all that is natural, innate to the person as originally created by God (e.g., a virtuous
life centered on a natural recognition of God and conformed to the
moral laws of the created world). Graced human existence, on the other
hand, is that dimension of human persons insofar as they are healed and
elevated to an end exceeding natural human capacity. Among other considerations, the distinction served to protect divine freedom. If God had
created in such a way that human nature would remain incoherent and
frustrated without the additional gift of grace, then, at least according to
scholastic arguments, creation would make a claim on God; it "deserved"
something from God because of the way God created it. The gratuity of
God's decision to send the Son would then be compromised.[2] To prevent
this, scholastic theology proposed a natural beatitude as a way of showing that human existence, at least in its prelapsarian form, would not be
inherently frustrated or incomplete apart from the additional work of
Christ.

Unfortunately, the argument also seemed to suggest that the human person could be satisfied apart from a relationship with God and was thus neutral in its disposition to the gift of grace. Human nature was self-sufficient, complete in itself without an eternal destiny in Christ, and grace was, correspondingly, "extrinsic, accidental, foreign, and an unintelligible super-added element."[3] In response to these concerns, post-conciliar thought has more explicitly embraced the view that "natural" humanity (i.e., humanity as it would have existed apart from the fall) has always been oriented toward a relationship with God; in the language of Henri de Lubac, it has a natural desire for God.[4]

With this emphasis on humanity's fundamental orientation toward a relationship with God, contemporary Catholic thought has shifted toward what is called a "supralapsarian" view. In the traditional Catholic account, God had originally intended to create a world of natural flourishing and only subsequently decided, in response to human sin, to send the Son. No sin, no Incarnation. Instead, many contemporary theologians, both Protestant and Catholic, argue that God has always intended to offer humanity a graced, personal relationship.[5] The fulfillment offered in Christ has always been the goal of creation, and at work within it.[6] Appealing to the themes of chapter 2, we can say that God's desire to be in a covenantal relationship with creation has guided the divine labor for the world from the beginning.[7]

If we are right to believe that creation has always been oriented toward Christ, then an organic link binds the world in its inception to God's eschatological plan for it. The import for our discussion is that it would seem strange—assuming that God's primordial plan for creation was always guided by God's covenantal intent—that some aspect of creation's primordial beginning (i.e., nonhuman creatures) had no relevance for creation's eschatological destiny to relate all things in Christ. The organic unity of God's intent across creation and eschatological fulfillment would be sundered, at least as far as nonhuman creatures go. Furthermore, two of the core commitments driving the nature/grace debate, though applied principally to the case of *human* nature and grace, have an inner logic that pertains to creation broadly considered. First, the present eschatological destiny of humanity is a possibility newly effected in Christ and not merely a continuation of the work of creation (even if always intended). A radically different future is made possible in light of the Incarnation and the paschal mystery. Though we typically emphasize how God's act in Christ is a new expression of God's love, the work of Christ is equally an expression of God's power. God accomplishes what creation is itself powerless to do. This creaturely impotence vis-à-vis God's goal for creation applies both to its human and nonhuman beings. In Christ, creaturely powerlessness is transformed into its exultation. It is a gift that, should God choose, can be shared with animal natures.

Second, in the traditional language of Aquinas, the "more" that Christ effects elevates and does not destroy nature. It does not replace humanity with a new model but rather perfects what humanity has always been. The Catholic tradition is deeply committed to the enduring integrity of nature—human nature, but also creation more broadly—even as grace transforms that nature. In redeeming humanity, God does not produce a different creature but brings humanity to a potential to which it was always oriented, even if never able to actualize through its own efforts. The respect that God gives to nature is such that even in the transformed life to come, human nature will remain *human*. This means, additionally, that the present form of human existence is no creaturely sham to be supplanted by a radically different, "truly real" existence awaiting us on the other side of death's door. Again, the present is organically linked to the eschatological future.

Although we cannot imagine exactly what our transformed existence will be like in the age to come, it will be a human one (i.e., corporeal, limited, passionate, intelligent, and social).[8] Given the goodness and significance of our relationships with other creatures in the present world and their relationships with each other (pets, nature walks, awe and wonder before the diversity of creation, ecological systems, etc.), it seems reasonable to hope that God's commitment to preserving the integrity of nature would include nonhuman creation, inasmuch as we are so profoundly connected to it. Human life would be radically different in the age to come were it not to remain embedded within, and even partly co-constituted by, our creaturely surroundings and the web of connections present within them. As the *Catechism of the Catholic Church* states, "God wills the *interdependence of creatures*"—certainly in this age but also, we can argue, in the age to come (emphasis in the original).[9]

God's love for the creatureliness of creation and the free decision by God to draw creation beyond itself to a new destiny expresses what I call the divine *magis*. God, whose immanent life is the eternal movement of triune "excess," continues to be this eternal excess of self-giving to the other as God creates what is beyond God and other than God, cherishes this otherness, and ultimately chooses to embrace it in its creatureliness with inconceivable closeness. The decision by God to do the impossible, giving humanity a destiny exceeding its natural capacities and doing so in a way that preserves its distinctive creatureliness, reveals that God loves creation qua creation—that is, as finite, limited, corporeal, varied, and individualized. God's commitments to creation—to the goodness of the creaturely, to the covenantal relationship, and to creation's fulfillment—together urge us to look beyond the circle of the human and consider how the divine *magis* might be directed toward all creation. The *Exsultet*'s proclamation that "heaven is wedded to earth" should also be celebrated as good news for animals; and fortunately, a number of important voices in Catholic thought, both historical and contemporary, have encouraged us to do so.

VOICES FOR ANIMAL REDEMPTION

The question of animal redemption is one part of a comprehensive eschatology that also includes other questions—such as God's intent in creating, the eschatological life of the saints, and the form of cosmic redemption. Until the recovery in the late nineteenth and early twentieth centuries of the centrality of the kingdom of God in Jesus's preaching, however, eschatology had been relegated to a peripheral concern (a stance that continued to dominate Catholic thought until Vatican II). In the wake of the medieval exclusion of nonhuman creatures from the age to come and the soteriological debates of the Reformation era, eschatological reflection became focused primarily on the individual and the spiritual consequences of his or her earthly choices; otherwise, eschatology was a reality irrelevant for interpreting human lives and actions in the present.[10] With the neglect of Scripture's eschatological horizon, animal-friendly eschatologies, such as Isaiah's image of a peaceable kingdom (Is 11:1–9), were also ignored. By restoring the kingdom of God to the core to Jesus's preaching, scholars brought new attention not only to the eschaton but also to its significance for the present. The kingdom of God was inaugurated in Christ, is at work in the present age, and will be brought to its fullness when Christ comes again. The eschaton is not just a future event but is already emerging in the present and must, therefore, be included as part of the interpretive framework for understanding the present and God's labor within it. If this eschaton is to include animals, Christians must also consider how the eschatological destiny that God has planned for animals might be inchoately realized in the present age.

Much of post-Reformation Christianity has denied or ignored the possibility that animals will be restored. The Catholic tradition, following Aquinas's lead, has been fairly unanimous in that regard, but notable exceptions appear in the Protestant tradition.[11] The Anglican curate Richard Dean, for example, defended the resurrection of animals in his book *An Essay on the Future Life of Brutes* (1767), out of theodicy concerns. Like us, animals suffer. We should not, therefore, deny animals the same hope we have, "the Thought of a future and a better World; a World where all Pain is excluded, and all Tears for ever wiped away."[12] This view, however, was not the norm in Protestantism, and all the less so in Catholic thought. In contrast, early Christian thinkers typically expected that Christ's redemption would include all creation. Given the hope of many like myself that the Church's theology of animals and its corresponding ethics will continue to develop, the support for an inclusive eschatology found in those early voices (many formally designated as theological "doctors" by the Catholic Church) provides a welcomed encouragement for revisiting the Church's theology of animal life.

Among the post-apostolic thinkers supporting an eschatological destiny for all creation, the figure who has drawn the most interest among ecotheologians is Irenaeus, the second-century bishop of Lyon (d. 202, martyr). Irenaeus's eschatology centers on the deutero-Pauline theme of Christ as the endpoint of all creation. From the beginning, God planned to bring creation to its fulfillment under the aegis of Christ, "summing up all things in Himself" and drawing "all things to Himself at the proper time."[13] In this way, creation will be, Irenaeus maintained, "restored to its primeval condition."[14] Similarly, Ephrem the Syrian (d. 373; doctor of the Church) states in his *Hymns on Paradise* that in the eschaton, God will renew both heaven and earth, "liberating all creatures, / granting them paschal joy, along with us."[15] Athanasius of Alexandria (d. 373; doctor of the Church) is also a promising resource as demonstrated in Denis Edwards's *Partaking of God*. Athanasius appeals to the divinization theme common in Eastern Christianity. Humanity will be deified, and other creatures, through their common bond with humanity, will share in this divinization.[16]

John Chrysostom (d. 407; doctor of the Church) likewise ties the redemptive fate of nonhuman creatures to humanity. In his homily on chapter 8 of Romans, Chrysostom makes two arguments that such creatures will share in humanity's redemptive transformation. First, he argues that just as creation became corruptible due to human sin, so also creation will, like the human body, become incorruptible when God redeems humanity. Second, he appeals to the example of a nurse caring for a child who is destined to become king. When he is so elevated, the nurse will also be elevated and thus share in his joys and blessings. Similarly, nonhuman creatures, who are made to serve humanity, will also be lifted up when God transforms creation so that humanity's joys will overflow to include all creatures. Thus, "creation is to come to the enjoyment of all those good things" that God has planned for redeemed humanity.[17]

Augustine of Hippo (d. 430; doctor of the Church) had a different interpretation of this Romans passage. He was one of the earliest Church thinkers to interpret Paul's discourse about "creation's groaning" as referring not to nonhuman creatures but to aspects of human nature; in so doing, he championed a view that was to become common in the Western Church. Nonetheless, Augustine also praised creation for providing us with sacramental signs of the Creator's glory, and he believed that it would continue to do so in the age to come. In the eschaton, he tells us, humanity will see God in "the whole creation as it then will be."[18]

Like Irenaeus, Maximus the Confessor (d. 662; described as "the great Greek Doctor of the Church" by Pope Benedict XVI) saw the integration of all things in Christ as the fundamental goal of creation.[19] God's creative intent for each creature, expressed in terms of what Maximus calls the *logoi*, is that it be harmonized and joined together as one within the Logos. The array of creaturely life forms, which might appear to us as randomly diverse, are expressions of the one Logos and as such will be drawn into an eschatological unity in Christ.[20]

What is particularly helpful for us in Maximus's thought is that through his concept of the *logoi*, he grounds the existence of individual creatures not in creation (which might imply that individual creatures are merely secondary expressions of the divine act of creating) but rather in God's eternal wisdom and creative intention *for that particular creature*.[21] Individual creatures, not a generic creation, are the objects of God's creative labor. Maximus's stress on God's eschatological intent for the individual creature contrasts with what I refer to below as an "epic eschatology," in which creation is redeemed *collectively* and not in terms of individual creatures.

These are significant voices in the tradition, and their affirmation of a creation-inclusive eschatology is remarkable in its contrast with the tradition that followed in Aquinas's wake.[22] Thinkers of the patristic era supported some form of a nonhuman restoration because Scripture, they rightly recognized, attests to such a future. Although contemporary biblical commentaries follow different methods and have different starting assumptions, their interpretations broadly affirm the creation-inclusive eschatologies that appeared in the post-apostolic age. In the previous chapter, we noted some of these passages. The Noahic covenant of Genesis 9 is made with "every living creature" and would last "for all ages to come" (Gn 9:10, 12). The prophet Hosea describes a covenant that God will make "with the wild animals, with the birds of the air, and with the things that crawl on the ground" (Hos 2:20). These passages indicate a "future restoration" that God will accomplish "by mediating a covenant between Israel and creation."[23]

Similar eschatologically-inclusive passages appear in Zechariah and Ezekiel. Zechariah's vision is of a future Jerusalem that "will be unwalled, because of the abundance of people and beasts in its midst" (Zec 2:8). Chapter 36 of Ezekiel, an extended meditation on the substance of Israel's eschatological hope, includes the blessing of fertility for animals and an abundance of crops. Other prophetic texts also make a connection between Israel's salvation and the earth's flourishing.[24] Particularly significant for a creaturely inclusive eschaton is Isaiah's depiction of a peaceable kingdom filled with creatures in harmony with one another (Is 11:6–9), a sign that divine justice will be established over all creatures.[25] The dominant message to be derived from Old Testament texts is that the eschaton will be more creature-inclusive than assumed by Thomistic thought:[26] "In the end, the Old Testament anticipates that salvation will be as wide as creation."[27]

An initial perusal of Jesus's teaching might not seem encouraging as his proclamation of the kingdom does not specifically address the question of animals' place within it. And although Jesus regularly challenges his disciples to exercise compassion and generosity in the face of human suffering, we never find him directly delivering a similar challenge about care for nonhuman creatures. Nonetheless, his teachings and practices assume as binding, without any need to defend, the traditional Jewish belief that animals should be treated with kindness.[28] We see this compassion in Jesus's commendations of efforts to relieve animal suffering on the Sabbath against narrow interpretations of the Torah's prohibition of Sabbath labor (Mt 12:11–12; Lk 13:15–16; Lk 14:5) and in his observation of the providential care that God gives to all creatures and to each and every creature (Mt 6:28–29, 10:29–31; Lk 12:6–7, 12:24).[29]

With regard to Jesus's views toward animals, skeptics might appeal to the troubling account of the Gadarene demoniacs and their expulsion into a herd of swine (Mt 8:28–34, Mk 5:1–20, and Lk 8:26–39). In it, Jesus allows (Mark and Luke) or commands (Matthew) that demons leave the afflicted human(s) and enter the swine, which are then drowned, leaving one to wonder whether Jesus had any concern for the perished animals. However, the story should be interpreted in terms of both its textual and cultural contexts. In all three Gospels, it occurs after Jesus's calming of the storm in a series of miracle stories, suggesting that the key point of the Gadarene account is to show that his "mighty deeds include both healings and displays of power over nature."[30] The story's use of pigs likely reflects the Old Testament's view of them as unclean.[31] Also, in the classic understanding, expelled demons would have sought out new hosts or returned to their previous ones, and thus Jesus had little choice but to provide the demons with a new vessel or dwelling place in order to prevent further harm to the human community.[32] We should, then, be cautious about allowing a secondary literary device (i.e., Jesus's use of pigs) to bear the weight of a revealed truth about the value of animals.

In contrast, an allusive indication that Jesus's redemptive work includes nonhuman creation is offered in the brief statement of Mark's Gospel, "Jesus was with the wild beasts." Placed in the context of the biblical narrative, the statement intimates "the messianic Son of God embarking on his mission to inaugurate the kingdom." "Jesus goes into the wilderness precisely to encounter the beings of the nonhuman world," so that he can "establish his messianic relationship" with those creatures before preaching the kingdom to the human world.[33]

We already saw in chapter 2 that explicit New Testament support for nonhuman redemption appears in the deutero-Pauline texts. The passages foretell a cosmic restoration that has been effected through "the resurrection and exaltation of Christ."[34] Allan Galloway believes that we find a similar cosmic restoration theme in John's appeal to Jesus as the Logos-Word. The beginning of John's Gospel "is tantamount to the assertion that in and through Christ the whole universe is reaching its maturity and returning to its perfection."[35] Because of the theme's presence in Pauline and Johannine writings, along with related apocalyptic imagery appearing in other parts of the New Testament, Galloway concludes that "the cosmic work of Christ, in one form or another, pervades the New Testament."[36]

The *locus classicus*, however, in support of an inclusive, cosmic redemption occurs in chapter 8 of Paul's letter to the Romans:

> For creation awaits with eager expectation the revelation of the children of God; for creation was made subject to futility, not of its own accord but because of the one who subjected it, in hope that creation itself would be set free from slavery to corruption and share in the glorious freedom of the children of God. We know that all creation is groaning in labor pains even until now; and not only that, but we ourselves, who have the firstfruits of the

Spirit, we also groan within ourselves as we wait for adoption, the redemption of our bodies. (Rom 8: 19–23)

Only with Augustine did the tradition begin to interpret this passage,
against both the plain sense of the text and post-apostolic readings of it,
to exclude nonhuman creatures. Unfortunately, what had been an atypical
reading eventually became the ecclesial norm. An essay by Cherryl Hunt,
David Horrell, and Christopher Southgate provides an overview of the
convoluted interpretive history of the text.[37] Modern scholarship through
the middle of the twentieth century tended to minimize or even reject
creation-inclusive interpretations, and only in the last fifty years or so have
these views begun to change.[38] The essay's conclusions about the ecological significance of the passage are cautious. Romans 8:19–23, it argues,
does far less "than its status as a 'mantra for Christian environmentalism'
would suggest."[39] Because the text is "brief and allusive," any attempt to
understand the nature of creation's futility or its liberation simply on the
basis of this text alone is unwise.[40]

Nonetheless, the text affirms some form of an eschatological destiny
for nonhuman creatures. It underscores the "intrinsic worth of creation"
and links "human redemption and creation's liberation."[41] Though it is
"hard to deny a certain anthropocentrism" in the text,[42] the authors suggest that it can be seen as a "chastened and humble anthropocentrism,"
one that accepts the importance of the human person while also rejecting
the view that "there is no value or eschatological purpose for the rest of
creation."[43]

Conciliar and post-conciliar teachings on creation have progressed, if
haltingly, toward a comparable eschatology, one that similarly entails a
"chastened and humble anthropocentrism"—at least in comparison to
earlier views—while also giving "value and eschatological purpose" to nonhuman creation. Five principles that regularly appear in official Church
statements during the period from Vatican II up to the publication of Pope
Francis's encyclical *Laudato Si'* express the Church's newly complicated
position regarding humanity, creation, and the eschaton. The first two principles espouse traditional views. First, and most emphatically, the human
person, distinct from all other creatures, is made in God's image, and as
such is the primary focus of God's work of creation and redemption. The
person is the "center and crown" of all things on earth,[44] and "is the only
creature on earth which God willed for itself."[45]

Second, creation is a gift from God, one of whose purposes—if not the
main or sole purpose—is the well-being of humanity: God made creation

"on man's account."[46] This commitment pervades post–Vatican II teaching. However, in the context of a growing ecological crisis, it has been frequently deployed, with unintended irony, as an argument against environmental misuse: Abusing nature is wrong because it is not good for us. By an "ill-considered exploitation of nature," we risk becoming "the victim of [nature's] degradation."[47] We must respect "the particular goodness of every creature" to avoid "contempt of the creator" and "disastrous consequences for human beings."[48] Self-interested environmentalism was a regular theme in Pope John Paul II's 1985 address to representatives of the United Nations in Kenya:[49] "It is a requirement of our human dignity . . . to exercise dominion over creation in such a way that it truly serves the human family. . . . All created goods are directed to the good of all humanity. . . . *God is glorified when creation serves the integral development of the whole human family*" (emphasis in the original).[50] "The Catholic Church approaches the care and protection of the environment from the point of view of *the human person*" (emphasis in the original).[51]

With the third principle, however, a decidedly new note—at odds with the biotically sparse world of the Thomistic eschaton—is sounded: Creation will share in the redemption of humanity. The documents do not develop this commitment beyond two intertwined suggestions: Creation will be renewed, and its renewal will be linked to that of the human person—"At that time, the human race *as well as the entire world, which is intimately related to man and attains to its end through him*, will be perfectly reestablished in Christ" (emphasis added).[52] "*Man, and through him all creation, is destined for the glory of God*" (emphasis in the original).[53] We will have occasion to develop this principle, and also the next, fourth principle, in chapter 4.

Fourth, God calls on the human person to participate in the work of creation and in its redemption and restoration. As "created in the image of God," the human person shares "*in the activity of the Creator*, and . . . in a sense continues to develop that activity" (emphasis in the original).[54] The human person has been given "a mandate to relate himself and the totality of things to Him Who was to be acknowledged as the Lord and Creator of all."[55]

Finally, the documents of this era are increasingly marked by emphatic denunciations of environmentally abusive practices and by moral exhortations toward greater environmental care. As I noted above, these appeals sometimes reference human self-interest; but in other instances, they are grounded in theocentric claims similar to those I noted in the last chapter. God, not humankind, has established norms for creation, its integrity, and its proper treatment. Humanity must put aside "pride and deranged self-love" and receive creation as a gift from God with respect, reverence, and gratitude.[56] Humanity's exercise of dominion must "remain subject to the will of God, who imposes limits upon [the] use and dominion over things,"[57] and "is to be accomplished within the framework of obedience to divine law."[58]

MOVING BEYOND AN "EPIC ESCHATOLOGY"

There are praiseworthy developments in these texts but also some weaknesses. They replace the almost cavalier attitude toward animal suffering found in early twentieth-century writings with stringent exhortations to respect nonhuman creatures. They not only affirm that creation will be restored but also, as we saw above, appeal to inclusive phrases (e.g., "the entire world," "all creation," and "the totality of things") to describe that restoration, suggesting that it will encompass creaturely life in all its biotically diverse array. Some weaknesses in Vatican documents before *Laudato Si'* include an exaggerated emphasis on creation's service to humankind, an insufficient attention to the organic solidarity of all creatures, and a limited interest in nonhuman creatures' particular forms of flourishing, independent of human needs.

Of significant concern for our discussion, however, is that the renewal of creation discussed in these texts does not explicitly move beyond an "epic eschatology." I use this term to refer to those views that describe creation's eschatological renewal in terms of a collective narrative that in the end devalues the individual nonhuman agents living in the present age. An epic eschatology of creation might propose, for example, that salvation history leads up to a new creation composed of new forms of nonhuman life but not the particular animal creatures that have lived and died in the present order. Such an eschatology would not so much restore nonhuman creation as create a new version of it. The "objective redemption" approach advocated by some ecotheologians is effectively an epic eschatology. Creatures are remembered as part of God's creation; but their subjective existences, as individual creatures with agency, are lost. In one version of this approach, all that occurs in evolutionary history, including its "suffering and tragedy . . . is 'saved' by being taken eternally into God's own feeling of the world." Here, creatures "abide permanently within the everlasting empathy of God," and thus are "redeemed from absolute perishing."[59]

I do not believe this approach is adequate to the biblical view of creation; yet I also recognize that the hope that God will restore the subjective existences of each and every creature is problematic. As I noted in chapter 1, it is difficult to understand what it would mean to restore a creature (e.g., a fly) that, based on what we know now, has no sense of self-identity. Thus I am sympathetic to the both/and, variegated approach suggested by Denis Edwards and others: "It may be, then, that while it is appropriate for some creatures to share in the resurrection with a transformed individual existence in God, it is at least possible that God may find it appropriate for other creatures to be taken up into divine life in another way—in the living memory of the divine Communion."[60] This book's argument focuses on the former possibility, with the claim that at least some animals have a sufficient sense of self-identity to be recipients of a resurrected life, should God choose to grant such a gift.

Generally speaking, early Christian writers, even those who favor a creation-inclusive redemption, are not clear as to whether the new creation of the eschaton will include the restoration of the specific, nonhuman creatures that live and die in the present age. Nonetheless, we can note three concerns that argue against the idea of a new creation populated with wholly new, replacement creatures. First, such a view falls short of the redemptive love revealed in Christ's life, death, *and* resurrection. This Christological inadequacy is evident in proposals like that of Holmes Rolston and Lisa Sideris. Rolston allows the possibility that "the fauna and flora" that perish in the present age might "be regenerated in an age beyond our own,"[61] but his favored view is that the Spirit redeems creatures by their "sacrificial suffering through to something higher,"[62] and he appeals to the cross as a symbol of such redemptive suffering.[63] Such a claim, however, would make sense only if Christ's redemptive suffering on the cross were the terminus of the Christian narrative instead of the resurrection, with its hope of new life ("And if Christ has not been raised . . . empty [is] your faith"; 1 Cor 15:14). Sideris likewise argues that the good achieved through the struggles of evolutionary history redeems its corresponding pain. She suggests that concerns about the suffering of particular creatures might be the product of false sentiment: "Environmental ethicists ought to be more circumspect about censuring nature—or God—for processes that fail to match human preferences." It is possible that God is concerned about "the *supervival* of the system as a whole . . . rather than the survival of each and every individual part" (emphasis in the original).[64] In both of these situations, an epic narrative is used purportedly to redeem, in the sense of making meaningful, the cosmic history of individual creatures and their eternal demise.

However, the idea that God cares primarily for the *whole* of creation and not its individual creatures goes against a commonsense understanding of what it means to love: "It is individuals who personally feel pain and suffer, not species,"[65] and one would expect that a salvific God would respond to suffering in the mode in which it occurs—that is, in the individual creature. It is not enough to redeem the whole creation and not the parts as well, "if the love of God is anything like that of an all-loving parent."[66] In response to Sideris's question of whether God's love for nature aligns with human sentiment, Scripture offers the view that "not one of [these creatures] has escaped the notice of God" (Lk 12:6).[67] Moreover, though it is true that all human language about God is inadequate, when it comes to virtuous categories like love, mercy, and patience, Scripture portrays a God whose goodness *exceeds* human assumptions—"For as the heavens tower over the earth, so his mercy towers over those who fear him" (Ps 103:11); "God . . . is generous in forgiving. For my thoughts are not your thoughts, nor are your ways my ways, says the LORD" (Is 55:7–9); "If you then, who are wicked, know how to give good gifts to your children, how much more will the Father in heaven give the holy Spirit to those who ask him?" (Lk 11:13). Our inability to grasp fully God's love is not so much because it is a different goodness than that supposed by our moral instincts but because it is an infinitely greater one.

A second reason for rejecting an epic eschatology is that the individual creature, qua individual, evidences a distinctive goodness beyond the general goodness associated with its species identity—and, we can hope, it is a goodness that God loves precisely in its particularity. This is another point on which the philosophical assumptions of Aquinas's arguments need to be challenged. In arguing against the renewal of individual animal life in the eschaton, Aquinas states that "all animals of the same species operate in the same way."[68] Because the life of any member of a species unfolds in accord with the same instincts common to the entire species, there are no relevant distinctions, he believed, between one member of a species and another; the inclusion of any particular representative of that species would suffice for the restoration of God's creation.[69] The goodness and beauty of the world to come would be indifferent to which particular representative of an animal species is present in it—a resurrected animal or newly created one would serve creation's goodness and the divine glory equally well.

The question raised by Aquinas's argument, then, is whether the differences between individual members of a species are substantial enough to endow a particular animal with an individualized and, we might say, inimitable goodness. Contemporary animal studies indicate that animals—dogs, cats, elephants, great apes, dolphins, and the like—are individual subjects with distinctive personalities (lazy, aggressive, aloof, nurturing, curious, playful, sweet, shy, mellow, excitable, etc.), and are thus rightly to be seen as more than interchangeable instances of a species.[70] The naming of companion animals—which personalizes them as distinct, and distinctly beloved, members of our household—is no anthropomorphic projection but rather a truthful sign of the animal's creaturely reality; that is, each of them has its own integral subjectivity, identity, and character. Because they are agents with particular personalities, they elicit in us particular reactions of enjoyment and affection. We are able to love these individual animals distinctively because they are good in distinctive ways. What is true in these experiences also holds for any member of a developed species: Each is distinct in its personality. The loss of their particular goodness in death is a loss for creation and would be an impoverishment of the beauty and goodness of God's new creation. God could, no doubt, fill in the aesthetic gap, so to speak, with other forms of creaturely goodness, but it would not be the same goodness that God had willed and loved into existence as part of the present order of creation.

Finally, because the creatures of this world are embedded within manifold and complex relationships with both human and nonhuman creatures, we can imagine that just as the God of the covenant cherishes the goodness of these interrelationships, so too does God cherish the individual creatures that now compose them. In a covenantal eschaton, creatures can be saved because creatures can relate. Furthermore, because personhood and relationship are coextensive in the triune life, it seems reasonable to believe that God would have a specific regard for creatures of the present order precisely insofar as they are at once particularized *and* related to other creatures.[71]

The failure to recognize the depth of creation's capacity to relate contributes to the decision by New Testament scholar Gerhard Lohfink to deny subjective redemption to nonhuman creatures and adopt instead an epic eschatology. He recognizes that the biblical witness requires that we affirm the redemptive solidarity of all creation.[72] However, Lohfink maintains that animals have no agency vis-à-vis God, and thus they can have no salvific interrelationship with God.[73] Indeed, against the assertions of numerous Old Testament texts, he believes it to be "obvious" that nonhuman creatures are not able to praise God on their own. In a strained defense of his view, Lohfink argues that creatures praise God "only because human beings again and again look at the world penetratingly, attentively, and with astonishment, appreciating the power and beauty of creation and making themselves its voice."[74] Thus forced to reconcile two commitments—that humans alone have a relationship with God and that all creation is to be redeemed—he proposes an intensely anthropocentric version of an epic eschatology: Nonhuman creatures live on only in the memory of resurrected humanity.[75] Even the redemption of cognitively sophisticated, pre-human hominids will entail nothing more than their continuation as "part of [humanity's] cultural memory."[76] Ironically, when it comes to humans, Lohfink rightly recognizes that such a redemption would utterly fail to satisfy our longing: "I don't want to live on in the hearts of my countrymen; I want to live on in my apartment."[77] Though God created animals to be agents with subjectivity and personality, the ultimate destiny of that agency, for Lohfink, is that it cease to exist as part of God's creation except as a humanly remembered past.[78] Animals of the present order are trinitarian and covenantal; in Lohfink's view, their redemption fails to reflect either.

Because of the Creator's trinitarian imprint, nonhuman creatures have a far richer potential for relationships than is acknowledged by Lohfink. Following the theology of Hans Urs von Balthasar, I argue that this trinitarian imprint appears in what can be called "creaturely bipolarity": The individual identity of each creature, human and nonhuman, is established and formed through its encounters with other creatures. John Haught, following Teilhard de Chardin, views this individuality in relationship as part of the providential teleology directing evolutionary history. "True union or convergence," Haught states, "simultaneously individuates and differentiates." Creation's "ultimate unity . . . coincides with creation's maximum differentiation, which in the human sphere means maximum *personalization*" (emphasis in the original).[79] Though Haught focuses on the human implications of this evolutionary development, I believe they logically extend to other creatures once we reject a binary interpretation of creaturely life (i.e., that humans are absolutely distinct from every other creature). The movement of creation and its creatures toward God (imagined as a union that individuates, to use Haught's terms) is realized not only in the human person but also in the interchanges of individual animals and their communities.

We will further explore the possibility of creaturely agency vis-à-vis God later in this chapter and in the next one. My argument here, however, has been that we have good reasons to reject an epic eschatology. These reasons are based on a desire to affirm that God's redemptive love is addressed to the creature in its particularity; to recognize that a unique, inimitable goodness is found in individual creatures; and to preserve the covenantal agency of creatures that is already at work within the relational bonds of the present order.

POPE FRANCIS'S *LAUDATO SI'*
AND ANIMAL REDEMPTION

Pope Francis's encyclical *Laudato Si'* is an important advance in Catholic understanding of animal eschatology and, more broadly, its theology of creation.[80] (Henceforth in this section, *Laudato Si'* is abbreviated as "*LS*," followed by the corresponding paragraph number.) It is the first encyclical to have the environment as its main theme. The encyclical does not discuss nonhuman creation in isolation but continues the practice of Catholic social teaching of examining contemporary problems in terms of the moral failures of individuals and the cultures they inhabit—in this case, disdain for the poor (who suffer most from the effects of climate change), rampant consumerism (the "throwaway culture"), technocratic instrumentalism, and a general disregard for God's plan for creation. It affirms the traditional teaching that not "all living beings [are] on the same level" and that human beings have "unique worth" (*LS*, 90). The pope also makes theocentric appeals ("We are not God," *LS*, 67)—with the hope of restoring "men and women to their rightful place" and "putting an end to their claim to absolute dominion over the earth" (*LS*, 75).

Although the main source for matters germane to our topic can be found in the document's second chapter (*LS*, 62–100), where the pope develops his theology of creation, relevant themes reappear throughout the document. If a theme's recurrence denotes its importance, then the encyclical must be seen as a passionate plea that we recognize our embeddedness within creation and our fundamental solidarity with all its creatures. "Francis's theology of the communion of creation" is, as Denis Edwards suggests, "the integrating center of the encyclical."[81] Throughout the document, the pope pointedly and repeatedly declares that "everything"—*everything*: humans, animals, plants, all creation—is "connected," "in communion," "interrelated," and "interconnected" (*LS*, 16, 42, 70, 76, 91, 117, 120, 137, 138). The fundamental interconnectivity of all creatures reflects their trinitarian origin:

> The divine Persons are subsistent relations, and the world, created according to the divine model, is a web of relationships. Creatures tend towards God, and in turn it is proper to every living being to tend towards other things, so that throughout the universe we can find any number of constant and secretly interwoven relationships. . . . Everything is interconnected, and this invites us to develop a spirituality of that global solidarity which flows from the mystery of the Trinity. (*LS*, 240)

It is not possible to be truly human without relationships that encompass not only God and our fellow humans but also nonhuman creatures: "The human person grows more, matures more and is sanctified more to the extent that he or she enters into relationships, going out from themselves to live in communion with God, with others and with all creatures" (*LS*, 240).[82] Thus, when the text speaks of our interconnection with the rest of creation, it implies something more than just an elective relationship or ecological codependency (though those are also included). Humanity's connection to creation is fundamental to the human identity.[83] We are all "linked by unseen bonds and together form a kind of universal family" (*LS*, 89) and are "joined [with the rest of creatures] in a splendid universal communion" (*LS*, 220). "Human beings too are creatures of this world" (*LS*, 43). Our connection with other creatures is so profound that we can feel "the extinction of a species as a painful disfigurement."[84] Echoing the universal Noahic covenant examined in chapter 2, Francis describes creation as "woven together by the love God has for each of his creatures and which also unites us in fond affection with brother sun, sister moon, brother river and mother earth" (*LS*, 92).

Less obvious (though ultimately more impactful for our topic) is the *particularity* with which the pope discusses nonhuman creatures. Against the traditional practice of using collective terms to denote nonhuman life (e.g., "brutes," "irrational creatures," "creation"), the pope's reflections regularly refer to the particular, concrete creature: "Each [creature] must be cherished with love and respect" (*LS*, 42). God has a loving plan for "every creature" (*LS*, 76). "Even the fleeting life of the least of beings is the object of [God's] love, and in its few seconds of existence, God enfolds it with his affection" (*LS*, 77). The fact that the human person is uniquely the *imago Dei* "should not make us overlook the fact that each creature has its own purpose. None is superfluous" (*LS*, 84). The "importance and meaning of each creature" is found "within the entirety of God's plan" (*LS*, 86). The pope appeals to Scripture to exhort us to care for the individual creature: "With moving tenderness," Jesus reminded his disciples, "that each one of them is important in God's eyes" (*LS*, 96). In light of these texts, I question Celia Deane-Drummond's statement that Francis's "overall approach tends to prioritize the protection of the ecosystem rather than individual creatures."[85] She is right to highlight the encyclical's attention to ecosystems; but the document also underscores, repeatedly and emphatically, that God cares for creatures in their individuality.

The most groundbreaking development in Church teaching, however, is the inherent worth that the encyclical attributes to nonhuman creatures.[86] The pope pointedly rejects the view that the primary value of animals and plants lies in their service to humankind. "The ultimate purpose of other creatures is not to be found in us" (*LS*, 83); rather, the value of each living being lies "in God's eyes" (*LS*, 69) and in this sense is extrinsic to the proximate needs and goals of the human person. With this statement, the pope undercuts the traditional Thomistic understanding of animal life and its anthropocentric teleology. Though service to humanity may well be *part* of the reason that animals were created, their "telos," the end toward which they are directed, is not to be found in such service. And, if the value and purpose of animals in this life does not depend on human need, there is no reason to believe that their presence in the next life will depend on whether or not they will be needed by humanity.

The pope connects his theocentric valuing of creatures to creation's capacity to praise God, citing the *Catechism*'s statement that "by their mere existence," creatures "bless [God] and give him glory."[87] Similarly, he tells us, the Canadian bishops "rightly" point out "that no creature is excluded from this manifestation of God: 'From panoramic vistas to the tiniest living form, nature is a constant source of wonder and awe. It is also a continuing revelation of the divine.'"[88] In the light of Christ, the world becomes sacramental: "Thus, the creatures of this world no longer appear to us under merely natural guise because the risen One is mysteriously holding them to himself and directing them towards fullness as their end. The very flowers of the field and the birds which his human eyes contemplated and admired are now imbued with his radiant presence" (*LS*, 100). Because the creatures of the world radiate the divine, "there is a mystical meaning to be found in a leaf, in a mountain trail, in a dewdrop, in a poor person's face" (*LS*, 233).

On the question of whether the document moves the tradition beyond an epic eschatology, the document does not provide a clear response, but one can find support for such a view in its text. Francis is insistent that redemption will include nonhuman creatures: "The ultimate destiny of the universe is in the fullness of God" (*LS*, 83), and "all creatures are moving forward with us and through us towards a common point of arrival, which is God, in that transcendent fullness where the risen Christ embraces and illumines all things" (*LS*, 83). The text's reference to "creatures" (i.e., plural, individual entities, not creation in general), reflects the pope's emphasis on the concrete and the particular. Moreover, the phrases "with us" and "a common point of arrival" suggest a salvific journey for nonhuman creatures that is similar to that of humans. The commonality of this journey is further underscored by the statement's Christological and covenantal language: "Christ embraces and illumines *all things*," not just humans but each and every creature (emphasis added). The phrase "through us" continues the idea we saw above (in the second section) that humans share in the task of creation's restoration. An eschatological inclusion of animal creatures has, as I continue to argue, practical implications for how we value and treat nonhuman creatures, and thus Michael Northcott is right to describe Francis's eschatological inclusiveness as his "boldest intervention in the Church's response to the ecological crisis."[89] Nonetheless, because the document does not develop a specific theory of the redemption of individual nonhuman creatures, and because the idea is relatively new, at least in the recent doctrinal tradition, I am cautious about claiming that the document endorses a non-epic view of redemption—that is, one that includes the particular creatures that are part of the present age.

Weakening the encyclical's teaching on animal redemption is its lack of a sustained reflection on the "dark side of nature," a criticism raised by both Deane-Drummond and Edwards.[90] The document does not examine the creaturely costs of the evolutionary process but instead assumes a "somewhat romanticized focus on creation theology,"[91] and too often portrays "God's creation as a harmonious ordered cosmos without acknowledging the violence, pain, and death of the natural world."[92] Because the encyclical does not examine creation's fallenness and the theological implications of its primordial wound, it is not impelled to consider how Christ's redemption might address the suffering endured by nonhuman creatures. Pope Francis appreciates the need for a final, redemptive resolution of life's tragic undertows when discussing *human* salvation, and we can hope he is similarly inclined with regard to animal redemption. "How wonderful," he exclaims, "is the certainty that each human life is not adrift in the midst of hopeless chaos, in a world ruled by pure chance or endlessly recurring cycles!" (*LS*, 65). He is right, of course, but if we were to reject an individual redemption for nonhuman creatures, we would be left with a world where the overwhelming majority of creatures live lives that are virtually meaningless, "hopeless," and "ruled by pure chance."

Even though the document's soteriology of nonhuman creatures does not expressly affirm a non-epic eschatology, its language indicates sympathy for such a view. In order to give this implicit suggestion a theological basis, I turn to Hans Urs von Balthasar. Not only do his theological commitments align with some of the themes raised in Pope Francis's encyclical, but, in addition, the various arguments that he marshals in defense of creation's integrity will help us see how the covenantal goods present in creaturely existence (as suggested in chapter 2) can provide building blocks for a theology of creaturely redemption.

BALTHASAR AND CREATION

Balthasar's theology of creation is scattered throughout his corpus, but three locations are particularly important for introducing its core themes. In the first volume of his *Theological Aesthetics*, he develops a theory of human agency that grounds the agent's response in his or her perception. Insofar as creaturely existence is good, it displays a beauty, and our perception of this beauty/goodness elicits our response. This natural dynamic is transformed in Christ: God uses the language of creation to reveal divine glory, and the appearance of this glory, in turn, calls forth the response of the disciple.[93]

Second, in his *Theology of Karl Barth*, Balthasar identifies what he sees as a fundamental limitation in Barth: his failure to appreciate that creation has its own "*eidos*," that is, creation's innate but relative meaning that is taken up in Christ to serve as the instrument of divine revelation. "The Incarnation demands that there be a relatively solid content of meaning that cannot be totally robbed of its substance when we provisionally abstract from our supernatural goal," Balthasar writes.[94]

Third and finally, in the first volume of his *Theo-Logic*, he confronts the question of how creaturely existence can become a vehicle for divine revelation. God's appearance in the Incarnate Son, he argues, presumes that creation is fundamentally disposed to its transformation by God into a site of divine revelation. Indeed, creation is fashioned with just such an end in mind.

Together, these and other sources show the importance of creation's integrity and relative autonomy in Balthasar's theological project while also underscoring, as he repeatedly states, that creation's ultimate meaning is found in Christ. The result is a theology of creation that preserves both the integrity of creation and its ultimate destiny in Christ and thus embodies the two core commitments of Catholicism's nature/grace interplay.

For Balthasar, three dynamics appear in a creature's relationships with other creatures. The "object-other" manifests itself—that is, its identity, integrity, individuality, and particularity—to the "subject-perceiver." The perceiving subject is in turn moved beyond itself, ek-statically, by this self-expression of the perceived other. The perceiver and the perceived each realize "self" in the inter-agential encounter between the two. These three dynamic phases—object-expression, subject-reception, and the bipolarity of self-realization—together realize creation's fundamental openness to a deeper incorporation into God's triune life.

Turning to each of these three phases of relationality, I note, first, Balthasar's claim that God gives all creatures the ability to manifest themselves without exhausting their inner richness. This expressive hiddenness is obvious in the case of human persons, who can choose to reveal or hide various aspects of their identity in speech and action but Balthasar claims that something similar occurs in nonhuman life as well. The inner richness of animals is exemplified in the fact that though they are able, as subjects, to express themselves, their full subjectivity remains hidden from us. Plants strike wonder in us in their capacity to grow, heal, bloom, and yield fruit. Even inanimate objects defy perfect transparency. Balthasar recognizes, of course, that observation and scientific study can uncover much about the creatures of our world. Balthasar's point here is that no matter how much we learn about them, creatures will always retain hidden, often alluring depths that resist empirical understanding—the paradigm for which is found in the beloved, who can always surprise us with new expressions of his or her inexhaustible goodness in words and acts.

The veiled goodness that appears in the world's creatures leads us to the mystery of being itself: the simple but unanswerable question of why something is. In light of this mystery, every creature becomes a "theophany," a reflection of the Creator within creation. In the contingency and beauty of creaturely existence, we perceive an ultimate freedom (it does not need to exist) and, in turn, experience a giftedness (its presence to us is not only freely bestowed but also attractive and thus experienced as gift). We are thus drawn into a shared experience of our fellow creatures and of the God who freely brought them into existence.

This brings us to the second aspect of creaturely relationality: the responding subject. We are, by divine intent, receptive to the manifestation of the other. The subject for Balthasar "is *as such* a being with windows, a being hospitable to other realities," and thus the other affects the beholder.[95] Balthasar appeals to the quality of beauty (a quality that is, along with truth and goodness, shared by all creatures insofar as they exist) to indicate the capacity of all creatures—human, animal, plant, and inanimate object—to elicit an agent's response. The appearance of the other draws the perceiving subject beyond herself, making a claim on her, that she allow the other to "be": to be able to manifest itself, to be true to its identity, and to share this identity with others. Balthasar's aesthetics proposes that truly perceiving our fellow creatures, both human and non-human, requires more than a disengaged observation of their factual features. Rather, we must allow ourselves to be moved beyond ourselves (ek-stasis) and surrender to the other, providing the other with an acting space to be its own "self." Moreover, as we "let be" the other in its self-expression, we form ourselves into responding agents, and in so doing, express our own identity.[96]

This subject/object bipolarity, our third element, takes any number of earthly forms (e.g., wonder before creation, dialogue, I/Thou encounters marked by genuine freedom, and erotic love). Balthasar believes bipolarity to be fundamental to the created order. Indeed, we *are* only insofar as we are also in relationship. The human person is not a creature who, through external circumstances, has various relationships with the world and its creatures. Instead, the human creature *is* through these relationships; she gains self "only on account of having been communicated."[97]

In each of these three dimensions of creaturely relationality—the expressive other, the ek-static subject, and the bipolar/dialogical character of all encounters—Balthasar sees a reflection of creation's innate disposition toward receiving a covenantal relationship and "an echo, however distant, of [God's] infinite, majestic freedom."[98] Our development of an inclusive eschatology will depend on Balthasar's argument that creaturely existence reflects the *triune* God of Christian revelation. For "just as the Divine Persons are *themselves* only insofar as they go out to the Others (who are always Other)," so also creatures are "*themselves* only insofar as they go beyond themselves . . . [and] surrender themselves for their neighbor" (emphasis in the original).[99] The truth of the Trinity revealed in Christ, "the fact that 'the Other' exists is *absolutely good*," by analogy "also applies to creation" (emphasis in the original).[100] The otherness of the creature is treasured by God; the creature can be drawn into the divine life because, like the triune God, it is fundamentally open to the other.

Balthasar's claims here align with contemporary theologies of the Trinity that see human relationality as a reflection of God's triune life. The International Theological Commission's document "Communion and Stewardship" (examined in chapter 2) notes that "God is not a solitary being, but a communion of three Persons" and, therefore, the human orientation toward relationships "is founded essentially on the Trinity of divine Persons." Never alone, the human person "is always constituted with others and is summoned to form a community with them."[101] Similarly, Walter Kasper maintains that "the ultimate and highest reality is not substance but relation." "The meaning of being is therefore to be found not in substance that exists in itself, but in self-communicating love."[102] Catherine Mowry LaCugna likewise argues that "person not substance is the ultimate ontological category."[103] Particularly influential on this point has been the Orthodox metropolitan and scholar John Zizioulas: "*To be* and *to be in relation* becomes identical" (emphasis in the original).[104] The Finnish theologian and Lutheran minister Veli-Matti Kärkkäinen concludes that, among the important developments in recent theologies of creation, "probably none surpasses the importance of the shift from substance ontology . . . to relationality and holistic explanations."[105]

My appropriation of Balthasar's approach to creation's relational ontology comprises three elements. First, creation's relational inclination is the nature upon which grace builds. Second, the meaning and value of the concrete, individual creature is preserved and redeemed within the one economic drama between God and creation. And third, the relational drama that unfolds in a creature's life is a particularizing and personalizing form.

Examining each of these, I suggest, first, that the attributes of expressiveness, receptivity, and relational bipolarity are common, albeit in varied ways, to all creatures and act as covenantal building blocks. Together, they form the "nature" upon which trinitarian grace builds. All beings have a fundamental commonality with one another (because all share in created *esse*, being) and display capacities (covenantal traits) that are differentiated incrementally rather than in a binary of human and all-else. These attributes suggest that though the universe is unfolding dynamically, it does not do so aimlessly. The universe displays certain qualities, linked to its covenantal disposition, and these will not (in a Christian theological view) be cast off in the course of creation's biological development. Even in their most basic act of existing and expressing themselves before the other, creatures manifest their trinitarian disposition toward the covenant. The nature on which grace builds is not simply that of the human person but rather the ontological reality shared by all creatures and characterized by expressiveness, receptivity, and relational bipolarity. We can take Balthasar one step further and suggest that through the gift of grace, the creatures of the world can and, we hope, will be unfolded within the trinitarian drama because, however diverse and varied, they are, nonetheless, covenantally inclined.

The second element of my appropriation of Balthasar is his strategy for guarding the particular and the finite within the salvific drama. A fundamental goal of his theo-dramatic theory is to show how human dramas (e.g., the lives of individual persons, with all their particularities) are given eternal value in salvation history and not reduced to transitory contingencies within an overarching drama between God and creation. "Theodrama" is the term that Balthasar gives to salvation history as this history fulfills—reinterpreting without overturning—the native meanings of finite, concrete dramas. Salvation history protects the person's integrity by taking her story and giving it a new, christomorphic reach and meaning. Balthasar's antagonist on this point is Hegel, whose philosophy of an all-encompassing historical drama, he believes, effaces the singular importance of the individual, creaturely drama. He praises Maximus and Aquinas for preserving "the essence of every thing—or better, [for setting] each thing's *integral completeness* within an openness and a readiness for union that allows it to be elevated and brought to fulfillment" (emphasis added).[106] His concern here is similar to that found in critiques of totalizing discourses: frameworks, metanarratives, or linguistic constellations that effectively obscure the distinctiveness of the concrete other. In this vein, Rowan Williams, reflecting on Balthasar's contribution to contemporary theology, astutely observes that theology's "reflections on otherness within the divine life and the peculiar otherness between the divine and the human in the identity of the Saviour, demand, in our present context, to be read afresh, as attempts to think through otherness so as to avoid totalization."[107] For Balthasar, the "otherness" that is already part of the triune essence allows God to draw the dramatic life of the human person into the dramatic life of the Godhead without either erasing her distinctive identity or compromising divine unity. We will further develop this idea of a dramatic inclusion below.

This brings us to our third element of appropriation. For Balthasar, the drama appearing in the life of the individual person can be understood as an integral and personal form. That is, it expresses, without exhausting, a particular wholeness that identifies the individual as *this* person and not another. This dramatic form, however, remains inchoate and broken as it develops across the individual's earthly life. It needs redemption and receives it through its inclusion in the dramatic life of the Godhead. Balthasar's focus is on the human person and her life story, but on the basis of his view that covenantal dispositions are to be found in all creatures, we can hope that the divine *magis* extends to include nonhuman creatures. The meanings of animal lives would remain indeterminate and incomplete apart from the theo-dramatic fulfillment that comes only through their inclusion in the divine economy.[108]

Thus, the specific challenge that I hope to address by appealing to Balthasar's notion of the theo-drama is to show how the one divine drama appearing in salvation history can integrate—drawing to itself and preserving—the earthly drama of the *individual* creature as it unfolds "horizontally" (i.e., within the earthly domain). The virtue of Balthasar's approach to drama as a theological category is that it shows how the individual dramas of the creaturely order find their ultimate meaning within the whole of the salvific narrative without losing their individual particularity. Balthasar's theology of creation draws our attention to the fundamental and constitutive role that the drama of encounter plays in forming the identity of each creature. These micro-dramas are teleologically insignificant on an evolutionary scale but, for the creatures within them, are vitally momentous. Although earthly encounters as they occur among animals do not, generally, have the quality of free choice, they are analogous to free and dramatic encounters in their expressiveness and receptivity. Their stories can be elevated, in Christ and through the Spirit. Like the drama of human life, they can be realigned with the divine-creature encounter of the salvific narrative and as such be included within that salvific drama.

We begin our exploration of how Balthasar's theo-drama understands this salvific inclusion by first examining the redemptive work of Christ. We will complete this study in the next chapter, where we incorporate the work of the Spirit.

BALTHASAR AND *HUMAN* REDEMPTION

Though Balthasar does not specify the nature of nonhuman redemption or how exactly it fits within his approach to human redemption, he asserts, repeatedly and ardently, that all creation shares in the redemption of humanity: "Scripture nowhere says that God's plan is to redeem the Church; it is always a case of redeeming the world."[109] He condemns as "egotistical" Christian hope for one's own salvation that does not also "hope for the salvific transfiguration of the whole cosmos and its tragic history."[110] He attacks Aquinas's judgment that animals and plants will be excluded from the eschaton as "cruel;" such a view "contradicts the Old Testament sense of solidarity between the living, subhuman cosmos and the world of men."[111] The task of making theological sense of these affirmations, however, is left to us. In undertaking it, I first examine briefly Balthasar's understanding of human redemption and then turn to consider how such a view might be developed into a theology of nonhuman redemption.

Maintaining that "Scripture clearly says that the events of the Cross can only be interpreted against the background of the Trinity,"[112] Balthasar constructs a theological approach whose every aspect depends conceptually on the doctrine that God is triune and not a monolithic unity. Revelation allows us, and even compels us, to apply the idea of interpersonal relations to the triune life of God.[113] The dramatic and interpersonal language with which Balthasar describes the interchange of the divine processions is, of course, analogous, but he believes it is necessary in order to portray the vital and dynamic mystery of divine love as found in revelation.[114]

The clearest reflection of this dramatic, triune life occurs in the interchange between the Father and the forsaken Son. For Balthasar, Good Friday is not the expression in time of some static love that God has for creation.[115] Rather, it is an irruption into the world of the eternally dramatic exchange between the Father and the Son, an interchange in which something new happens in the history of God's labor for the world ("Good Friday is not just the same as Easter"; God "acts dramatically in the Son's Cross and Resurrection").[116] The exchange between the Father and the Son reveals the shape of God's love. It is one of life-giving surrender to the other—the Father's self-giving to the Son and the Son's return of all to the Father. The mutual giving of Self between the Father and Son manifests a divine receptivity that grounds the possibility of God's engagement with humanity. God's immutability is not threatened by receiving, accepting, and answering humanity's response, because God is, in God's very Self, self-surrendering and interpersonal love.[117] Again, the inclusion of the creature in the divine life is possible because in God there is already an "Other."

The Father confronts sinful humanity in the person of his beloved Son. Good Friday expresses the Father's wrath toward sin, while Easter manifests God's decision to envelop even the human "no" into the divine life through God's all-encompassing love.[118] For some critics, Balthasar's language is excessive here, as when he ties the Son's suffering to the Father's wrath against sin, ostensibly projecting discord into the Godhead.[119] However, Balthasar's point is to underscore the lengths to which God goes to redeem. The alienation endured by Christ is not ultimate; it is an appearance within earthly time of the costliness of sin. This event is no threat to divine unity, because it is bounded by the love and absolute oneness of the Trinity, as shown on Easter, when the eternal fullness of the Father's love for the Son is revealed. The human condition in all its brokenness and sinfulness now finds a home, *in Christ* (i.e., in the One who took on our condition), within the divine life because the Father has, in embracing Christ, embraced sinful humanity.

In the Father's acceptance of Jesus, God determines Godself to be a God who welcomes the sinner. In Jesus's surrender (as one like ourselves) to the Father and in the Father's acceptance of Jesus (and thus of humanity), an "acting space" is opened up for the human person within the triune life. It is, Balthasar repeatedly states, a spacious, open area, made possible by the distance [*Abstand*] that stretches between the Father and the Son on the cross and the enclosure of that distance in the loving bond of the Spirit.[120] This spaciousness is such that it can include our individual identities and creatureliness as they are encircled within the life of the triune God.[121] I believe Balthasar's appeal to the metaphor of "space" is a helpful way of imagining God's covenantal and redemptive embrace of humanity. Humanity now occupies the "space" where the divine has embraced creation (i.e., in Christ), and humanity is, in Christ, turned to the Father as its Father.

In the dramatic exchange between God and the human person, each individual is called to a personalizing mission that bestows on her and her life story a Christological character. In her response to the call, even when imperfect, she fashions her life story, which is ultimately redeemed and incorporated into the drama of the triune life. Each follower of Christ is called to a distinctive mission, not so much a single, lifelong task but rather a complex life story that comprises her responses to Christ's call. It is Christological in form and faithful to the individual's identity and personhood, adapting to her strengths and weaknesses. Through this individual, personalizing mission, each of us shares in the eternal exchange between the Father and the Son (in which the Father calls forth the Son and the

Son surrenders all to the Father's will). Balthasar takes seriously Paul's description of the Christian as "in Christ." The Christian, like Christ and in Christ, stands before the Father in union with the Spirit. For Balthasar, there is no "generic elevation of the person into divine life," but rather "God's work in Christ incorporates the Christian into the *particular* relatedness of the Son as he faces the Father" (emphasis in the original).[122] It is not surprising, then, that we see in Balthasar's portrayal of the Christian life some of the same features that mark the life of Christ (e.g., loving self-surrender to the Father). We are, like Christ, given a mission from the Father that is, like Christ, self-constituting.

ANIMAL REDEMPTION

Balthasar locates humanity's salvation in the acting space established by the reciprocal Father–Son kenosis; it is capacious enough to include our creaturely stories without overturning them. Can this human soteriology be expanded to include animals? To my knowledge, the closest Balthasar comes to addressing the "how" of nonhuman redemption appears in his *Epilogue*.[123] Christ's incarnation in human form offers redemption to all creation "because the whole of the cosmos is indivisible from man, and because man himself emerged and developed from that same cosmos."[124] Balthasar's argument here reflects what I referred to in the last chapter as a "Chalcedonian incarnationalism." In contrast to a "deep incarnationalism," a Chalcedonian incarnationalism stresses the fact that Jesus became *human* (and not simply enfleshed—the emphasis of deep incarnationalism) and through his *humanity*, all creation shares in his redemptive death and resurrection. At the same time, for Balthasar it is not the assumption of human nature per se that effects creation's redemption. Alluding to the recapitulation theme noted above, where all things are drawn together in the "cosmic Christ," Balthasar argues that creation waits "not for the specific Incarnation of Jesus, but for its fulfillment in his Mystical Body."[125] As we will see in the next chapter, creatures are incorporated into this mystical body through the labor of the Spirit, whose task it is to "universalize" Christ.

Though a complete development of a creation-centric soteriology must wait until that discussion, here I can identify three of its elements, each derived from the relational ontology of creation introduced above (i.e., relational polarity is the nature upon which grace builds; in its redemption, the meaning of the creature is preserved; and the creature's life drama is a personalizing form). First, all creatures, albeit inchoately and in varied ways and degrees, already foreshadow in their lives the form which their salvation will take in Christ Jesus. It is a salvific form that will incorporate the three relational qualities shared by all creatures: the objective goodness of the creature's "otherness" before God; the innate capacity of each creature to express itself before God, others, and the world; and the constitutive role of relationality in forming the identity of the creature. Second, because of the capacious acting room within the Godhead established by the paschal mystery, the Godhead can embrace the finite creature as other, in its integral wholeness. Third, the individual life story of the creature becomes completed and fulfilled in its new relationship with God in Christ. This narratival completion of the creature's story occurs as Christ gives its distinctive goods a new Christological meaning. Grace builds upon nature, redemption upon creation: "It is not a matter of throwing over the created world and making another."[126] With these three pieces, I suggest that we can imagine the nonhuman creature, with its innate trinitarian disposition, being included in the life of the Trinity, specifically in the metaphorical "space" established by the Trinity's Second Person through the drama of the cross.

As I have noted, it is a fundamental principle in a Catholic view of nature that God respects the integrity and identity of each creature. Thus, redemption, which we can understand now as the drawing to fulfillment the creature's triune, covenantal disposition, will look different for each creature (and, we can add, for those creatures with moral agency, it will look different depending on their moral responses). As Jay McDaniel suggests in an often-quoted phrase, "If there is a pelican heaven, it is a *pelican heaven*" (emphasis in the original).[127] Given this variety of creaturely capacities, it is hard to imagine the eschatological life of all animals simply in terms of the resurrection of each and every one of them. I suggested in chapter 1 and again earlier in this chapter that some creatures (e.g., those with no capacity for memory or a sense of self) do not seem to have a sufficient continuity or sense of personhood for us to understand how their resurrection could have any meaning for them or on what basis they would be the *same* animals that previously existed on earth. As C. S. Lewis comments, "If the life of a newt is merely a succession of sensations, what should we mean by saying that God may recall to life the newt that died today? It would not recognize itself as the same newt."[128] My argument is not that all creatures will share in a resurrection similar to ours (though I am not excluding that possibility) but only that we can hope that at least some of them will.

NATURE/GRACE REVISITED

Contemporary theology has cast a critical eye on approaches to grace that presumed to protect the gratuity of grace by proposing some sort of "natural" fulfillment of human nature apart from Christ, as if our lives would have been complete without God's intervention in history. The earlier prominence of the infralapsarian view that Christ would not have come absent human sin has been increasingly challenged by a supralapsarian view. God created with the intent of expressing the divine *magis*, displaying the radicality of divine power and love in Christ and reorienting all creation toward the covenant in Christ. The "two divine ways of acting," creation and redemption, "are intimately and inseparably connected" and have always been intended to be so by God.[129]

There remains, nonetheless, an interest in Catholic thought of preserving a sense of creation's own integrity and autonomy—albeit a relative, not absolute autonomy, in line with what Rahner referred to as a "remainder concept" (*Restbegriff*). Translating the Aristotelian category of a natural end into more contemporary terms, we can suggest that creation has (or would have had, apart from the fall) an innate *meaningfulness*. It is meaningful in itself, in part because it has its own stable laws and intelligibility, and thus we can form a relatively correct understanding of it without forcing it into a christomonistic mold.

Balthasar's way of negotiating these issues—the relative meaningfulness of creation and, simultaneously, its fundamental orientation toward grace—is to interpret salvation in terms of God's economic drama fulfilling and completing the "merely" human drama. In a "well-crafted drama," two things are true: "The plot is so constructed that it could have no other satisfying conclusion, and at the same time the conclusion is altogether surprising and unforeseen."[130] Something similar characterizes humanity's inclusion in the salvific narrative. We can see in retrospect that when human agents, in all their earthly choices and stories, are invited to share in the story of Christ's death and resurrection, it is the only event that can draw "the tangled threads" of their lives "into a meaningful resolution." However, nothing about human existence—our nature, our personal histories, our longings—allows us to anticipate "the shape of that gift" until we actually receive it.[131] The drama, as seen in Christ's life and displayed most prominently in the events of the paschal mystery, brings fulfillment to human lives but does so in a way that incorporates, not overrides, all that forms us into who we are—our relationships, choices, histories, longings, and even our failures. Each person's life drama is not expunged but rather given new meaning and fulfillment in and through its participation in Christ. We will explore in the next chapter how this theo-dramatic structure can also be applied to the lives of nonhuman creatures.

I believe the notion of a meaningful life drama is more helpful for understanding the nature/grace distinction in our contemporary context than Aquinas's abidingly influential notion of a rational creature uniquely capable of spiritual elevation. The distinction Aquinas makes between animal nature (which does not need an enduring life to be fulfilled) and human nature (which does) is instructive. We briefly noted in chapter 1 how Aquinas (or his student), in arguing against animal restoration in the eschaton, addresses a potential critique of his position. Because animals want to live and it is their *nature* to so desire, it would be "unseemly" if God, who created them with the natural desire to live, allowed this desire to be frustrated.[132] His answer relies on an outdated cosmology. The animal's natural desire for life endures only as long as the heavenly bodies continue to move (because their movements govern the lives of plants and animals); however, because the heavenly bodies will no longer move in the world to come, animals will no longer be driven by the instinct to live.[133] With animals now divested of these life-preservation instincts, God does them no injustice in denying to them what God grants to humans: unending life. In hindsight, we recognize this explanation as a case of bad science supporting bad theology. Our fellow creatures, loved into existence by God, yearn for life, and this instinct is always frustrated in the present order. My point, however, is to underscore that Aquinas's argument, however wrong in its progression, is grounded in a very Catholic instinct about the integrity of nature: "a natural desire cannot be in vain."[134] Thus, the force of Aquinas's argument, given contemporary understanding, now points us in a different direction. If God respects nature's integrity, can we not assume that God also protects its creaturely meaningfulness, preserving it from the tragedy of being "adrift in the midst of hopeless chaos," to use Pope Francis's words? The divine *magis* is expansive enough to preserve nonhuman creatures from this fate, as it does human ones.

NOTES

Epigraph: United States Conference of Catholic Bishops, *Roman Missal*, 208.

    1. All references to the *Exsultet* can be found in the United States Conference of Catholic Bishops, *Roman Missal*, 207–09.

2. It is understandable, then, that Henri de Lubac's suggestion that the human person has a "natural desire" for God seemed to threaten the gratuity of Christ, leading Pius XII to implicitly condemn de Lubac in *Humani Generis* for "destroying the true gratuity of the supernatural order." Dych, *Thy Kingdom Come*, 64. Edwin Christiaan van Driel believes the connection between creation and divine responsibility to be the mainstream view: "Most Christian theologians agree that the act of creation comes with a form of divine commitment to God's creatures." Van Driel, *Incarnation Anyway*, 137.

3. Duffy, *Graced Horizon*, 56.

4. For a recent discussion of this debate, see Mansini, "Henri De Lubac."

5. E.g., "We are presupposing, then, that the goal of the world is God's self-communication to it, and that the entire dynamism which God has implanted in the process . . . is already directed towards this self-communication and its acceptance by the world." Rahner, *Foundations*, 192. Similarly, Karl Barth: "God anticipated and determined within Himself . . . that the goal and meaning of all his dealings with the as yet non-existent universe should be the fact that in His Son He would be gracious towards man, uniting Himself with him." Barth, *Church Dogmatics*, vol. II.2, 101.

6. Van Driel explores three contemporary versions of supralapsarianism in his *Incarnation Anyway*.

7. The infralapsarian approach, that the Incarnation was not part of God's original plan, was the dominant position of post-Tridentine Catholicism. It was Aquinas's preferred view, though he allows that there are different opinions on the topic. Aquinas, *ST* III.1.3 *ad.* 3. Nevertheless, important historical voices argued for supralapsarianism, among them Alexander of Hales (d. 1245), Albert the Great (d. 1280), Duns Scotus (d. 1308), and Francisco Suárez (d. 1617). For a brief history of the arguments, see van Driel, *Incarnation Anyway*, 171–75.

8. "The deification of humanity is not about changing human nature into something other than it is, but about becoming fully human in a way that is faithful to God's intention." Edwards, *Partaking*, 44.

9. Catholic Church, *Catechism*, no. 340.

10. Burrell, "Creation," 97.

11. Preece provides a helpful survey of historical attitudes toward animal redemption during the modern period, including people from various walks of life (e.g., theologians, priests, philosophers, and poets). Preece, *Brute Souls*, 156–72.

12. Dean, *Future Life*, 17.

13. Irenaeus, *Against Heresies* [III.16.6], 443.

14. Irenaeus [V.32.1], 561.

15. Ephrem, *Hymns* [IX], 136.

16. "Therefore, it is in the Spirit that the Word glorifies creation and presents it to the Father by divinizing it and granting it adoption." Athanasius, "Letters to Serapion on the Holy Spirit," 1.25, in *Athanasius*, ed. Anatolios, 225, cited in Edwards, *Partaking*, 48.

17. John Chrysostom, *Chrysostom: Homilies* [homily XIV], 445.

18. God "will be spiritually perceived by each one of us in each one of us, perceived in one another, perceived by each in himself; he will be seen in the new heaven and the new earth, in the whole creation as it then will be; he will be seen in every body by means of bodies." Saint Augustine, *City of God* [book 22.29], 1087.

19. Benedict's statement on Maximus appears in *Spe Salvi*, no. 28.

20. Hiuser, "Maximizing Animal Theology."

21. "At one level, the *logoi* constitute the divinely premeditated and exemplary plan of created beings. They are ontological 'codes' that establish the salutary interconnections and interactions between creatures spiritual and material, grand and minute, macrocosmic and microcosmic, and that situate those beings in networks conducive to their peculiar development and thriving, and to their participation in the uncreated Logos." Blowers, "Unfinished Creative Business," 144. See also, Thunberg, *Microcosm*, 77–80.

22. By the Middle Ages, most theologians were ambivalent about the idea of animals in the next life and typically rejected it. Santmire, *Travail*, 75–77.

23. McCarthy and Murphy, "Hosea" [12], 221a.

24. For examples of this connection, see Is 35:1–2, 6–7; Ez 47:12; Jl 4:18; Am 9:13–15; and Zec 8:12; 14:8.

25. Blenkinsopp, *Isaiah*, 265.

26. Murray, "Cosmic Covenant," 29.

27. Middleton, *New Heaven*, 108.

28. Bauckham, "Jesus and Animals I," 33.

29. Bauckham, 37–42.

30. Harrington, *Gospel*, 115.

31. "They have cloven hooves but no ruminant stomach." Harrington, 120.

32. Harrington, 121.

33. Bauckham, "Jesus and Animals II," 54–55.

34. Lohse, *Colossians*, 59, commenting on Col 1:20.

35. Galloway, *Cosmic Christ*, 54.

36. Galloway, 55.

37. Hunt, Horrell, and Southgate, "Environmental Mantra?"

38. Hunt, Horrell, and Southgate, 549–55.

39. Hunt, Horrell, and Southgate, 572.

40. Hunt, Horrell, and Southgate, 573.

41. Hunt, Horrell, and Southgate, 573.

42. Hunt, Horrell, and Southgate, 574.

43. Hunt, Horrell, and Southgate, 575. Joseph Fitzmyer similarly argues that Paul's statements should be interpreted as an affirmation of nonhuman redemption. Redemption "is no longer considered from an anthropological point of view; it is now recast in cosmic terms. Human bodies that are said to await such redemption (8:23) are merely part of the entire material creation." Fitzmyer, *Romans*, 505. "Hence Paul is affirming a solidarity of the nonhuman world with the human world in the redemption that Christ has wrought." Fitzmyer, 506.

44. Vatican Council II, *Gaudium et Spes*, no. 12.

45. Vatican Council II, no. 24.

46. Vatican Council II, no. 39. Cf., God created "the visible world . . . for man." John Paul II, *Redemptor Hominis*, no. 8. "The whole of creation is for man." Paul VI, *Populorum Progressio*, no. 22.

47. Paul VI, *Octogesima Adveniens*, no. 21.

48. Catholic Church, *Catechism*, no. 339.

49. John Paul II, "United Nations (Kenya)."

50. John Paul II, no. 2.

51. John Paul II, no. 4.

52. Vatican Council II, *Lumen Gentium*, no. 48.

53. Catholic Church, *Catechism*, no. 353.

54. John Paul II, *Laborem Exercens*, no. 25.

55. Vatican II, *Gaudium et Spes*, no. 34.

56. Vatican II, no. 37.

57. John Paul II, *Sollicitudo Rei Socialis*, no. 29.

58. John Paul II, no. 30.

59. Haught, *God after Darwin*, 47. Haught here is describing a process theology approach to redemption, not specifically his own view.

60. Edwards, "Every Sparrow," 119.

61. Rolston, "Does Nature Need to Be Redeemed?" 227–28.

62. Rolston, 220.

63. Rolston, 221.

64. Sideris, "Censuring Nature," 41.

65. Bekoff, *Why Dogs Hump*, 37.

66. McDaniel, *Of God*, 41.

67. "For you love all things that are and loathe nothing that you have made; for you would not fashion what you hate." Wis 11:24.

68. Aquinas, *SCG*, II.82.2.

69. This is a view assumed by much of the Western philosophical tradition. Giovanni Pico della Mirandola, for example, states that animals, "from the moment of their birth, bring with them . . . all they will ever possess." Pico della Mirandola, *Oration*, 8.

70. Carere and Maestripieri, *Animal Personalities*; Gosling, "Personality"; Stamps and Groothuis, "Development."

71. For a helpful examination of a relational understanding of personhood and how identity is constructed in dialogue, see McFadyen, *Call*.

72. The "entire cosmos" gains its "perfection" in Christ. Lohfink, *Is This All There Is?* loc. 3063–64 of 5403, Kindle.

73. David Meconi is rightly critical of such denials of the relational agency of nonhuman creatures. Neither God's address to nonhuman creatures in the biblical texts nor the accounts of the saints engaging creatures in "second-person" relationships is "hyperbolic jargon," he writes. Meconi, "Establishing I/Thou Relationship," 219–20.

74. Lohfink, *Is This All There Is?* loc. 3096–97 of 5403, Kindle.

75. Lohfink, loc. 3749–51 of 5403, Kindle.

76. Lohfink, loc. 3747 of 5403, Kindle.

77. He cites Woody Allen here: Lohfink, loc. 547–51 of 5403, Kindle.

78. The redemption of animals, he tells us, is similar to that of "books [that] have become part of my personal development" or a "garden I have planted." Lohfink, loc. 2908–10 of 5403, Kindle.

79. Haught, *Resting*, 69. He appeals to Teilhard de Chardin, *Human Phenomenon*, 186. Balthasar finds a similar idea in his study of Maximus the Confessor. In a relationship that appears "throughout the whole edifice" of creation and reflects creation's triune origins, unity and diversity are realized together in a "paradox of synthesis." Balthasar, *Cosmic Liturgy*, loc. 1086–92 of 8806, Kindle.

80. Francis, *Laudato Si'*.

81. Edwards, "Sublime Communion," 385.

82. The Genesis creation accounts, Francis writes, "suggest that human life is grounded in three fundamental and closely intertwined relationships: with God, with our neighbour and with the earth itself." *LS*, 66.

83. And if our connection to other creatures is so deep, then, one can argue, such must also characterize our life to come if human nature is to continue being human.

84. *LS*, 89. He cites himself: *Evangelii Gaudium*, no. 215.

85. Deane-Drummond, *"Laudato Si',"* 397. She refers to the encyclical's section on biodiversity. *LS*, 37.

86. See the section "The Value of Nonhuman Creatures in Themselves" in Edwards "Sublime Communion," 380–83.

87. *LS*, 69, citing the *Catechism*, no. 2416.

88. *LS*, 85. He cites the Canadian Conference of Catholic Bishops, "You Love All That Exists," no. 1.

89. Northcott, "Planetary Moral Economy," 898.

90. Edwards, "Sublime Communion," 380.

91. Deane-Drummond, *"Laudato Si',"* 414.

92. Edwards, "Sublime Communion," 379.

93. In his five-volume *Theo-Drama*, Balthasar develops this "aesthetic" response to include the dramatic; the economic drama revealed in Christ elicits the dramatic response of the Christian and gives new meaning to her life story.

94. Balthasar, *Theology of Karl Barth*, 362.

95. Nichols, *Say It Is Pentecost*, 16.

96. No one "can really behold who has not also already been enraptured, and no one can be enraptured who has not already perceived." Balthasar, *Glory*, vol. 1, 10.

97. Balthasar, 21; cf. "It is proper to every living being to tend towards other things." *LS*, 240.

98. Balthasar, *Theo-Logic*, vol. 1, loc. 1294 of 4502, Kindle. Even the "ability to interpret nature, the flowers and birds, the powers of the elements, the whole of being as it makes its appearance has its root in God." Balthasar, *Glory*, vol. 2, 347.

99. Balthasar, *Theo-Drama*, vol. 5, 76. The human person "bears the stamp of the *imago trinitatis*" in that he or she can "only be and become a person by relating to the other persons." Balthasar, 302.

100. Balthasar, 81.

101. International Theological Commission, "Communion," no. 41. "It is precisely this radical likeness to the triune God that is the basis for the possibility of the communion of creaturely beings with the uncreated persons of the Blessed Trinity." International Theological Commission, no. 25.

102. Kasper, *God*, 156.

103. LaCugna, *God*, 14.

104. Zizioulas, *Being*, 88.

106. Kärkkäinen, *Creation*, 102.

106. Balthasar, *Cosmic Liturgy*, loc. 1118–20 of 8806, Kindle.

107. Williams, "Afterword," 174.

108. I do not explore the possibility in this book, but perhaps this idea of a creaturely drama that is completed in Christ's story could be used to develop a soteriology that includes even those creatures without a rudimentary sense of self.

109. Balthasar, *Theo-Logic*, vol. 3, 255.

110. Balthasar, Balthasar, *Theo-Logic*, vol. 2, loc. 6411n50 of 7072, Kindle.

111. Balthasar, *Theo-Drama*, vol. 5, 421. In Christ's "definitive form he takes up into himself all the forms of creation. . . . This holds for the forms for nature, concerning which we cannot say (as in medieval eschatology) that they will at some time simply disappear, leaving a vacuum between pure matter and men." Balthasar, *Glory*, vol. 1, 679.

112. Balthasar, *Theo-Drama*, vol. 4, 319.

113. Against those critical of using "persons" to describe the hypostases of the Trinity, Balthasar maintains that the Christian tradition and Scripture—which regularly ascribe personal, agential qualities not only to God but also specifically to the Father, Son, and Spirit—provide ample justification for the continued use of the term. In contrast, see Rahner, *Trinity*, 103–15.

114. Thus, God's life is not static in itself; it does not only acquire "its dynamism and its many hues by going through a created, temporal world." Balthasar, *Theo-Drama*, vol. 4, 326.

115. The "mission of Jesus" is not "a mere, symbolic *illustration* of something that already *is the case* anyway" (emphasis in the original). Balthasar, *Theo-Drama*, vol. 3, 240.

116. Balthasar, *Theo-Drama*, vol. 4, 362.

117. Balthasar, 319–28. For a fuller treatment of how immutability and receptivity are reconciled within the triune God, see O'Hanlon, *Immutability*, 121–24.

118. The "Son's eternal, holy distance from the Father, in the Spirit, forms the basis on which the unholy distance of the world's sin can be transposed into it, can be transcended and overcome by it." Balthasar, *Theo-Drama*, vol. 4, 362.

119. I defend Balthasar on this count in chapter 4.

120. Christopher Hadley explains and defends Balthasar's use of the metaphor of distance. See Hadley, "All-Embracing Frame."

121. "Existence in all its gravity can be embraced and kept safe by God's sphere." Balthasar, *Theo-Drama*, vol. 4, 134.

122. Steck, *Ethical Thought*, 45.

123. Balthasar, *Epilogue*, in particular, the section "The Word Becomes Flesh," loc. 1251–1410 of 1687, Kindle.

124. Balthasar, loc. 1306–7 of 1687, Kindle.

125. Balthasar, loc. 1302 of 1687, Kindle.

126. Balthasar, "Some Points," 262.

127. McDaniel, *Of God*, 45.

128. Lewis, *Problem of Pain*, 123.

129. Francis, *Laudato Si'*, no. 73.

130. Yeago, "Drama," 98–99.

131. Yeago, 98.

132. Aquinas, *ST* Supplement-III.91.5 *arg.* 5.

133. See Aquinas, *ST* Supplement-III.91.2.

134. "The intellect apprehends existence absolutely, and for all time; so that everything that has an intellect naturally desires always to exist. But a natural desire cannot be in vain." Aquinas, *ST* I.75.6.

CHAPTER 4

SANCTIFICATION

The Spirit's Cosmic Embrace

Creation is permeated with redemptive sanctification, even a divinization.

—Pope John Paul II

IT HAD been virtually axiomatic that Christian theology has too often ignored the distinctive role of the Holy Spirit.[1] If the pneumatological appeals of ecotheologians are any indication, that negligence has been remedied. The role of the Spirit, as the ubiquitous presence of God poured out upon the world, has been particularly important for ecotheologians seeking to interpret evolution theologically. The Spirit shepherds the evolutionary process, acting as a nurturing guide and comforter for creation as it suffers the travails of its growth toward fulfillment.

The danger in some ecotheologies, however, is that the Spirit's work in history is so integrally interwoven with evolution that salvation history threatens to become indistinguishable from evolutionary history itself. Christ's primary accomplishment is incarnating the ideal endpoint of evolutionary history, not effecting a gift that is irreducible to that history. Against this view, I argued in the last chapter that in Christ, God effected something new, giving humanity a destiny beyond what could have been achieved through natural processes: It has been invited to share in the very dynamics of the triune Godhead. The role of the Spirit, I argue here, is to expand this achievement so that it includes all creatures. I refer to this inclusion of nonhuman creatures as their "sanctification," as distinct from "redemption," which I view as a broader category but associate primarily with the work of Christ. The two are, of course, only different aspects of what is ultimately the one economic labor of God to draw all creation into a covenantal relation.

GROUNDING SOTERIOLOGY IN CHRIST
AND THE PASCHAL MYSTERY

A recent and important work by Jack Mahoney offers an example of the approach I want to avoid. He suggests "that there is no longer a need for the doctrine of atonement," because it is tied up with "traditional beliefs in original sin and the fall," with which we can now, in light of evolution, dispense.[2] In response to the question, What is the "positive purpose for the death of Jesus"? he proposes that the answer is "impressively provided by reflection on modern evolutionary theory."[3] Jesus, "in his accepting death as a human being and in his rising from the dead, . . . achieved a new phase of evolutionary existence for the human species, into which he could then usher his fellow humans."[4] Mahoney, unfortunately, does not explain exactly *how* it is that Christ does this or how his accomplishment is connected with "his accepting death as a human being." I believe we again confront a place where too much heuristic weight has been given to evolutionary dynamics. What is missing is a comprehensive soteriology that includes a clear exposition of exactly how the Christ event effects creation's advance (however that is understood). We can affirm, with Mahoney, that "Jesus's return from the dead . . . had cosmic repercussions," but we are left to wonder how exactly "the resurrection of Jesus" accomplished a "breakthrough for humanity," one described by Mahoney as "evolutionary."[5] A similar ambiguity appears in the writings of other ecotheologians. John Haught, for example, describes Christ as "a fully incarnate deity who suffers and struggles along with all of life" and is able to save "the cosmic drama by weaving it everlastingly into the divine life."[6] I agree, but it is not clear what exactly it is about Christ's life and death that accomplishes that weaving.

Given that, in a trinitarian framework, the work of the Spirit is intimately and indivisibly united with that of Christ, it is not possible to develop a comprehensive understanding of the Spirit's role in an evolutionary world without also understanding Christ's contribution in redeeming that world. The risk is that, unmoored from its Christological grounding, the Spirit's labor becomes the ad hoc facilitator of everything we believe to be good in the evolutionary process—for example, newness, creativity, progress, and development—along with comforter of all those creatures who endure its painful effects. Those are, of course, appropriate roles to associate with the Spirit, but God's acts in the world are always at once the act of all the triune Persons, and thus our interpretation of the Spirit's work is incomplete until tied specifically to Christ's paschal mystery.

Inarticulacy about the soteriology of nonhuman life also impairs our ethical responses. I have argued that Scripture's eschatological horizon, especially its understanding of God's ultimate plan for creation and how this plan affects the present, is necessary to adequately illuminate creation's goods and values. Until we clearly articulate the nexus linking Christ, the Spirit, and the redemption of creatures, our theological vision of creation will be deficient. As a result, our perception of creation's sacramental luster will be obscured, and its capacity to evoke our passionate response to its needs will be diminished. This is similar to a critique made by Willis Jenkins of ecotheologians in his *Ecologies of Grace*. Their response to contemporary issues, he argues, has been "garbled" in part because they "downplay talk about salvation."[7] Creation theologies "share in a common task" of responding to the global crisis. "Why not," he asks, "do that by engaging soteriology," because "that seems to be where the problem lies?"[8] However innovative Mahoney is with regard to "the traditional doctrines"—dispensing with the need for the "doctrines of original sin, the fall, human concupiscence, and the views of the Last Supper and Calvary as propitiatory sacrifice to God to atone for the fall"—he writes as an anthropocentric traditionalist when it comes to the *scope* of Christ's redemptive work.[9]

Balthasar's soteriology can provide the kind of environmental resource encouraged by Jenkins. We saw in chapter 3 that he uses the metaphors of "distance" and "space" to imagine how Christ effects humanity's reconciliation and incorporates it into the divine life. Taking on the lot of sinful and suffering humanity in obedience to the Father, Jesus stretches the relational "distance" between the Father and the Son (though this distance is always, absolutely, and lovingly transcended, as Balthasar repeatedly emphasizes), so that a "space" within the Godhead is established for creatures who are broken and sinful. Creating such an acting space that can embrace humanity's sinful "no" is, in Balthasar's view, necessarily costly.

By partially tying Christ's achievement to his suffering, Balthasar's approach is vulnerable to the critiques of the theory of atonement attributed, often inaccurately, to Anselm and his heirs. This theory seems to portray a petty god who requires divine due before there can be any possibility of mercy or forgiveness. Balthasar, of course, never proposes such a crude quid pro quo, and it is doubtful that it fairly reflects Anselm's view. Recent commentators have offered more nuanced and sympathetic interpretations of Anselm, and some of their insights likewise apply to Balthasar's approach. Lisa Sowle Cahill, for example, argues that Anselm "focused not on the death of Christ or on divine appeasement but on Jesus's unbreakable relationship with God as restoring the harmony of creation."[10] "God's honor," which Christ restores, "refers not to individual personal dignity, but, as in feudal society, to an integrated system of relationships, revolving around an authoritative benefactor." Mercy and justice are joined together in God's determination "to restore to the entire creation the beauty, harmony, and rectitude for which it has been created, and which participates in God's own supreme goodness."[11] The cross is not necessary to "mollify an angry God"; rather, "it is Christ's unbreakably close relation to God throughout his life that rectifies the human situation."[12]

Balthasar shares Anselm's view of redemption as the restoration of relationship, and so it is no surprise that many of the commendable features Cahill identifies in Anselm's theory—Jesus's unbreakable relationship with God, concern for the harmony of creation, an integrated set of relationships, and God's determination to restore creation's beauty—also appear in Balthasar's theory. Balthasar's approach focuses on the establishment of a new covenantal relationship in Christ that is able to encompass even sin and the world's brokenness. There is no payment of a debt; Christ's suffering is the expression in time of the divine kenosis, God's self-giving surrender to humanity in its sinfulness, and concomitantly, God's corresponding relational embrace of it. For Balthasar, each moment in the divine economy is always oriented toward relationship—the establishment of the conditions for it, its restoration, and its eschatological fulfillment.

Understanding Christ's soteriological role is a prerequisite for understanding the work of the Spirit. The bond between Christology and pneumatology must be preserved, given that the economic acts of the triune Persons are always one. I argue here that the task of the Spirit is to facilitate creation's appropriation of Christ's achievement. However, before turning to explore this role, we need first to understand a bit more about the trinitarian context of Balthasar's soteriology in order to address some of the concerns that have been raised against it.

THE TRINITARIAN FRAMEWORK
FOR BALTHASAR'S SOTERIOLOGY

The most controversial aspects of Balthasar's soteriology center on his view that as the Son takes on the burden of human sin, he experiences the full depth of human alienation from God. A "distance" erupts between the Father and Son that is overcome only by the ever-greater love of the triune relations. In welcoming the Son, the Father also welcomes the dramas of human sin and suffering into the triune life.

The concern of Balthasar's critics is that he has entangled the transcendent Godhead in the pathos of the world's sin and suffering. Of Balthasar's trinitarian theology, Karl Rahner complains that his own desire to be released from "[his] dirt and mess and [his] doubt" cannot be realized if God "is just as dirty."[13] Denis Edwards maintains that Balthasar is "in danger of appearing to undermine" the divine communion by pushing "the economic suffering and the self-emptying of the Word back into the eternal trinitarian relations, apparently making suffering and self-emptying essential to trinitarian life."[14] Celia Deane-Drummond similarly protests, "To put it rather more simply, he has failed to keep his trinitarian epistemology sufficiently qualified and has introduced unnecessary complications on the premise that God has to experience in Godself something like human experiences of sin, suffering, and death."[15]

Given the cumulative weight and authority of these and other critical voices, they merit a response. Their concerns are understandable. Balthasar's reflections are unsystematic, and his speculative imagery and analogies are excessive at times, to be sure.[16] Nonetheless, the excess serves a good theological end (whether intentionally or not): not to pierce the mystery of the immanent Godhead but to reinvigorate it. Balthasar effectively unfocuses and complicates our tidy, theological instincts about God—challenging the idea of a static God with one that is dramatic, of a passionless God with one that overflows with divine pathos, and of a unitarian Godhead with one that is actively triune. Additionally, Balthasar insists on three theological guideposts: (1) God is absolute mystery and always exceeds human understanding (in classical language, *si comprehendis, non est deus*); (2) though descriptors of the creaturely realm can never be applied univocally to God, they must nonetheless be used as analogous claims; and (3) the economic Trinity (God as God labors within the world) reveals the immanent Trinity (God's life within the Godhead).[17]

This last point is a crucial axiom for Balthasar's theology. To be faithful to the God revealed in Christ, the goods associated with human relationships—for example, spontaneity, word and response, creativity, and drama—can and should be used analogously to understand the tri-une processions. Even the "fundamental philosophical act, wonder, need not be banished from the realm of the Absolute."[18] And, as Rowan Williams argues, "If divine difference were the negation of all finite predicates," God would be subsumed into "a discourse about the world."[19] That is, absolutely excluding the validity of any and all descriptors of God would still lead to God being defined by the world's categories, though now as their antithesis. Even ascribing "emotions" to God is not always inappropriate. The early Church recognized this, as Paul Gavrilyuk observes. In its response to heresies about Christ's divinity, it did not reject attributing all passions to God, only those unworthy of God. The "qualified divine impassibility" supported by orthodox theologians allowed for "certain God-befitting emotions."[20]

Regarding the concern that his soteriology seems to interject alienation within the Godhead, thus compromising the divine unity, Balthasar recognizes that he is pushing theological boundaries ("To think in such a way is to walk on a knife edge")[21]. But his use of seemingly unbefitting attributes for God is at least partially redeemed when placed in the broader context of his arguments. He employs spatial and temporal terms like "distance," "separation," and "super-time" as metaphors to underscore that there is "space" within the Trinity for real interchange and dialogue. Thus he says that something "like infinite 'duration' and infinite 'space' must be attributed to the acts of reciprocal love so that the life of the *communio*, of fellowship, can develop."[22] "God's 'abiding forever' must not be seen as a 'non-time' but as a super-time that is unique to him."[23] As these quotations show, Balthasar frequently uses inverted commas and the prefixes "supra-" and "super-" as a way of acknowledging that "none of these attributes can be ascribed univocally to God."[24] They allow us to understand imaginatively, if ever so inadequately, the complexities of the divine response—which according to Scripture, includes passions such as anger, sorrow, regret, rejoicing, compassion, and mercy—by ascribing these varied and even contradictory passions as analogous moments in the divine exchange of love. Thus, Balthasar argues "that the God-forsakenness of the Son during his Passion was just as much a mode of his profound bond with the Father in the Holy Spirit as his death was a mode of his life and his suffering a mode of his bliss."[25] He continues: "The reciprocal self-surrender of Son and Father appear 'as something so strong and so good that everything involving separation and suffering and obligation and obedience that is taken up into this is totally absorbed into love, indeed itself becomes love, as if it had never been anything else.'"[26]

Because Christ stepped out of eternity into time, what is always experienced within the Trinity as perfect, immediate love among the divine relations is perceived in the temporal world as a sequence of moments, where suffering appears in one instance and the delight of fellowship in the next. Whatever "distance" is displayed in Christ's suffering, it is ultimately transformed and revealed to be the ever-greater power of infinite, triune love.

There is a danger with projects, like this one, that try to systematize and explain Balthasar's thought; doing so effaces its multiple perspectives, qualifications, and, we might even say, creative inconsistencies that make it such a deep and rich resource for theological reflection. That said, I believe a thought experiment can help us here. We can call to mind the way a novel's entire drama, even with its lows and points of despair, ultimately provides us with satisfying consolation and joy. If we could imagine the essence of such a novel—everything about it that delights us as we read it across a period of time—being distilled into a goodness whose entirety can be experienced immediately by us, we would begin to have a glimmer of insight into the difference between God's experience of dramas (in the eternal present) and our own (which always unfolds across a succession of moments). The one drama of Christ's death and resurrection, properly interpreted, does not threaten divine unity, even though it includes a moment in earthly time in which the Son is "distant" from the Father. Rather, such a moment, in the context of the eternal Father, becomes immediately part of radical and absolute love: "As the three in one, God is so intensely everlasting love, that within his life temporal death and the hellish desolation of the creature, accepted out of love, can become transmuted into an expression of love."[27]

We know of earthly analogues of such a transforming love. Parenting, for example, involves what might otherwise be unpleasant experiences—perhaps for some, an example would be listening to an elementary school musical production. Loving bonds transform these experiences if not into joy at least into an experience that includes joy. The analogy is inadequate, but we can imagine something similar regarding Balthasar's view of God. God's transcendence is not threatened by engaging creaturely drama because the Father always lives within the eternity of time, where what in a human perspective appears as a series of discrete and varied moments is transformed—"transmuted," to use Balthasar's term—immediately and eternally into the joys and ek-stases of boundless, creative love.

It is interesting, then, to note a similar struggle that Pope John Paul II faced in negotiating the paradoxical themes of a God who is transcendent and perfect and yet who, because of the perfection of the divine love, is affected by human sin and suffering. Although we must, he wrote, exclude "from God any pain deriving from deficiencies or wounds," we must also recognize with Scripture that because of the Father's love, he "feels compassion" for humanity, "as though sharing in [its] pain." Moreover, "this inscrutable and indescribable fatherly 'pain' will bring about above all the wonderful economy of redemptive love in Jesus Christ," in which love reveals itself "as stronger than sin."[28] We might add to his reflection that the *joy* God experiences through God's love for creation shows itself stronger than whatever "inscrutable and indescribable" pain accompanies this love.

My argument that God desires a covenantal relationship with non-human creatures does not depend on Balthasar's particular understanding of the triune processions (i.e., God's immanent life). However, I appeal to Balthasar's trinitarian framework because it offers a way to give some flesh to the astounding idea that God establishes a genuine covenantal relationship with that which is not God—that is, humanity and other creatures. Its provocative metaphors can deepen and enliven this covenantal conviction as something more than an abstract assertion. Balthasar's metaphors of divine "distance" and a capacious acting "space" between the Father and the Incarnate Word, absolutely united in the Spirit, offer a way of imagining how God's economic labor, specifically the offer of the covenant, truly expresses and reveals *who* God is. God undergoes no essential change in offering the covenant because God has always been, in God's very self, dramatic receptivity of the "other." The "space" within the triune life, whose vibrant and dramatic contours are fundamentally open to what is "other," has, through the costly events of Christ's cross and resurrection, been made expansive enough to include the distinctive particularity and life drama of the creaturely other. Thus, the creature need not become something different in order to be embraced by God and included in the very depths of God's triune life.

Balthasar's belief that God has revealed Godself to be dramatic, triune life also has the virtue of providing a trinitarian grounding for an ethical theme to be developed in the last chapter: the receptive quality of Christlike love. To love is to receive the gift of the other by letting the other "be" (i.e., be its true self, express its self, and flourish as God intended); it is an active letting be, one that empowers and enables.[29] In actively receiving the gift of the other, we, in turn, express our own identities. Love in its truest form is mutual receptivity and expression—that is, it is trinitarian.

BALTHASAR AND THE HOLY SPIRIT

Though Balthasar is known for his soteriological hope for humanity ("no one has argued more forcefully for the possibility and necessity" of the hope that all will be saved),[30] he is also hopeful, as we saw in the previous chapter, about the inclusion of all creation in God's redemptive plan. Central to both hopes is the work of the Spirit.

Balthasar's pneumatology is one of his theology's most creative and daring moments, as is shown in how far he is willing to allow the Spirit's mission to emerge as a distinctive aspect of God's one economic labor. He portrays the agency of the Spirit in ways analogous to that of Christ in order to expand our imagination about how this third Person of the Trinity fully participates in God's economic activity. The Spirit is not a ubiquitous, impersonal force enhancing our moral abilities but is rather God's personal, creative, and dialogical bond with creation. The Spirit's task is to adapt God's work in Christ to endlessly new circumstances by molding the agents who operate within them. The Spirit accomplishes this through the Spirit's unique presence to the world. The Spirit acts as co-subject/agent and object/bond, expressing God's penetrating openness to the free, autonomous, and even sinfully marred choices of humanity.

As in the case of Christ's economic role, the form of the Spirit's labor in creation reflects the life of the Godhead. God does not change as God acts within creation. Although the Spirit is, like all the hypostases of the Trinity, a "person," the particular way in which the Spirit is personal makes theological reflection on the Spirit difficult. The Spirit is, as Balthasar states, the "least objective mystery," the one who is "eternally beyond all objectification."[31] As the personal and active uniting of the Father and Son, the Spirit has a "twofold face." On the one hand, as the One who "is breathed forth from the one love of the Father and Son as the expression of their united freedom," the Spirit is the personal realization of their joint subjectivity. On the other hand, the Spirit is also their objective bond, "the objective witness to their difference-in-unity or unity-in-difference."[32] Thus, the Spirit who proceeds from the Father and the Son can be described as both subject and object: the *subjective* bond uniting them and also the *objective* expression of this bond.

Balthasar finds support for the Spirit's active role in the salvific economy in a number of canonical texts: in the Johannine passages that speak of the Spirit's active presence in Jesus's ministry, in the Synoptic passages that describe Jesus being led by the Spirit, and in the creedal formulae that portray the Spirit as an agent in salvation history (e.g., the Spirit "speaks through the prophets" and through the Spirit Jesus "was incarnate"). Together, these passages indicate, in however a fragmentary manner, the mystery of a volitional distinction that appears within the divine economy and that is actively mediated by the Spirit.[33]

Like the Incarnation, the resurrection is a new act of the triune God and, like all acts of the Godhead, it leads to a new modality in the Spirit's labor. The Son's return to and welcome by the Father is a new event of love within the divine processions, and as such it issues forth in a new, objective expression of that love, the outpouring of the Spirit on creation. As one of the Father's two hands, the Spirit first mediates the Father's will to the earthly Jesus and is then sent by the Father and the Son to continue Christ's work after his ascension.

We can see then how in his portrayal Balthasar allows the Spirit the kind of personal agency that the Christian tradition has generally attributed to the Father and the Son.[34] The roles and agency of the Father and the Son in the divine economy are more substantive and clearer to us because we associate them directly with specific, historical events, whereas the Spirit's labor is more hidden (the Spirit is the "mysterious Someone," to use Balthasar's phrase).[35] For Balthasar, the Spirit's economic labor is not simply the diffused expression of the Father's universal will, but—in a way that reflects the Spirit's procession as "illuminating the most intimate love of the Father and Son"—it is a distinctive expression of divine agency, we might even say initiative, in the drama of salvation history.[36]

Balthasar attributes newness and creativity to the loving and dialogical space of the Godhead. Of course, these qualities have an essential temporal aspect in our experience, and this aspect must be "kept at a distance" from our concept of God. But if God is love in Godself, then there must be "an acting area" in the Godhead, within which something analogous to our experiences of love can find expression (e.g., the "joys of giving and receiving"). Eternal fruitfulness lies at the heart of God's triune love.[37] All the Persons of the Trinity share in the newness and creativity of love, but Balthasar sees these qualities as particularly appropriate for the Spirit. The Spirit proceeds from the love of the Father and Son, not as an echo of that love but as a new act of divine creativity and fruitfulness. Because the Spirit's procession is the eternal emergence of newness from within the love of the Father and the Son, Balthasar sees the economic labor of the Spirit as the expression of God's essential openness to what is other and new.[38] He appeals to the metaphor of time's futurity to characterize the Spirit's procession and, correspondingly, the Spirit's distinctive economic labor: "There is no doubt that, when created time begins, the fact that the future stands open beyond the present is a particular parable of the Spirit."[39]

These features that Balthasar associates with the Spirit—autonomy and freedom, the expression of interpersonal bond, and agent of new futures—serve to support a claim that is essential to Balthasar's understanding of how the saving mission of the concrete, historical person Jesus Christ expands to include all times and places: The Spirit's distinctive mission in the divine economy is to universalize Christ (to "liquefy" Christ, to use Balthasar's phrase).[40] In this distinctive mission, the Spirit labors—in accord with the Spirit's "twofold face"—as *co-agent* with creation and as the *objective bond* between creation and the Godhead, acting as God's receptive adaptation to the dramas of creation.

Though distinctive, the Spirit's mission is absolutely rooted in and joined to the work of the Son; the Spirit works to align creation with Christ, making Christ appear in ever new ways within creation. Because the Spirit is free, however, this universalization of Christ is not merely repetitive or derivative but is a creative adaptation in accord with the concrete possibilities present in the world. Even today, theology "has not paid attention" to how "Christ has released us," Balthasar maintains, into "the daring adventure of Christian freedom."[41] The failure to recognize the Spirit's gift of freedom creates an additional problem. We ossify Christ, and in so doing, we undermine the possibility of a genuine Christian eschatology where something new can arise—something that emerges out of the encounter between God and God's creatures. Indeed, Balthasar sets the term "dramatics" in contradistinction to related terms like "history" and "story" to underscore that salvation history (and, by association, the lives of individual agents) is affected and effected by decisions—both divine and creaturely—that are dialogical and not simply the unidirectional expression of God's eternal, changeless will.[42]

Even while underscoring the openness of human history, Balthasar maintains that it has received its definitive shape and destiny. The freedom of God's work in the Spirit will not compromise the determinative work of Christ. Thus, whatever the shape that the eschaton ultimately takes, it will be the creative embodiment of the form of Christ. Balthasar uses the term "Christ form" to refer to "the person and story of Christ" and "everything in salvation history that relates to him" and is "interpreted in light of him."[43] Apart from the Spirit, this story appears simply as a tragic drama or an absurd series of events, but the Spirit helps us to perceive in the drama of Christ and the whole of salvation history a narratival meaningfulness that centers on the self-surrendering love of the Son for the Father (who accepts the Father's will and takes on the burden of sinful humanity) and the Father's love of the Son (expressed in his acceptance of the Son's offering). With the paschal event as its center, the Christ form draws together all the narrative pieces of salvation history—dramatic events such as sin leading to mercy, reconciliation, and fellowship; discouragement eliciting the promise of a hope-filled future; and the Father's call bringing forth saintly witness. All these earthly, concrete, and historical elements are part of the Christ form, and, in the Spirit, they become touchstones for interpreting our historical lives and for discovering the broad, Christological arc that gives them meaning.

Because what is revealed is not a fixed code but rather a covenantal drama whose *form* is to be creatively and concretely embodied, there is no tension between the revealing work of Christ and the Spirit's labor of calling forth new and creative crafters of the Christ form. The New Testament is "equally a word that journeys, proceeding once for all along the path from the earthly Jesus to the exalted Christ—and yet, in the Holy Spirit, it is new at every moment for everyone who hears it."[44] And because the form revealed in Christ is rich and complex, the Spirit can inspire countless ways of discipleship in the followers of Christ. Each generation—each person, each creaturely agent—can, under the inspiration of the Spirit, renew the mystery of Christ through actions that embody his form in new ways. Thus, the creaturely response called forth by the Spirit will be more than "variations" on the same old "theme" of the events of Jesus's life.[45] Christians become empowered to renew the freshness of the Gospel as their "most intimate acts of believing, loving, and hoping, [their] moods and contacts," are "penetrated" by the Spirit.[46]

Thus, Balthasar associates the Spirit with three economic roles: co-agent within creation, bond between it and God, and facilitator of creativity and newness. Balthasar is not alone in making these pneumatological associations. Even though Balthasar's pneumatology is grounded in what some view as excessive speculations about the immanent triune life, its conclusions are similar to those drawn by other theologians. Denis Edwards, for example, describes the Spirit as the "interior presence of God to all creatures."[47] The Spirit "is ultimately the source of all novelty in creation"[48] and "brings every part of our universe into a creaturely communion with God."[49] Similarly, in *Women, Earth, and Creator Spirit*, Elizabeth Johnson portrays the Spirit as the "creative origin of life," "immanent in the historical world,"[50] and the bond "between God and the world."[51]

Edwards and Johnson introduce two wrinkles in the Spirit's three roles of immanence, communion, and creativity that helpfully supplement Balthasar's pneumatology. First, the Spirit is "the power of becoming at work in evolutionary history."[52] Balthasar's focus is on the agency of the creature, but the Spirit's work is also directed toward the development of the world itself. As I noted in chapter 2, I do not attribute creaturely freedom to evolutionary history as a whole, but I agree that the Spirit directs the development of our broken world, bringing forth new forms of goodness within the relatively autonomous workings of the natural order and leading it toward its eschatological fulfillment in Christ.[53] Second, the bonds established by the Spirit include not only those between God and God's creatures, which is Balthasar's emphasis, but also the bonds of relationship among creatures themselves, both human and nonhuman. The Spirit "weaves a genuine solidarity among all creatures."[54] Including these two dimensions underscores the "horizontal" dimension of the Spirit's labor, that the Spirit facilitates not only the God–creation relationship but also the unfolding of creation itself and the bonds of creatures within it. Again, however, we can note that though creative, the labors of the Spirit are never formless. The Spirit always strives to imprint Christ on the forms of the world, working to integrate all the "words" of God's creatures so that they all come to speak of the one Word, Christ.[55]

THE SPIRIT: GOD'S OPENNESS TO CREATION

This pneumatology provides the basis for a soteriology of nonhuman life. As the universal agent who shepherds the diverse particularity of all things into the particularity of Christ, the Spirit is poured out onto all creation and labors in all the spaces and corners of creaturely life, breaking down barriers between the sacred and the earthly, the divine and the creaturely.[56] Omnipresent in the world, the Spirit acts as "the ultimate unity of the world of creation and the world of the Church."[57] The Spirit binds whatever is good and loving in creaturely responses while perfecting their "discrepancies," so that nothing worthy in creation may be lost, and encompassing in love that which is not God. The love revealed by God contains such a "vastness" that it allows "the tragic and apocalyptic differences between God and the world, God and hell, [to] be fully expressed within [God's] own all-embracing differences."[58]

Given the astonishing depth of God's openness to creation, we can hope that God would seek to welcome all creatures, not just humanity. I argue here that through the work of the Son and Spirit, the Father is able to do just that, encompassing even those creatures without the kind of agential freedom that is the focus of Balthasar's soteriology. All creation is oriented toward the dialogical, a view that I attribute to creation's innate trinitarian disposition and its openness to relationality. This ur-dialogical capacity provides the earthly ground for the Spirit's "liquefying" of the Christ form (i.e., making it appear within the dramas of creation) and, through the co-agency of the Spirit, can become the creaturely basis for the recapitulation of all things in Christ. Just as the Father expresses himself in the Son, so also every creature in some way speaks a word that expresses itself to the other.[59] Because of the vastness of the "space" in God for that which is other, there is also a place for these many creaturely expressions. Through God's economic labor, the complex and diverse forms of goodness, brokenness, suffering, and even sinfulness that mark creaturely lives can be sanctified, enveloped into the loving bonds of God's triune life. Although we cannot know exactly how this embrace will transform God's creatures, Balthasar's theology of the Spirit offers us a way of imagining that it is possible.

THE SPIRIT AND ANIMAL SANCTIFICATION

As I noted above, although Balthasar pointedly affirms the inclusion of all creation in the eschaton, he does not explore how such nonhuman sanctification might occur or how exactly it relates to the rest of his theology. Our exposition of the soteriological tasks that Balthasar attributes to the Son and the Spirit, however, suggests a couple of possibilities for redressing this lacuna. The first focuses on the individual, nonhuman creature and reflects on how the labor of the Spirit incorporates it into God's triune life. The second appeals to the solidarity between nonhuman creatures and humanity, effected in the celebration of the Eucharist, as an argument for the inclusion of nonhuman creatures in the eschaton. The two are complementary—the individual and the communal—and elements of both appear in the Christian tradition and recent Catholic thought. We consider each one in turn.

Animal Salvation: Theo-Drama and Individual Creatures

The challenge facing the idea of God drawing nonhuman creatures into participation in God's triune life, at least within the Balthasarian framework I have described, is that they are unable to be Christ-like agents. That is, they cannot freely perform acts of self-giving love, in Christ and in response to the Father. And because they cannot act in Christ-like ways, these creatures cannot, it would seem, be incorporated into the christomorphic acting space established by Christ and therein share in the triune life of God. Perhaps they will be granted an eschatological restoration in some other way, but they cannot, in Christ and with the Spirit, say "yes" to the Father's call, which for Balthasar is the goal and summit of the divine plan—God's "astounding masterpiece," as he calls it.[60]

However, three aspects of Balthasar's theology help us surmount this obstacle. First, Balthasar highlights the active quality found in the simple fact that a creature *appears*, and in so doing expresses itself. "God has given to all created things their own operation," Balthasar maintains, "and this includes a spontaneity in manifesting themselves outwardly, an echo, however distant, of [God's] infinite, majestic freedom."[61] "Every flower, every mountain, every man speaks of this freedom."[62] Each creature is an irruption in time and space of the free and personal choice of God for that creature; its life is not simply a "being-there," to use Heidegger's term, but a movement outward from its hidden source. In being what it is—in its appearance to the other—a creature is active and thus has a kind of agency. This natural agency also appears in the fact that all creatures have been given the power to elicit a response from the other. The beauty of each creature and the goodness it offers call forth the other's answer, and in this sense every creature is an agent within God's creation.

Second, we saw above that the Spirit acts as both subjective co-agent with creaturely life and as objective bond to the Godhead. If the Spirit is indeed immanent in all creation, it seems appropriate to suggest that the Spirit can also act as co-agent in animal activity and as the bond between animal-agents and the divine life. The creature's fundamental disposition to express itself can become, through the co-labor of the Spirit, a form of obedience to the divine will, a possibility that Aquinas recognized as part of God's providential working within "irrational" creation.[63]

Third and finally, Balthasar interprets Christ's work as a dramatic narrative, and this move allows us to expand the possibilities of how creaturely activities can be Christ-like (and thus how the creature can participate in the acting space established by Christ). Christ's *dramatic* narrative encompasses more than individual moral actions; the Christ form incorporates the whole complex web of earthly, quotidian dramas as they unfold across time and among human and nonhuman creatures, bestowing on these stories, individually and collectively, a new, Christological meaning. In the denouement of a good drama, every character and subplot is provided with a new meaning. Analogously, Christ reveals the ultimate meaning of the entire drama of salvific history. It is a meaningfulness that can encompass all of the micro-dramas of creaturely existence: the complex interchanges that entail basic experiences such as surprise, love, violence, sin, disappointment, transition, future hope, regression, loss, anxiety, fear, joy, and friendship. In the Christ form, all the creaturely dramas that precede Christ historically and all that follow find their final, coherent, and creaturely meaning because God desires a covenantal relationship with the entirety of creaturely lives in all their dramatic wonder. As Balthasar expresses it, God has taken "the drama of existence which plays on the world stage and inserted it into his quite different 'play' which, nonetheless, he wishes to play on our stage. It is a case of the play within the play: our play 'plays' in his play."[64] In Christ, the dramas of creaturely lives become a Christological response to the Father. This is what Balthasar calls the "theo-drama": the drama of God's life that is expressed in the salvific narrative and that reconfigures the ultimate meaning of human and, I argue, creaturely lives.

God can bring about the inclusion of creaturely drama into the divine life because God's very Self is dramatic. Because "change and surprise" reflect God's life, Balthasar suggests, they were included in God's act of creation so that "finite time" could be "an image of the infinite time that is his."[65] Our experiences of time—moments following moments, acts leading to counter-acts, change creating new possibilities—are creaturely analogues of the loving interchange within the divine life. For Balthasar, creaturely existence will continue to be dramatic in the eschaton, with "open space for creativity," "newness," and "surprise." An eschatological life without something like time and the change it entails would be "hellish." There would be no "room for life, action, and love."[66]

My appeal here to Balthasar's concept of the "theo-drama" has some similarity to that taken by Celia Deane-Drummond, but there are also instructive differences. Deane-Drummond is one of the most significant contributors to the field of ecotheology, and her works reflect a rich and fruitful engagement with Balthasar's theology. My use of Balthasar's concept of the theo-drama centers on how Christ bestows on earthly dramas a christomorphic meaning that builds on, without overturning, the relative, creaturely meaning of those dramas. Deane-Drummond applies the concept in order to preserve the contingency of inter-creature acts and their significance vis-à-vis God. We are both concerned with preserving creation's integrity but emphasize different aspects of it—for me, the innate meaningfulness of creaturely actions and for Deane-Drummond, the contingency of those actions and of the horizontal, inter-creature dramas in which they occur. The "advantage of theodrama as a metaphor for God's working in the world," she argues, "is that it allows God to be present to creation . . . without violating the freedom of creatures or the contingency of individual events and encounters."[67] In contrast, an approach that focuses solely on the salvific metanarrative is unable to attend to the "exceptions to the rules, resistances to explanation, and densities of meaning" that appear within the encounter between God and creation history.[68]

In addition, a theo-dramatic approach underscores that the dramatic dimension of salvation history includes more than the divine-human encounter. There are "different ways of God acting" in the world, and "different scenes call for rather different players, even if the Director is the same."[69] In another volume, she offers a concrete example by exploring the concept of "niche construction" in terms of a theo-dramatic approach. A niche construction refers to any complex system of multiple creatures (human and nonhuman) marked by various forms of interaction and mutual dependencies—including altruism, cooperation, symbiosis, parasitism, and predation. A theo-dramatic view is able to incorporate this entanglement of human and creaturely lives by highlighting the fact that "the natural environment is not some blank stage," but is itself "woven into the fabric of the drama into which human lives are situated." Other creaturely agents, beyond the human, "come more clearly into view in a dynamic, ecologically vibrant theo-drama."[70]

Again, I think the difference between us is one of emphasis. My question regarding her application of Balthasar's category of the theo-drama is whether her stress on God's respect for dramatic contingency and the autonomy of earthly events leaves their eschatological meaning underdetermined. Her approach underscores the dramatic complexity of the horizontal order, but it is not clear how this order's meaning is transformed in the vertical irruption of God into history. She appeals to Christ as the Wisdom of creation as a way of reading the drama of creation Christologically.[71] The "language of wisdom is helpful," she states, because it "*connects* Jesus with his history on earth" and resists detaching Christ from history "in an epic seemingly remote from his ordinary experience" (emphasis in the original).[72] I agree that the Wisdom of Christ—or what Balthasar refers to as the Christ form—can appear within different contingent and historical forms, but I also want to underscore (and I suspect that ultimately Deane-Drummond does also) that in Christ the world's dramas have been given their ultimate and irrevocable meaning.

Balthasar preserves this both/and between contingent and universal meanings by appealing to the role of an interpretive horizon; *all* dramas are interpreted in light of some tacit or explicit horizon. The countless stories of our world in all their myriad forms—for example, the interplay of human love, the development of human culture across time, and the violence of predator and prey—imply contingent, possible meanings that can be resolved definitively only in light of a transcendent, interpretive horizon. For the Christian, the revelation of Christ provides the ultimate backdrop against which every earthly drama must be interpreted, leading the "ambiguities of world theatre beyond themselves to a singleness of meaning that can come only from God."[73] Through his idea of the theo-drama, Balthasar defends both the ultimate christomorphic form of crea-turely reality and its innate, meaningful solidity, the fact that it has its own *eidos*. The I/Thou relationship with God is at the center, but the meaning-fulness of horizontal interactions is preserved: "Whatever positive elements the world has known, at any of its stages of development, will be worthy to participate in God's eternally new event."[74] As David Yeago explains in his examination of Balthasar's theory, "Nothing in human experience and human culture is outside the interpretive range of the story of Jesus Christ, which is the universally and unsurpassably redemptive resolution of the whole drama of creation."[75]

As an illustration of just how capacious God's dramatic life is for includ-ing creaturely life, we can consider the troubling and pervasive reality of predation. In a widely cited letter to the botanist Asa Gray, Charles Dar-win expressed doubt that God could have brought into being a world as violent as our own: "I cannot persuade myself that a beneficent & omnip-otent God would have designedly created the Ichneumonidæ [wasps] with the express intention of their feeding within the living bodies of caterpil-lars, or that a cat should play with mice."[76] We can well understand his aversion. How can the drama of Christ redeem such brutal dramas?

In response, I suggest that we not view predation as wholly or abso-lutely the consequence of the world's cosmic fall; even in predatory acts, there endures a trace of the Creator's goodness. Predation's concrete form *is* marked by the fall, and its goodness is distorted by it; but because it nonetheless also reflects a creaturely goodness, God can and, we hope, will redeem and sanctify it. Animal predators are, of course, more than their predation, but I focus on that aspect because it seems most opposed to any inclusion in the dramatic form of Christ. My goal is to show how, as Christopher Southgate puts it, "the eschatological fulfillment of creatures relates to their protological natures, how they were in the old creation."[77] Is predation fundamental to the nature of these animals and God's original intent for them (i.e., their protological nature), and if so, what happens to that predatory character in the eschaton? How can it be incorporated into the divine life as revealed in Christ?

The reason for excluding predation from the eschaton, if not predatory species themselves, is fairly obvious. Violence of any kind is antithetical to Christian hopes for the kingdom, as shown by its conspicuous absence in Isaiah's imagery (Is 11:1–9), where wolves, lions, and bears have been transformed into socially gentle creatures. Their transformation into non-predators is not, some argue, a violation of their natures or an eradication of their distinctive goodness. David Clough, for example, rejecting the idea that predation is essential to an animal's divinely intended nature, argues that just as the identities of martyrs in the eschaton will not depend on the "continued existence of their enemies," so also the identity of what we now know as predator animals will no longer depend on their violent practices here.[78] In both cases, we are dealing with an aspect of an individual's identity that, in the present age, is contingent on the world's fallen condition. Though I agree with Clough that violence will not be part of the eschaton, I resist his conclusion regarding predation in the eschaton because I am not as convinced that it is so marginal to the animal's nature. As Willis Jenkins observes, "Were the wolf tamed or the lion pacified, it would no longer intelligibly be wolf or lion but something else."[79] Predators thus would not be *sanctified* so much as replaced—presumably by tamer, blander versions—and with this blandness, the diverse goodness and beauty of creation would be diminished.[80] The diversity of outward appearances might be preserved, but those appearances would be superficial shells for a newly universal "Bambi" personality.

Other ecotheologians, especially those who eschew the idea of a cosmic fall, argue that predation is a positive good, if not inherently at least instrumentally so, because through it God diversifies the goodness and beauty of our world. Richard Cartwright Austin thus claims that "to be eaten" can be "part of the blessing of God."[81] Matthew Fox appeals to the fact that "even Divinity gets eaten in this world" to define his "Eucharistic law of the Universe."[82] Rolston sees a reflection of the paschal sacrifice in predation: "The abundant life that Jesus exemplifies and offers to his disciples is that of a sacrificial suffering through to something higher. There is something divine about the power to suffer through to something higher."[83] However, as I noted in the last chapter, no understanding of a creature's Christological redemption is complete if sacrifice has the last word. The *resurrection* of the One who suffered to give life is the essential culmination of the drama revealed in Christ.

The challenge that confronts us here is a different version of the grace/nature distinction examined in the last chapter: Can God transform predatory creatures into christomorphic participants in the eschaton without violating their natures? What we need, I believe, is to negotiate a position between the essentialist transformation of predation proposed by Clough and the mere reinterpretation of it offered by Rolston. I have referred to this position as a "transformed continuity," in which creation, including animal nature, is preserved even as it is elevated into a new eschatological existence. We cannot comprehend what the eschatological life of animals will be any more than the glorified life of the saints, but in order to justify our belief in the possibility of such a transformed continuity (and make some sense of it), it would be helpful to imagine how such an eschatological life might be realized.

The approaches of Clough and Rolston both take seriously the Christian commitment that the eschatological life is an embodied one. Following Balthasar, I suggest that we imagine two aspects of such an embodied life. First, like God's own life, it will include those dimensions we associate with drama: interchange, newness, and creativity. Second, our eschatological lives will reflect the triune processions of self-giving relationality. God's triune life is the eternal giving of Self to the Other and the reception of Self from the Other; our participation in God's life will also share in that co-determinative movement of self-giving and self-realization. The suffering that self-giving often entails in the present order is a consequence of the fall, and thus that negative dimension will not be present in the age to come. Yet, if our eschatological lives are to genuinely share in the life of the triune God, they must continue to be marked by a trinitarian rhythm of self-giving and self-reception.

We have intimations in our present lives of self-giving acts that are also joyful and life-giving: the delight in having a beloved child beat us at a game, the joy of sports among friends even in defeat, the communal delight of a game of charades. These examples are all instances of competitive play where the experience of winning and losing matters less than the joy of seeing the other happy and the delight in being with them. They can help us imagine an eschatological transformation of predation in which the drama of play and self-giving "loss" is experienced as joyful, life-giving, and self-realizing. My suggestion is that the predator/prey tragedy reflects, however distortedly, the self-sacrificial drama of Good Friday and that it can be transformed, not simply annulled, in the resurrected life of Easter. James Dickey famously describes such a new creation in his poem "The Heaven of Animals." It is a bloodless heaven, yet it contains predators endowed "with claws and teeth grown perfect." The hunted "feel no fear, / But acceptance, compliance. / Fulfilling themselves without pain." When "They fall, they are torn, / They rise, they walk again."[84] I believe Dickey goes too far in including the destruction of other creatures, even if temporary, as part of the eschaton, but his suggestion presents the possibility that once pain, violence, and destruction are removed, the predator/prey dynamic could become a reflection of the self-giving life of the Trinity, an eschatological reflection of the complete drama of Good Friday *and* Easter Sunday. The suggestion is, of course, speculative (and very much so). I offer it not to forecast what the eschaton will actually be like but only to help us imaginatively understand that there are other possibilities for the eschatological life of predators besides either their continued violence or their unrecognizable transformation.

As illuminated by Christ, the drama between the predator and its prey can be seen as a shadow, though imperfect and flawed, of God's kenotic life. Given the importance Balthasar places on kenosis as fundamental to the life of the Godhead, and thus to the created order made to reflect this life, it is not surprising that Balthasar likewise sees in the drama of predation a dispositive christomorphism:

> Today we have a much deeper insight into how the successive formations of matter constitute the substratum of the [human]. . . . Or perhaps we could see in the whole of this progressive fashioning, which reveals a "disposition" of simpler forms to be incorporated into, and engulfed by, more highly organized ones—from matter, variously transformed, on and up through the plant and animal forms—a sort of self-effacing readiness to be disposed of, a self-oblation for the sake of the end that was intended from the very beginning. . . . If so, it is only in this sacrificial shape that man would be both the embodiment of the universe as well as its dispositive opening to the "loving sacrificial death" that occurs once for all when the Word of God becomes incarnate—the death that eucharistically fills up the cosmos with triune life.[85]

In the brutal earthly dramas of lives being sacrificed for others throughout evolutionary history, we see an incipient foreshadowing of the form that the divine life will assume within a broken and fallen world, manifested paradigmatically on the cross. The Christian is called, Balthasar argues, to live "freely and knowingly" the same "sacrificial process of nature" that animals live out "unconsciously."[86]

Both Balthasar and Rolston suggest that a similarity of dramatic form exists between Christ's self-offering and animal predation; however, unlike Rolston's truncated version of animal redemption (Good Friday without Easter Sunday), Balthasar recognizes that the brutality of nature requires a next act—that is, a divine response:

> What, then, is this whole climb through millions of years of "nature" supposed to mean? For we should recall that this is a nature that could only develop because every living thing (however well equipped with defensive shells or other evolutionary mechanisms for self-defense) must necessarily offer itself to the sustenance of other "higher" creatures. And, on that allegedly higher level, what is the unspeakable history of mankind's butchery also supposed to mean? (Hans André speaks of "nature's great sacrificial triumphal march.") What can we say about human history, this grinding, pulverizing witches' millhouse of blood and tears, unless all these baffled, uncomprehending, and stunned victims finally come before God, embedded inside a final, conscious, and all-encompassing Victim?[87]

The only answer—not so much an explanation but a response—that can be given to the myriad "stunned victims" of the world's brokenness and sin is their inclusion in the saving work of Christ.[88] Interpreting the story of suffering in terms of the cross and resurrection does not ennoble that suffering or explain it away. Against Rolston, however, I believe we cannot find a Good Friday among creatures without also hoping for their Easter joy. The meaningfulness of God's world is at stake, and, as John Haught states, the only way forward is if "the series of events that make up the life-story and the larger universe . . . flow into the bosom of an everlasting compassion that saves it all from final nothingness and that rescues it from eventual incoherence."[89]

My point, of course, is not that re-narrating the lives of animals in itself "saves" them. Rather, the capacity to see in animal lives a reflection of the story of Christ helps us make some sense of the claim that the Spirit can genuinely bind their dramatic stories to the drama of the Godhead without threatening the integrity of either. Through the economy, God has determined that the drama of triune life will be such that God's "story" now includes our stories. In Christ, our stories and God's story align. The divine story is expansive enough to embrace the widespread exchanges of creaturely violence in a way that preserves the creature's integrity, even while leading it to its Easter transformation. Because the cross gives us a way to interpret the drama of predation and prey Christologically, we can hope that, like the lives of Christians, animal agents within these stories can be sanctified, included within the triune life, so that their lives, now liberated from the distortions of the fall, can unfold in life-giving interchange with God and the rest of creation.

Animal Salvation: Redemptive Solidarity

As we noted in chapter 3, Western Christianity has until recently given little theological attention to the place of creation in the eschaton. The Eastern tradition—perhaps because its history was free of the post-Reformation debates about human salvation and was shaped significantly by creation-friendly theologians like Irenaeus and Athanasius—has better preserved the place of creation in the divine economy and has correspondingly been critical of Western Christianity's neglect of it.[90] Fortunately, those critiques are increasingly less apt today, even if further progress is needed. Pope Benedict, who has been called "the green pope," was disquieted early in his life as a priest by what he saw as the narrowing of Catholicism's focus on *human* salvation.[91] "Perhaps the Christianity of the last century had actually restricted itself a little too much on [the issue of] the spiritual salvation of the individual found in the afterlife, and had not proclaimed loudly enough the salvation of the world, the universal hope of Christianity." Because of this failure, he maintained that Christianity must take on the task of "thinking through these thoughts anew," developing "a new, positive interpretation of the world as creation bearing witness to God's glory and, as a whole, destined for the salvation in Christ."[92]

As part of Western Christianity's course correction regarding creation, two important soteriological themes have received new attention. First, the human person acts as the bond of the cosmos's unity, either as its symbol or as the agent that, in Christ, effects that unity. Second, the cosmos—and all creatures therein—is marked by a fundamental solidarity, both in its creation and in its final redemption.

Historically, the unitive role of the human person was viewed in terms of the Greek notion of the person as "microcosm." Based upon the generally accepted cosmology found in Plato's *Timaeus*, classical thinkers understood the human person to contain all the structures of the created order and thus function as its microcosm. Among the Greek Church fathers, the idea of the human person as microcosm was "so well known" that they deemed "it superfluous to add any explanation."[93] Basil of Caesarea (d. 379), for example, "combines, as do most of the Greek fathers, the biblical idea of the human as created in the image of God with the idea from the *Timaeus* that the human is a little cosmos" (i.e., reflecting the cosmos "in miniature"). According to Basil, humanity acts as the "bond of the cosmos," such that "the fate of the cosmos" is tied to it.[94] Maximus the Confessor (d. 662) also constructed his soteriology around the microcosm theme. God intends to "unite creatures' own voluntary inclination to the more universal natural principle of rational being through the movement of these particular creatures toward well-being." This will bring harmony to their relations with one another and with the whole universe.[95] Humanity was to have been "the natural bond of all being," thus drawing creation into that unity, but it is now "the cause of separation." "The only solution is the Incarnation," which overcomes the divisions of creaturely existence and brings about the harmony that had always been intended.[96]

The eschatological solidarity of all creatures is a common theme in the Old Testament, some examples of which we reviewed in the last chapter. Ezekiel 36, for example, describes a common deliverance for both the earth and humanity.[97] Other expressions of the "principle of a common fate" appear in Isaiah 11:6–9, 43:19–21, 55:12–13; Ezekiel 34:25–31; Hosea 2:18; and Zechariah 8:12. Nature exults in humanity's success and suffers in its sin. Thus it is cursed as a result of Adam's disobedience (Gn 3:17–19) and rejoices in Israel's liberation from captivity.[98] The solidarity theme is also implied in the New Testament idea of the cosmic Christ and in the important passage of Romans 8. With regard to the latter, Brendan Byrne argues that Paul's argument "hinges around the principle that, because human beings were created along with the non-human created world and given responsibility for that world, they share a common fate with that world. When human society deteriorates, so does that of the rest of creation and, vice versa, when we do well, creation shares in the blessing."[99]

Although the idea of the human as a micro-cosmos comprising all levels of reality does not play much of a role in contemporary Christian thought, the idea of a human-mediated or human-symbolized soteriology does (though not without criticism). Characteristic of this approach is the view that the human person exists in fundamental solidarity with creation (both protologically and eschatologically) and, in Christ, acts as its unitive principle. Those who advocate for this view often appeal to the evangelical role of the human person as priest, broadly understood. For Linzey, God has called humanity to a life of "service and self-sacrifice" and has commissioned it to exercise a priesthood "not just for members of [its] own species, but for all sentient creatures."[100] T. F. Torrance, a Reformed theologian and disciple of Karl Barth, states that the "priestly role of man must take on a redemptive form—that is how we should view man's relationship to nature. It is his task to *save* the natural order" (emphasis added by Linzey).[101] Zizioulas sees this role expressed in the Eucharist: "The priest . . . takes the world in his hands to refer it to God, and . . . in return, brings God's blessing to what he refers to God. Through this act, creation is brought into communion with God himself." It is only the human being who can "unite the world in his hands in order to refer it to God, so that it can be united with God and thus saved and fulfilled."[102] Jürgen Moltmann provides the theme with its proper ecclesial breadth: "The church has to represent the whole cosmos, so it must bring before God the 'groanings of creation' (Rom 8.19ff.) as well as the hope for the coming of God to everything created."[103]

Not all agree, however. Richard Bauckham, for example, considers the idea that humanity has a priestly role for creation an "arrogant assertion." The view that "only through human mediation can the rest of creation be itself in relation to God" finds no evidence in Scripture. In the world of the Old Testament, "creatures have their own relationships with God quite apart from humanity and fulfill their God-given existence without human interference (e.g., Ps 104; Jb 38–39)."[104] His critique is correct as far as it goes: Creatures do praise God and do so without human mediation. However, his argument does not address what I believe to be at the heart of contemporary appeals to humanity's priestly role: creation's *Christological* redemption and the role that the Church, in the Spirit, plays in effecting it. Giving a priestly role to humanity vis-à-vis creation is consequent to the view that the Christian community has been called to share in Christ's redemptive labor for the world and to be an efficacious witness to the kingdom that he inaugurated. Humanity, as formed into the people of God, is to be the "steward" of the Gospel (1 Cor 4:1); and this divinely given task, however undeserved, gives it a distinctive role in creation's eschatological fulfillment.

A Catholic version of the theme of a cosmic solidarity centered in humanity appears in the writings of Karl Rahner. He develops the theme, however, in a way that ultimately undercuts the theological corollary of a *redemptive* solidarity. Rahner understands the human person as embodied in the world, arising out of matter and always tied to it. The person is "the existent in whom the basic tendency of matter to discover itself in spirit through self-transcendence reaches its definite breakthrough."[105] The emphasis on the human person's embeddedness in the cosmos is initially promising, and Rahner suggests, albeit cryptically, that "each creature according to its own kind, will (though we cannot imagine how) participate in the eternity of God."[106] On the whole, however, Rahner rarely treats nonhuman creatures on the individual level, and his ability to consider their redemption is inhibited by how he understands matter and spirit. For Rahner, humanity is the cosmic event of matter transcending itself.[107] This becomes problematic for animal redemption because of two additional moves he makes. First, in distinguishing sentient life forms, Rahner tends to assume a clear binary between those creatures that transcend matter (i.e., human persons) and those that do not (everything else).[108] Second, he views individuality in terms of matter coming to know itself, and thus individuality is limited to fully self-aware creatures.[109] Together, these commitments—ascribing transcendence and individuality exclusively to humanity—explain why Rahner avoids speaking about individual nonhuman creatures and frequently slips into a collective personification of the cosmos when discussing creation (e.g., in the human person, "the cosmos can become conscious of itself" and "the world becomes present to itself").[110]

In his own way, Rahner presents the person as "microcosm," though the person does not so much act as a metaphysical agent binding together human and cosmic salvation, but rather, in a severely attenuated form of cosmic redemption, human salvation precisely *is* the cosmos becoming saved: "The total, created reality of the world grows in and through persons having body and spirit, and the world is, in a certain sense, the body of those persons."[111] The "history of the cosmos as a whole will find its real consummation despite, in and through the freedom of man."[112]

Like Rahner, Balthasar upholds the idea of humanity's fundamental solidarity with creation.[113] The human person is at the center of the cosmos, the "natural focal point" for the communion of all beings.[114] But whereas for Rahner the redeemed person is the symbol and singular expression of the cosmos's salvific realization, Balthasar sees creation's redemption as distinct from, though nonetheless tied to, that of humanity; through human redemption, "the cosmos is being drawn" into its own redemption.[115] Two of the commitments noted above help Balthasar avoid the marginalization of nonhuman creatures that threatens Rahner's thought. First, Balthasar allows for gradations within creation, so his soteriology is not constrained by a bifurcation of creation into mere matter and matter transcending itself. Second, he insistently defends the distinctive dignity of the *individual* creature. Though Balthasar's principal concern is for the *human* individual, the expressive agency he attributes to each creature provides a foundation for including nonhuman creatures.

In responding to Bauckham's critique above, I alluded to another aspect of the contemporary links drawn between humanity and cosmic salvation: Like post-apostolic thought, they place the redemptive role of the human person within a context of substantial ecclesial and eucharistic commitments. In the paschal mystery, Christ initiated creation's restoration, and he will bring it to fulfillment when he comes again. Through the gift of the Spirit, the Christian community continues Christ's saving work in the present age, and in the Eucharist, its labor finds its fullest expression. It is an efficacious liturgy, in which heaven becomes present to earth in order to bring earth back to heaven.

The connection between creation's sanctification and the liturgy began to be expounded early in the post-apostolic age. The earliest reference to the "Lord's Day" as the day of the Christians' community celebration (what came to be known as the Eucharist) appears in the *Didache*, a document that scholars now date to the second half of the first century.[116] Worship on *Sunday* (as opposed to the traditional Sabbath) likely developed in association with the community's celebration of Christ's resurrection. Early Christian thinkers recognized the symbolic connection between Sunday (as the eighth day after the seven days of the first creation) and the new creation established in Christ.[117] For Eusebius of Caesarea (d. 339), Christians face eastward in their Sunday gatherings "as if to welcome Christ as the risen Sun of the new creation,"[118] whereas Gregory of Nazianzus (d. 390) suggests that "just as the first creation has its beginning on a Sunday . . . , so the new creation must begin again with the same day."[119] A text attributed to Athanasius (d. 373) maintains that "we honor the Lord's Day as a commemoration of the second creation. For he did not create another creation but renewed the original one and finished what he had begun to make." Sunday thus came to be celebrated as the renewal of creation, the "birthday" of the new cosmos.[120]

It is no surprise, then, that creation also became a theme in the eucharistic prayer. Irenaeus (d. 202) is the first known thinker to associate the gifts of bread and wine with an offering to God of the goods of creation:

> Again, giving directions to his disciples to offer God the first-fruits of His own created things. . . . He took that created thing, bread, and gave thanks, and said, "This is My body." And the cup likewise, which is part of that

creation to which we belong, He confessed to be His blood, and taught the new oblation of the new covenant; which the Church receiving from the apostles, offers to God throughout all the world, to Him who gives us as the means of subsistence the first-fruits of His own gifts in the New Testament.[121]

Through the epiclesis, the calling down of the Spirit, the bread that is "produced from the earth" now consists of "two realities, earthly and heavenly."[122] By including creation and the offering of its gifts in the Eucharist, Irenaeus, by implication, draws creation itself into the Christian community's mimesis of Christ's saving act.

The grateful celebration of the gift of creation recurs in the liturgies of early Christianity, particularly in the prayers directly preceding the *Sanctus*. Examples of this prefatory praise of and by creation can be found in the *Apostolic Constitutions* (written in the late fourth century), which exclaims how God, who created all things, "filled the world and adorned it with sweet-smelling and healing herbs, with many different living things, . . . the cycles of the years, . . . [and] the order of the seasons";[123] in the *Liturgy of Saint Basil* (parts of which date back to the fourth century), where God is praised as master of "all creation, visible and invisible";[124] and in the baptismal rite of Theodore of Mopsuestia (d. 428), in which the bishop exhorts that "praise and adoration be offered to the divine nature by all of Creation" and the people respond by repeating an abbreviated form of the *Sanctus*.[125] That these prayers directly precede the *Sanctus*, in which the assembly voices its exultant praise for God ("Holy, holy, holy, Lord of Sabaoth . . ."), suggests "an ingathering and an uplifting of creatures in worship of the Creator."[126]

The theme comes to full expression in the thought of Maximus the Confessor (d. 662). As we saw, for Maximus the goal of creation is the integration of all creatures, their *logoi*, into the unity of Christ the Logos. The human person, as composed of sense and intellect, was created to be the instrument of this cosmic unity; humanity's capacity to unite the cosmos, which was lost in the fall, was restored in Christ.[127] Maximus sees the Christian community's worship as a continuation of Christ's work, in that it is both a symbol of creation's unity and a movement toward its realization. Indeed, the Church itself is an image of the "sensible world."[128] The human person, as the "true priest of the world,"[129] "offers to God" creation as contemplated by human reason.[130] For Maximus, the Eucharist is thus a "cosmic liturgy," celebrating and symbolizing the eschatological unity that God intends for all creatures.[131]

The eucharistic prayers of the Eastern churches have preserved the ritual inclusion of creation in the salvific work of Christ. Until 1970, the Latin Rite of the Catholic Church exclusively followed the Roman Eucharistic Prayer (much of which dates back to the sixth century), in which the theme of creation scarcely appears. However, following the liturgical reforms of Vatican II, additional prayers were added, including Eucharistic Prayer IV, which is based on the *Apostolic Constitutions* and the *Liturgy of Saint Basil*. Unique among the Eucharistic Prayers of the Roman Missal (of which there are now ten), this Eastern-inflected prayer draws creation into the liturgy's ritual movement, lifting creation up in thanksgiving, praise, sanctification, and eschatological hope. Its "Preface" (which is specifically designed for this Eucharistic Prayer and must always accompany it) opens with a proclamation of God's goodness to humanity and creation and looks expectantly to the sanctification of both: "[You] have made all that is, so that you might fill your creatures with blessings and bring joy to many of them by the glory of your light."[132] With the angels, the human community gives "voice to every creature under heaven" and confesses God's name "in exultation."

After the *Sanctus*, the Eucharistic Prayer begins by praising God for fashioning all creatures "in wisdom and in love." The work of Christ is then recounted, and the theme of creation's sanctification is more explicitly stated. Christ "proclaimed the good news of salvation" and sent the Holy Spirit so that "we might no longer live for ourselves" and that God "might sanctify creation to the full." After the words of institution, the Church offers up to God Christ's "Body and Blood . . . which brings salvation to the whole world." At its close, the prayer looks with hopeful anticipation of the kingdom that is to come: "There, with the whole of creation, freed from the corruption of sin and death, may we glorify you through Christ our Lord, through whom you bestow on the world all that is good."

Balthasar follows this tradition of attributing a cosmic sweep to the eucharistic celebration. All creation is incorporated in its movement from sacrificial offering to sanctification. Consistent with Catholic understanding, Balthasar holds that the eucharistic liturgy "is identical, in the here and now celebration, with what was accomplished on the cross."[133] Through it, the Spirit assimilates us into the "mind of Christ, which is *eucharistia*, praise and thanksgiving to God,"[134] and gives us a share in the cosmic "work of Christ."[135] Through Christ's eucharistic body, "the life of the Trinity comes down from heaven and penetrates earth"; the universalizing Spirit gathers the world to itself and brings it to the Father.[136]

Balthasar places a eucharistic stamp on the Pauline idea of the cosmic Christ: All that the Son gathers to himself—all creation—is surrendered to the Father in the Eucharist. In the Church's celebration of the Eucharist, the world itself comes to share "in the divine exchange" (i.e., the Son giving all creation over to the Father), and the liturgy is thus empowered by the Spirit to take the gifts of the earth it has received from God and "return them to God as a divine gift."[137] In sum, the work of the Christian community in sanctifying creation is one of entering "into Christ's life and mission *by eucharistically receiving creation in its entirety as a gift that mediates and expresses the triune life*—thereby confirming and fulfilling God's original plan for the world" (emphasis in the original).[138]

We can distinguish two steps here, and both appear in recent papal writings: The cosmos shares in the salvation offered to humanity; and this salvation is celebrated and effected in the Eucharist. I have already noted that contemporary Church documents attest to some form of a cosmic redemption.[139] The scope of Jesus's mission "is the whole of creation, the world in its entirety."[140] Humanity's participation in Christ's mission to redeem creation includes a liturgical response centered in the Eucharist, which "unites heaven and earth" and "embraces and permeates all creation." Through the Eucharist, the Christian community celebrates and enters into the movement of Christ's redemptive labor, one in which Christ "gives back to the Creator and Father all creation redeemed"; "the world which came forth from the hands of God the Creator" is now returned "to him redeemed by Christ."[141] In the Eucharist, "creation is projected towards divinization" and "toward unification with the Creator himself."[142]

We will explore the ethical implications of these claims in the next chapter, but we can note here that the writings of recent popes have encouraged the Christian community to recognize its role, both liturgical and ethical, in the redemption and sanctification of creation. John Paul II stated that our service to creation is "ministerial, . . . a real reflection of the unique and infinite lordship of God," to be exercised "with wisdom and love."[143] Before becoming pope, Benedict XVI described Christian worship as the "soul of the covenant" that "not only saves mankind but is also meant to draw the whole of reality into communion with God."[144] Pope Francis challenges us to "be instruments of God our Father, so that our planet might be what he desired when he created it and correspond with his plan for peace, beauty and fullness."[145] Ultimately, we "are called to lead all creatures back to their Creator."[146] The boundaries are fluid between the liturgical and ethical, between the universal and the particular. Through the Eucharist, our prayer for creation's sanctification—our own and that of our fellow creatures—is given cosmic reach; in our daily lives, we labor for the concrete and particular that creation may better reflect its eschatological destiny. Yet, as Balthasar's pneumatology reminds us, these moments are not isolated operations; rather, the Spirit enfolds all of them into the one drama of Christ, binding together earth and heaven, the concrete and the universal.

CONCLUSION: AN INDIVIDUAL
AND COSMIC SALVATION

Balthasar's soteriology centers on the joint labor of the Father's "two hands," the Son and the Spirit. In order to expand his theology to include more explicitly the individual creature, it was necessary to supplement the Christology of chapter 3 with this chapter's pneumatology. God's actions in the world belong at once to all three Persons of the Trinity and to each individually in ways appropriate to that Person. For Balthasar, the economic expression of the Spirit's triune life continues the twofold role of subject and object within the Godhead. The Spirit, as both co-subject with the creature and as objective bond to the divine life, labors at liquefying Christ and making his form appear in the world.

I have sought to develop these ideas further through a set of reflections that have approached the issue from two directions—the sanctification of the individual creature and that of creation in solidarity with humanity. My hope is that these two different paths offer complementary portrayals. Starting with the individual creature, I have argued that the form of Christ's life, death, and resurrection is expansive in its capacity to include all creaturely dramas, even that of predation and prey. Christ illuminates the fragments of meaning displayed in such creaturely existence that are, through the work of the Spirit, made to reflect the redemptive drama and as such are included in the divine life. In the second approach to creation's salvation, I noted two themes that recur in early Christianity: the redemptive solidarity of all creation and the human person as the unitive agent and symbol of this solidarity. Though these themes ceased to have much traction in the post-patristic theology of the West, contemporary forms of them have been developed in recent decades as part of the Church's renewed commitment to a redemption that includes "the entire world."[147]

In general terms, Balthasar's thoughts and those of recent popes converge in affirming the dual themes of salvific solidarity and the human person as its bond. It is ultimately God's work, of course; but in the liturgy, the Christian community participates in this work by drawing creation into the event of its salvation. In offering the earthly elements of bread and wine, the Church lifts up all creation to the Father and joins the voices of creation in a grateful eucharistic praise. This sacramental expression of the eschatological life is, I argue in the next chapter, to be anticipated in our daily deeds beyond the Church's walls.

My goal in these two sets of reflections has been to imagine how the salvation of all creation is effected by the Father's two hands. I believe that the cumulative weight of the arguments warrants the hope that God's fidelity to creation will include the sanctifying embrace of its creatures. Finally, the reflections given above have underscored a privileged, ministerial role for the human person, one that integrates the ideas of humanity as servant steward and as coparticipant in creation's redemption. It is a weighty responsibility. In the final chapter, I develop a general framework for discerning how the Christian community is to realize its task of caring for creation.

NOTES

Epigraph: John Paul II, *Crossing the Threshold*, 22.

1. Elizabeth Johnson mourned that "the full range and activity of God the Spirit has been virtually lost from much of Christian theological consciousness." Johnson, *She Who Is*, 130. Walter Kasper similarly complained that "the Holy Spirit does not play an outstanding part in the average ecclesial and theological consciousness." Kasper, *God*, 198. Catherine Mowry LaCugna maintained that many of the theologies of the West are "christomonistic." LaCugna, *God*, 235n15.

2. Mahoney, *Christianity*, xi.

3. Mahoney, 91.

4. Mahoney, 50.

5. Mahoney, 65.

6. Haught, *Resting*, 120.

7. Jenkins, *Ecologies*, 12.

8. Jenkins, 13.

9. Mahoney, *Christianity*, 151.

10. Cahill, "Atonement Paradigm," 421.

11. Cahill, 422.

12. Cahill, 423.

13. Rahner, *Im Gespräch*, 245–46. English translation cited by Mongrain, *Systematic Thought*, 206n1.

14. Edwards, *Partaking*, 93.

15. Deane-Drummond, "Breadth," 51.

16. A theologian friend once quipped, "Balthasar wanders around in the inner life of the Trinity the way I walk around my apartment."

17. Cf., Rahner's famous dictum, "*The 'economic' Trinity is the 'immanent' Trinity and the 'immanent' Trinity is the 'economic' Trinity*" (emphasis in the original). Rahner, *Trinity*, 22.

18. Balthasar, *Theo-Drama*, vol. 2, 258.

19. Williams, "Afterword," 178.

20. Gavrilyuk, *Suffering*, 173.

21. Balthasar, *Theo-Drama*, vol. 4, 324.

22. Balthasar, *Theo-Drama*, vol. 2, 257.

23. Balthasar, *Theo-Drama*, vol. 5, 30.

24. O'Hanlon, *Immutability*, 80. It is interesting then to note that in critiquing Balthasar, Keith Ward neglects to include one of Balthasar's inverted commas. The original English translation reads "an absolute, infinite 'distance'" (i.e., with inverted commas around "distance"), whereas Ward cites him as stating simply "an absolute infinite distance." Ward, *Christ*, 215.

25. Balthasar, *Theo-Drama*, vol. 5, 257.

26. Balthasar, 258. He cites himself: Balthasar, *Sponsa Verbi*, vol. 2, 270.

27. Balthasar, *Two Say Why*, 53.

28. John Paul II, *Dominum*, no. 39.

29. Margaret Farley develops the idea of "active receptivity" as part of her examination of interpersonal commitment. Farley, "Fragments."

30. Sachs, "Current Eschatology," 242.

31. Balthasar, "Unknown," 112.

32. Balthasar, *Theo-Drama*, vol. 3, 187.

33. The Spirit has a "mediational form between the Father and the Son." Balthasar, 186.

34. As Balthasar says, the Spirit "as the common *fruit* of the Father and the Son, . . . can become autonomous in relation to them" (emphasis in the original). Balthasar, "Holy Spirit," 125.

35. Balthasar, "Unknown," 107. Cf., Kasper: "The Holy Spirit is the most mysterious of the three divine persons, for while the Son has shown himself to us in human form and we can form at least an image of the Father, we have no concrete grasp of the Spirit. Not without reason has he frequently been called 'the unknown God.'" Kasper, *God*, 198.

36. Balthasar, *Theo-Drama*, vol. 2, 257.

37. Balthasar, "Improvisation," 145; Balthasar, *Theo-Drama*, vol. 2, 257.

38. Balthasar, "Holy Spirit," 128–29n11. This "anonymous Spirit shows all the traits of the highest personal freedom and freedom of movement. . . . He is the unfathomable, incomprehensible freedom of the love of God brought near to us." Balthasar, 125–26.

39. Balthasar, "Improvisation," 146.

40. "By the power of the Holy Spirit, [Jesus] is 'liquefied' and rendered accessible to all times and places, without forfeiting his uniqueness." Balthasar, *Theo-Drama*, vol. 3, 38–39.

41. Balthasar, "Unknown," 109.

42. If there is to be a drama, there must be "some other, nondivine, created freedom." Balthasar, *Theo-Drama*, vol. 2, 62.

43. Steck, "Graced Encounters," 259.

44. Balthasar, *Theo-Drama*, vol. 2, 104–5.

45. Balthasar, "Improvisation," 152.

46. Balthasar, "Unknown," 114.

47. Edwards, *God*, loc. 841 of 1462, Kindle.

48. Edwards, loc. 922 of 1462, Kindle. Here, he refers approvingly to the view developed by Kasper, *God*.

49. Edwards, loc. 969–70 of 1462, Kindle.

50. Johnson, *Women, Earth, and Creator Spirit*, 42.

51. Johnson, 43.

52. Edwards, *God*, loc. 841–42 of 1462, Kindle.

53. Again, I do not believe the relatively autonomous workings of the natural order (which I affirm) can be characterized as "free" or "creative" in a way that justifies a "free process" theodicy.

54. Johnson, *Women, Earth, and Creator Spirit*, 43.

55. Balthasar, "Unknown," 113.

56. The task of the Holy Spirit "is to universalize the drama of Christ." Balthasar, *Theo-Drama*, vol. 2, 96.

57. Balthasar, "Counsel," 263.

58. Balthasar, *Theological Anthropology*, 71.

59. Balthasar follows Bonaventure in this. See Balthasar, *Glory*, vol. 2, 346.

60. Balthasar, *Theo-Drama*, vol. 1, 34. Clough and Deane-Drummond have both argued that we cannot exclude the possibility of a context-dependent form of moral agency in animals—i.e., some sense in which animals can say "yes" to God. Clough argues that there are no biblical or theological grounds for rejecting the possibility of animal sin. If a creature can sin, it would take a form "particular" to that creature and would "depend on the degree to which a particular creature is able to respond to God and to its environment." Clough, *On Animals: Volume One*, 119. Deane-Drummond similarly affirms "the possibility that at least some [animals] express forms of morality that are distinctive to their own social worlds." Deane-Drummond, *Wisdom*, 122. See also Deane-Drummond, "Are Animals Moral?" As I stated in chapter 2, I am not yet convinced that we can attribute genuine moral agency to any animal, though I accept it as a possibility and also acknowledge that moral agency can appear in other forms than that associated with human morality. However, even if it is the case that some animals *can* respond to the divine will, I want also to argue for the redemption of animals that do not have such a capacity.

61. Balthasar, *Theo-Logic*, vol. 1, loc. 1293–94 of 4592, Kindle.

62. Balthasar, loc. 1634–35 of 4592, Kindle.

63. In Aquinas's interpretation of the depiction in Psalm 147:9 of ravens who call on God, he states, "The young ravens are said to call upon God, on account of the natural desire whereby all things, each in its own way, desire to attain the Divine goodness. Thus, even dumb animals are said to obey God, on account of the natural instinct whereby they are moved by God." *ST* II.II.83.10 *ad*. 3. Also: "Irrational creatures neither partake of nor are obedient to human reason: whereas they do partake of the Divine Reason by obeying it; because the power of Divine Reason extends over more things than human reason does." *ST* I.II.93.5 *ad*. 2.

64. Balthasar, *Theo-Drama*, vol. 1, 20.

65. Balthasar, "Finite Time," 55.

66. Balthasar, 55.

67. Deane-Drummond, *Christ*, 283. Also, the theo-drama is "a theological way of reading history . . . that eschews the reductionism of an epic or grand narrative, and points to particular occasions and particular events." Deane-Drummond, *Wisdom*, 309.

68. Deane-Drummond, *Christ*, 199.

69. Deane-Drummond, 283n75.

70. Deane-Drummond, *Wisdom*, 235.

71. Deane-Drummond, *Christ*, 111ff.

72. Deane-Drummond, 54.

73. Balthasar, *Theo-Drama*, vol. 1, 20.

74. Balthasar, *Theo-Drama*, vol. 5, 418.

75. Yeago, "Drama," 104. Deane-Drummond echoes Balthasar's project on this point in her section titled "Christ, the Form of Beauty." There, she rightly notes that for Balthasar, Christ shows the inadequacy of earthly forms of beauty while also drawing these same forms to their fulfillment. Deane-Drummond, *Christ*, 138–43. Along with other interpreters of Balthasar, I believe we must see his theo-drama as an organic development of his theological aesthetics. The principles developed in his aesthetics (e.g., the form as necessary for perception, Christ as the form that fulfills and transcends earthly forms, and the ek-static response that the Christ form evokes) continue in his theo-drama, only now applied to the *dramatic* form. He develops the aesthetics of the beautiful form so that it can encompass, as a form, the drama of salvation and its culmination in Christ. His theological aesthetics then becomes, as it must, a theological dramatics, so that the "picture of Christ" will not "ossify into an icon." Balthasar, *Theo-Drama*, vol. 2, 21.

76. Asa Gray was a nineteenth-century botanist who believed that God guided evolution. For the letter, see Darwin, "To Asa Gray."

77. Southgate, *Groaning*, 86.

78. Clough, *On Animals: Volume One*, 161.

79. Jenkins, *Ecologies*, 144.

80. For a helpful theological reflection on diversity, see O'Brien, "The Sacramental Value of the Variety of Life," in *Ethics*, "The argument of this chapter could

therefore be summarized by saying that biodiversity has intrinsic, inspirational, instructional, survival, and economic value. However, the Christian tradition of sacramentality helps to articulate these claims in a particular way designed to resonate with those who believe that this world is God's creation." O'Brien, 72.

81. Austin, *Beauty*, 196–97, cited by Linzey, *Animal Theology*, 119.

82. Fox, "Green Spirituality," 14–15, cited by Linzey, *Animal Theology*, 119.

83. Rolston, "Does Nature Need to Be Redeemed?" 220.

84. Dickey, *Self-Interviews*, 108–9.

85. Balthasar, *Theo-Logic*, vol. 2, loc. 3096–106 of 7072, Kindle. He cites the third volume of Hans André, *Annäherung durch Abstand*, 225.

86. Balthasar, *Theo-Logic*, vol. 2, loc. 3121–24 of 7072, Kindle.

87. Balthasar, *Epilogue*, loc. 1316–23 of 1687, Kindle.

88. "The Son, as it were, actively gathers unto himself sins, but also the world's pains." Balthasar, *Theo-Drama*, vol. 5, 260.

89. Haught, *Making Sense*, 103.

90. Thus, the critique of Orthodox voices like the theologian Andrew Louth: "Western theology has become so concerned with the movement from fall to redemption that it has lost sight of the fact that all this takes place in the created environment, that rests on God's Word." Louth, "Between Creation and Transfiguration," 211–12. Similarly, the Orthodox metropolitan John Zizioulas stated that the West has "lost consciousness of the importance of the material creation." Zizioulas, "Priest of Creation," 277.

91. In addition to practical actions (e.g., installing solar panels at the Vatican), creation regularly appeared as a theme in the pope's homilies and writings. For a collection of his writings and addresses related to the environment, see Benedict XVI, *Garden*.

92. Ratzinger, "Kardinal Frings," 172–73, cited and translated by Vallery, "Pope Benedict XVI's Cosmic Soteriology," 177–78.

93. Allers, "Microcosmus," 321.

94. Louth, "Six Days," 52. Allers identifies six versions of the microcosm theme appearing in early Christian history. Allers, "Microcosmus," 321–37.

95. Maximus Confessor, *On the Cosmic Mystery*, 100.

96. Maximus Confessor, *Maximus the Confessor*, ed. Louth, 73–74.

97. Gowan, *Eschatology*, 101–2.

98. Nature puts on "a spectacular display in sympathy with Israel emerging triumphant from Egypt and from captivity in Babylon: the mountains leap for joy, the desert blooms, the rough places are made smooth." Byrne, "Creation Groaning," 197.

99. Byrne, 197.

100. Linzey, *Animal Theology*, 45.

101. Torrance, *Divine and Contingent Order*, 130, cited by Linzey, *Animal Theology*, 54.

102. Zizioulas, "Proprietors."

103. Moltmann, *Ethics*, 139.

104. Bauckham, *Living*, 152.

105. Rahner, *Foundations*, 181.

106. Rahner, *On the Theology of Death*, 36.

107. Rahner, "Christology," 160.

108. "It is clear that the lower always moves slowly towards the boundary line in its history which it then crosses in its actual self-transcendence." Rahner, 167.

109. "Starting from the original self-experience of the one man, however, it can be said that spirit is the one man in so far as he becomes conscious of himself in an absolute consciousness of being-given-to-himself." Rahner, 162–63. "The [human] soul is essentially more individual than the entelechies of the sub-human realm." Rahner, *On the Theology of Death*, 29.

110. Rahner, "Christology," 170, 176, respectively. Rahner does say that "the cosmos gradually becomes conscious of itself in man" (171), but I do not know of any place where he explores the possibility of gradations in matter coming to know itself.

111. Rahner, *On the Theology of Death*, 37.

112. Rahner, "Christology," 168. In humanity's corporeality, each person "communicates with the whole cosmos in *such* a way that through this corporeality of man taken as the other element of belonging to the spirit, the cosmos really presses forward to this self-presence in the spirit." Rahner, 170 (emphasis in the original).

113. "God's creation, in all its multiplicity, is one." Balthasar, *Theo-Drama*, vol. 5, 422. The human person "owes his existence as a bodily being to the cosmos." Balthasar, *Epilogue*, loc. 1314 of 1687, Kindle.

114. Balthasar, *Theo-Logic*, vol. 2, loc. 3141 of 7072.

115. Balthasar, *Epilogue*, loc. 1313 of 1687, Kindle. Also: "The whole created world (at least) has been drawn into the destiny of redeemed man." Balthasar, *Theo-Drama*, vol. 5, 420.

116. LaVerdiere, *Eucharist*, 128–31.

117. Blowers, *Drama*, 338–39.

118. Blowers, 339.

119. Gregory of Nazianzus, *Oracle* 44.5. Translation provided by Daley, *Gregory*, 157–58. cited by Blowers, *Drama*, 341.

120. Blowers, 338.

121. Irenaeus, *Against Heresies* [IV.17.5], 484.

122. Irenaeus [IV.18.5], 486.

123. *Apostolic Constitutions*, bk 8. Translated text provided by Jasper and Cuming, *Prayers*, 106.

124. "Liturgy of St. Basil." Translated text provided by Jasper and Cuming, 116.

125. Theodore of Mopsuestia, *Catechesis* 16. Translated text provided by Jasper and Cuming, 136.

126. Blowers, *Drama*, 351.

127. Maximus, *On Difficulties*, vol. II ["Ambiguum 41"], 103–21.

128. *Mystagogia*, chap. 3. Translated text provided by Stead, *Church*, 71.

129. Balthasar, *Cosmic Liturgy*, loc. 5403 of 8807, Kindle.

130. *Mystagogia*, chap. 4. Translated text provided by Stead, *Church*, 72.

131. The title of Balthasar's book on Maximus is *Cosmic Liturgy*. The Maximus scholar Lars Thunberg similarly interprets Maximus. Thunberg, *Microcosm*, 422–23.

132. United States Conference of Catholic Bishops, *Roman Missal*, 508–13.

133. Balthasar, *Theo-Drama*, vol. 4, 391.

134. Balthasar, 400.

135. Balthasar, 405.

136. Balthasar, *Theo-Drama*, vol. 5, 417.

137. Balthasar, 521.

138. Healy and Schindler, "For the Life of the World," 51.

139. "Revelation affirms the profound common destiny of the material world and man." Catholic Church, *Catechism*, no. 1046.

140. Benedict XVI, *Jesus of Nazareth: Part Two*, 100.

141. John Paul II, *Ecclesia*, no. 8.

142. Benedict XVI, "Homily: Sacred Body."

143. John Paul II, *Evangelium Vitae*, no. 52.

144. Ratzinger, *Spirit of the Liturgy*, 27.

145. Francis, *Laudato Si'*, no. 53.

146. Francis, no. 83.

147. Vatican Council II, *Lumen Gentium*, no. 48.

CHAPTER 5

ETHICS

Ministers of the Eschatological Covenant

There are no unemployed people in the Kingdom of God.

—Pope Francis

THIS FINAL chapter examines the ethical implications of the theological structure developed in the previous chapters. Nonhuman creatures are not nameless extras in the salvific drama, unnoticed in their absence when the eschaton's final act begins. They are part of the drama, genuine objects of God's creative and redemptive care. The argument has been that God wills not only the redemption of humanity and the general renewal of the earth but also the restoration of at least some of the individual nonhuman creatures who exist or have existed in the present age (e.g., those individual creatures with something like a subject-identity that endures across time). Because these creatures have an eschatological destiny, our response to them should be instructed by Christianity's vision of that future life. Christ inaugurated the kingdom of God in human history, and the Spirit now calls forth laborers to make its presence real.

The eschatological kingdom does not directly generate specific ethical norms for animal care. As is the case with other ideals of the eschaton (e.g., nonviolence, hospitality toward the stranger, communal sharing of one's goods), those associated with a renewed *animal* kingdom (e.g., the ideals reflected in Isaiah's image of a peaceable kingdom) cannot be converted into detailed and comprehensive norms for the present. Factors like human finitude, limitless needs, and the difficulty in discerning values within a world of diverse life forms contribute to our inability to translate ideals into concrete norms. But encompassing all these is the fact of our

world's fallenness. The Christian commitment to embodying the kingdom's ideals must be tempered by an eschatological reserve, one that
acknowledges the enduring brokenness of creation and the impossibility
of realizing in it all our deepest hopes and ideals.

In the chapter's first section, I situate animal ethics within the theological framework of the already / not yet of the kingdom of God. Because
the labor for the kingdom is integral to the Church's mission, I then make
the case that care for animals, and for creation more broadly, is a fundamental task of the Church. These two considerations—animal ethics
within the already / not yet of the kingdom and the ecclesial mission to
work for animals and creation—complicate our attempts to identify concrete norms for animal care. I examine this complexity in terms of three
tensions: the conflicts that arise between the competing goods of the
present order and the ideals of the kingdom, the differences between the
Church's social hopes and conventional social norms, and the creative
tension between universal obligations and God's often more demanding
call to the individual Christian. Finally, I propose a set of general principles as a framework for animal ethics. In order to show examples of a discernment informed by these principles, I briefly examine two topics that
have generated significant ethical debates: eating factory-farmed meat and
using animals in experiments.

THE KINGDOM OF GOD

In chapter 2, I noted the importance that the kingdom of God had in
Jesus's preaching. If one includes cognates of the term (e.g., "the kingdom
of heaven"), references to the kingdom of God occur "over one hundred
times in the Synoptic Gospels (50 times in Matthew, 15 times in Mark,
and 39 times in Luke)."[1] Contemporary scholarship, beginning with Oscar
Cullmann's *Christ and Time*, has generally interpreted Jesus's announce-
ment of the kingdom in terms of the "already and not yet." Through word
and deed, Christ inaugurated the kingdom of God, but its fullness will
appear only in the eschaton, when Christ returns and completes God's
plan.[2] Until then, the Christian lives between the times of the already and
not yet, within a broken world with the hope and expectation of a new era
appearing in its midst.[3]

The already / not yet tension is peculiar to the Christian worldview and
informs how we understand the Christian ethical response. The Spirit
helps Christians discern how to witness to the ideals of Christ's life and

teaching within the currents of their historical context, with its intermingling eddies of good and evil, blessing and tragedy. The vision of God's reign fundamentally structures the temporal horizon of Christian action in that the Christian lives oriented toward a future hope even while always alert for opportunities in the present to give visible form to that approaching era. Given this essential bond linking future hope and present praxis, Jürgen Moltmann is right to maintain that "every Christian ethics is determined by a presupposed eschatology."[4]

Nothing within our moral horizon is unaffected by the in-breaking of God's reign, but scholars often identify the task of restoring relationships as its heart. For example, John Thiel, building on the testimony of Scripture, invites us to imagine the eschatological life in terms of "bonds of reconciliation" that are "forged in the work of forgiveness, made and remade in acts of love"; these bonds "grace those who forgive as much as those who are forgiven."[5] James Dunn likewise describes the *"readiness to forgive"* as the "mark of discipleship and of the community of disciples" (emphasis in the original).[6] The work of restoring relationships has both interpersonal and social dimensions; the God of the covenant calls us not just to create and restore relationships with our brothers and sisters but also to transform those relationships into the bonds of community and, ultimately, into a people united in Christ within the reign of God.

This central eschatological task of forming and repairing relationships has been understood principally in human terms—centered on human relationships and human communities. However, in light of the Christian hope that animals will also share in the kingdom, this work of reconciliation should be understood to include "the renewal of all creatures in their interrelationship and interdependence."[7] The kingdom that Jesus proclaims is, as Pope Benedict observed, "universal; it embraces the whole earth"—and thus our work for it must be similarly inclusive.[8]

THE MISSION OF THE CHURCH

Vatican II taught that the mission of the Church is to continue the eschatological work of Christ, "to proclaim and to spread among all peoples the Kingdom of Christ and of God and to be, on earth, the initial budding of that kingdom."[9] This distinctive role given to the people of God is an unmerited privilege and has been abused any number of times; nonetheless, it remains the case that God has entrusted Christ's salvific work to a very human Church, albeit one also graced with the Spirit.[10]

I want to underscore this role of the Church vis-à-vis the kingdom, for two reasons. First, the Church's responsibility to animals is far more demanding and extensive than a conventional interest in the general well-being of the environment. Insofar as animals are to be drawn into the life of the kingdom, everything about their flourishing becomes an imperative of the Gospel and an appropriate object of ecclesial concern and responsibility. The Church, as the instrument of the kingdom, is called to recognize animals as fellow creatures of the kingdom and to act as a voice for them so that they might achieve the well-being intended by God and that their vibrantly varied lives might join in creation's praise of God. As agents of the eschaton, Christians are called to realize a harmony not only among humans but also between humans and animals, as stated in the Vatican-commissioned document "Communion and Stewardship."[11]

Moreover, as part of its responsibility to work for the kingdom, the Church's evangelical concern for animals extends beyond their well-being in the present age to include hope for their redemption. Thus, the Church can and should pray for animals—pray for them in their collective identity as nonhuman creatures and, in appropriate contexts, for each of them as individual creatures. The Church's formal prayers (e.g., "look not on our sins, but on the faith of your Church") and its rites (e.g., infant baptism) remind us that redemption is not fundamentally a matter of individual moral agency and autonomous choice but a gift that has been entrusted to a community and effected in its ritual acts. The Church participates in Christ's redemptive labor through these liturgical celebrations, foremost in the Eucharist. Worship, Cardinal Ratzinger rightly suggested, is "meant to draw the whole of reality into communion with God."[12]

It is unfortunate, then, that creation does not appear with any regularity as a theme in the Catholic liturgy, as I noted in chapter 4. This prayerful miserliness for creatures is shared by *A Book of Blessings*, an official collection of Catholic prayers published by the United States Conference of Catholic Bishops. It provides blessings not only for animals but also for homes, schools, libraries, offices, fishing gear, and technical equipment, among others. Its prayers for animals, however, do not evidence any direct concern for their happiness or well-being; rather, they only petition God that the animals serve us well.[13] In neither its formal rites nor its sacramental prayers do the Church's words express its full eschatological hopes.

My second motivation for reflecting on the Church's role in laboring for creation is that it allows me to explore an issue of contention among ecotheologians and to clarify my position regarding the Church's task in light of that discussion. The issue is whether or how humanity has been made creation's "steward." All agree that the granting of "dominion" (in Hebrew, *radah*, meaning "to rule") by God in Genesis 1:26—"let [human beings] have dominion" over the fish of the sea—does not give humanity unrestrained license to use other creatures indiscriminately. Rather, humanity is required to rule "in the same way as God," with benevolence and concern for animal well-being.[14] Even eating animals for food was not included in the original granting of dominion.[15] In part to moderate presumptions about humanity's prerogatives, Christian thinkers have turned to "stewardship" as the preferred term to portray our relationship with creation. In contrast to the language of "dominion," stewardship suggests the kind of nurturing governance exercised by God and has the additional virtue of reminding us of the task of cultivation given to humanity in Genesis 2:15, which depicts God placing Adam "in the garden of Eden, to cultivate and care for it."

Although critics recognize that stewardship is an improvement over the language of dominion, they believe that the term remains too readily co-opted by the same dynamics that led to the present environmental crisis. Specifically, the language of stewardship is vulnerable to four sinful undercurrents: a tendency to look at creation merely as an object to be used, an anthropocentrism that confers on humanity an exaggerated distinctiveness and superiority, a hubris that humanity can understand adequately and thus shepherd the complex workings of the world's ecosystems, and an arrogation of authority over creation that tends both to deny our own creatureliness and to infringe upon the unique authority of the Creator.[16] On the basis of these and other concerns, some scholars advocate the language of "kinship" or "community of creation" as better suited for describing our interdependent relationship with nonhuman creation.[17]

Given my emphasis on the covenantal relationship, my sympathy for the kinship model is unsurprising. I see it as an appropriate description of creaturely relationships in their ideal form. My reserve, however, is with its normative application to the present age. Until the kingdom comes in its fullness, there will continue to be, unavoidably so, real tensions and conflicts within creation ("enmity," to use the language of Gn 3:15). It is true that we participate in the world's ecosystems and have responsibilities to the creatures within them. These responsibilities require that we consider the needs of our fellow creatures and the effects that our actions have on them. But in tension with the sentiment conveyed by "kinship," we also allow ourselves to define the form and limits of our participation in the world's ecosystems—not absolutely so, but in significant ways nonetheless. With respect to webworms living in our pecan trees, wasps constructing a nest at a children's playground, pigeons hovering at the town square eateries, mice desiring the warmth of our homes, and ticks using us as food banks, we believe ourselves justified in refusing to share our goods with these nonhuman creatures and in treating them as something other than kin. Our homes are aggressively controlled eco-environments with sometimes lethal defenses against unwanted creaturely intruders. For the most part, these ecologically gated communities do not embody a kinship relationship with our creaturely near neighbors, and we need language that is able to reflect the moral legitimacy of that fact.

Because of the distinctive, eschatological task that God has bestowed on the Church, I believe it is appropriate to regard the Church as the steward of creation in this sense: As part of its labor for the kingdom, the Christian community has a distinctive role vis-à-vis the rest of creation. It is to care for creation in a manner that helps lead it to the eschatological destiny intended by God. Christians are called to be "stewards of the mysteries" (1 Cor 4:1). In response to the above concerns, I offer several observations. First, it is true that being a good "steward" of creatures can suggest using them for our own benefit (and doing so efficiently and productively). But the term can also mean, as it often does in Christian literature, caring for creatures in a way that serves God's interests, not our own. Second, there is broad support among Scripture scholars that humanity's "dominion" includes having a role of governance in creation that is linked to its status as *imago Dei*. Interpreted correctly, the mandate of Genesis rejects perverse forms of dominating governance but not dominion itself.[18] Moreover, even apart from this biblical mandate, it would be "unrealistic" to deny that humanity has a "special role and status within creation." We have a "unique power to affect most of the rest of creation on this planet. We cannot but exercise it, even if we do so by restraining our use of it."[19] The issue with which Christians must struggle is not whether humanity has a distinctive role within creation but how to act upon it within the limits and intent established by God.

Third, it is true that we do not clearly understand the operations of the natural world and the effects of our interventions within it. However, this does not eliminate our responsibility to care for creation. The work for the kingdom also includes endeavors to establish economic and social structures that are able to serve the needs of all, especially the disenfranchised. The fact that we do not fully understand social and economic systems or that they are beyond our capacity to ever control completely is not a reason to forgo that effort. Granted, the complexities of ecosystems are such that they are even less accessible to our understanding and control; nonetheless, we must apply our reason in trying to respond to their needs. At the very least, we should use our critical reason to surface and critique our operative assumptions about what is "good" for the environment and to better develop practical wisdom about whether, when, and how we might intervene. Neither ecological quietism nor an all-encompassing, technological governance expresses the responsibility that humanity has for creation as co-laborer with the Spirit.

Finally, not all forms of governance or hierarchy vis-à-vis creation entail an arrogant denial of our creaturehood or usurpation of divine rule. In the traditional Catholic understanding, earthly roles of governance and leadership are not lamentable developments necessitated by the fall and the threat of evildoers. Rather, because we are inherently social beings, we need individuals who will organize and lead so as to coordinate the various components of social existence and enable them to better serve the common good. Even in paradise, Aquinas maintained, there would have been some form of governance.[20] Correctly practiced, these socially embedded, vocational roles of authority and leadership—parental, political, pedagogical, and ecclesial—should encourage a stronger bond with creaturely existence, not an escape from it. Furthermore, recognizing that God has given humanity a distinctive role can and should *increase* our sense of concern for creatures that are vulnerable and have no other advocate. Because of the particular gifts and capacities that God has bestowed upon humanity, we have the privilege of doing what virtually no other animal is able to do: exercising the "kind of *servant leadership*" displayed in Jesus's life (emphasis in the original).[21]

Nonetheless, a glance at contemporary documents shows that the concerns raised by critics of the stewardship model are not without warrant. In spite of the Catholic Church's regular denunciation of environmental exploitation and its lauding of responsible care, some of its formal teachings on animals appear to be unaware of the problematic implications that could be drawn from them (e.g., the statements that "nature is not a sacred or divine reality that man must leave alone"[22] and that "God willed that man be the king of creation"[23]). Granted, such statements appear in tandem with reminders of humanity's moral limits and its fundamental duties toward God. However, it is scarcely reassuring that some of these moral constraints on animal treatment are themselves anthropocentric, such as when the *Catechism* states that our "dominion over inanimate and other living beings granted by the Creator is not absolute; it is limited by concern for *the quality of life of [our] neighbor, including generations to come*" (emphasis added).[24]

Worse in this regard is the egregious non sequitur that appears in the *Catechism*. After stating that "God entrusted animals" to humanity's "stewardship," the passage goes on to conclude: "*Hence* it is legitimate to use animals for food and clothing. They may be domesticated to help man in his work and leisure. Medical and scientific experimentation on animals is a morally acceptable practice, if it remains within reasonable limits and contributes to caring for or saving human lives" (emphasis added).[25] Given that the original conferral of dominion over animals did *not* include permission to use them for food, the logical inference drawn here between stewardship and a broad permission to use animals is unfounded. The fact that the compilers of the text believed that there is such a connection indicates why so many are uncomfortable with describing Christianity's relationship with creation as one of stewardship.

The challenge, then, is to portray positively the distinctive role that has been given to humanity while also precluding sinful justifications based on this role. Pope John Paul II uses the phrase "minister of God's plan," to describe humanity's relationship with creation,[26] whereas Pope Francis describes humanity as "protectors of God's handiwork."[27] Perhaps such language is able to avoid the negative connotations of stewardship while also affirming that a distinctive task has been given to humanity and the Church vis-à-vis the rest of creation.

THREE MUDDLING TENSIONS IN ANIMAL ETHICS

In developing a framework for animal ethics, I have placed our care for animals in the context of the kingdom of God and the Church's labor for it. This eschatological context complicates the endeavor to identify clear norms for Christian care of animals. We can break down this complexity in terms of three tensions: the tension between the goods of the present order, whose respective realizations are often in conflict, and the ideals of a kingdom that is yet unrealized; the tension between the Church's social hopes as inspired by the kingdom and conventional social norms that too often reflect an instrumentalizing view of nature; and the tension between general obligations that are binding upon all Christians and those moral norms that flow from God's personal call to the individual Christian.

The Tension between an Eschatological Care
for Animals and the "Not Yet" of the Kingdom

We have already touched on this first tension, related to the kingdom of God as already-but-not-yet, but it merits being further fleshed out. In doing so, I want to keep in mind the particular understanding of the moral response I developed in chapter 3. There, I discussed the subject–other encounter in which the other's goodness awakens the perceiver's response. My understanding of moral action builds on this view. Our moral response is shaped and elicited by the goods and values we perceive to be at stake in any given situation. As Iris Murdoch states, "I can only choose within the world I can *see*" (emphasis in the original).[28] More than a conceptual grasping of the moral object, the ethical task requires a discerning gaze that attends to the other with affect and reason in order to perceive holistically its value-soaked identity. Placed within the triune framework of the mutual self-giving of the Father and Son, this moral responsiveness to a perceived goodness can also be described as an agent's kenotic receptivity to the self-expression of the other. The moral life is a form of letting the other be—not a passivity before the other but an empowering of that other flowing from our creativity as prompted by the Spirit. Our moral agency reflects God's kenotic love for creation, "a calling to 'let be,'" and not a "flexing" of human will.[29] Thus our encounters with animals (especially when not overshadowed by the fall's distortions) should be graced relationships, ones that form us into divine images, creatures who give by receiving.[30]

I suggested in chapter 1, following Jay McDaniel, that we cultivate a "contemplative seeing" in order to develop the capacity to recognize other creatures "in their particularity, as subjects in and for themselves."[31] Such a recognition is the first step in forming ourselves as ethical agents vis-à-vis animals. Our rightly formed decisions about animal care entail a receptive agency drawn forth in us by the goodness of the animal other, not merely a rationally driven agency pushed outward, and thus a genuine perception of the animal other is essential. The challenge, however, is that such a perception requires a stereoscopic view of animals that we do not have—that is, an understanding of nonhuman creatures in terms of both their natural existence and their supernatural end. In the case of human neighbors, we have an initial sense of God's will for them, both in this life and in the one to come, through the teaching and example of Christ. We know that to be truly human is to be liberated from suffering and sin—in general, from all those forms of woundedness that prevent each of us from becoming an agent of and participant in a more harmonious, covenantal world. Consequently, we are able to understand how we should act toward our neighbor.

However, the situation for animals is epistemically different in two respects. First, and most basically, we know little about the nature of their eschatological transformation beyond the fact that our relationships with them and their relationships with other creatures will be harmonious (and some would even contest this claim). Second, and more importantly, even granting that the eschatological life of animals will entail harmonious, creaturely relationships, we do not know whether or how we should cultivate these relationships in the present. Thus, the connection between ethics and eschatology noted above is difficult to apply to our relationships with animals. It would seem that we do not know how to act as ministers of God's plan for animals, including whether or how to preserve nature as it presently is. What implication, for example, do the ideals of a harmonious, peaceable kingdom have for how we preserve (or not) the violence of predation in the present? Because of this uncertainty and the "not yet" of the kingdom, our ethical discernment will unavoidably be tentative and muddled, and our treatment of animals will include responses that are caring and harmonious *and* ones that cause animals suffering and death. The Christian vision requires that we see animals as co-citizens of the kingdom and respond to them in kind; but how do we do so? We have intimations of the implications that our eschatological vision has for relating to our fellow humans in the present age, but it is less clear in the case of animals.

The perplexities we face here are not absolute, but their extent can be brought into sharp focus by considering two broad categories of animal ecosystems: domesticated animals and wildlife. Domesticated animals are creatures with which we are in relationship and, we hope, are so in mutually benefiting ways. We believe that such relationships, good and life-giving in the present age for both humans and animals, will continue to be so in the age to come. The values of the kingdom can be translated into ethical norms more easily and knowingly than is the case for animals in the wild. The closeness of our relationships with these animals, along with the history of human experience about how to intervene helpfully in their lives and the managerial control we often have over their circumstances, mean that we are able to care for them with wisdom and knowledge, alleviating their fear, anxiety, and hunger and encouraging sociality and flourishing as appropriate to their species. Our response to these animals can be described as eschatological, in that by attending to the animals and to our relationships with them we anticipate the ideals of the peaceable kingdom. Nurturing care for domestic animals fosters the harmony we expect to be part of the eschatological life, and thus we can and should view such care as part of the Christian's participation in the labor for the kingdom.

Nonetheless, we should not idealize even this subset of animal relationships. In the limited ecosystems of domesticated animals, we still face difficult choices about how to care for such animals because of the "not yet" of the kingdom. Their interests and needs will sometimes conflict with those of humans, forcing a judgment between two goods that cannot both be realized (a conflict that appears in choices about using domestic animals for food, labor, enjoyment, experiments, etc.).

The more problematic case is that of animals in the wilderness. Based on the ideals of a harmonious kingdom, one might argue that we should work to transform wildlife into ecosystems more reflective of the life to come. God does not desire the suffering of animals, and, as Stephen Webb argues, it is hard to "imagine that the ultimate destiny of wild animals is to remain in the wilderness, turned against each other and against us in strife instead of living with each other and us in harmony and community."[32] Taking a cue from biblical imagery of paradise and of the eschaton, he offers the possibility of seeing pets as "the paradigm for the destiny of all animal life."[33]

My reservation in seeing companion animals as a paradigm, however, is that it places too great a speculative constraint on the diversity of animal goodness that God might desire for the eschaton. Though I agree with Webb that animal violence will not continue in the age to come, I also allow, as I argued in chapter 4, that predation might, albeit in a transformed version exceeding our present imagination. In addition, several cautions can be raised against attempts to reduce or eliminate ecological violence in the present. First, as I have noted, we do not fully understand the dynamics of ecosystems and the unintended consequences that our interventions might generate.[34] Second, we do not know what future, divinely desired goods might be lost in such an intervention. Though I do not believe that evolution is, without qualification, the way in which God intended to create the world, I also recognize that in the present order God has used it as an instrument for creating beauty and diversity. Our ambivalence about how God might be working in animal lives in the present recalls the problem noted above: We do not know how exactly the eschatological destiny of animals should inform our treatment of them in the present. This brings me to a third reason for caution: The transformation of these systems will ultimately be a work of grace, not human ingenuity.[35] For these reasons, I believe that Linzey is right to argue against interventions in the affairs of wildlife, tempered by a recognition of the exceptional case, one that "requires explicit justification and a much greater sense of humility."[36] A possible example of a justified intervention is the reintroduction of predators in order to restore ecosystems.[37] Such ecosystems are vital for producing diverse forms of goodness, and we can rightly believe that God desires such diversity and wants us to use our skills and abilities to consider how best to preserve them or restore them when adversely affected by prior human activity.

Some of our actions toward animals will reflect the "not yet" of the kingdom and thus a falling away from the ideals it represents. It is not possible in this world, because of human finitude and the conflicts between goods characteristic of a broken world, to actualize in any given act or set of practices all the values that we associate with the kingdom, and sometimes we will be forced to act in ways that are at odds with them. An example of these limits appears in the long history of human need for animals to survive, a need that sometimes—especially before the domestication of animals—unavoidably required hunting animals, thus inflicting significant torment and suffering on them. Our approval of such historical practices reflects a belief that there are circumstances where human well-being justifies the painful and deadly treatment of animals.

Nonetheless, in the more contained and manageable ecosystems comprising human and domesticated animals, we should recognize a unique opportunity to witness to the kingdom: to surrender, like Christ, our lordship and set aside our dominant place in the trophic hierarchy in order to create a space for the animal other "to be" and flourish; to see them in their comparative weakness, vulnerability, and voicelessness as God's poor; and to embrace them as members of our community.

The Tension between the Values of the Kingdom and Conventional Norms

Catholic moral thought emphasizes a continuity of values between the profane and the sacred, and the recognition of the kingdom's role in Jesus's preaching does not alter this instinct. Kingdom values are truly human values; thus, there is the possibility of what I have called a "transformed continuity" between creation in its present form and its eschatological destiny. Yet because cultural attitudes and social norms are often twisted by self-interest and sin, genuine human values will often be in tension with those assumed by the prevalent moral order, in ways minor and significant, and this tension will be all the greater when, in service to the kingdom, Christians strive to embody by anticipation eschatological ideals within a world still awaiting its restoration.

At the same time, it would be foolishly prideful, given the inadequacy of Christianity's historical response to animal and environmental abuse, to imagine our moral context in terms of a simple contrast, with the historical Church and the kingdom on the one side and culture and sin on the other. Though recent Church statements clearly denounce environmental exploitation and the false theology of domination that has been used to support it, we cannot assume that we have transcended our past and achieved evangelical clarity with regard to nonhuman creation. Christian understanding of humanity's relationship with other creatures is contested and in flux. In recognition of this fact, we must remain open to new insights from our own tradition and from those lying beyond it. In light of the unsettled questions we face, the Church should cultivate what Margaret Farley calls the "grace of self-doubt" and accept the limits of its own moral insight so that it "can more graciously acknowledge" its need for "the insights of others."[38]

The Church must listen, but it must also speak. Our culture requires an alternative way of envisioning the natural world, and the Church can help address this need. The dominant cultural instinct of our time is to use nature as a commodity. We live in a twistedly hominized world; all that exists has become interpreted and valued primarily in reference to humanity and its needs and desires. This entrenched view of nature operates as a "largely unstructured and inarticulate understanding of our whole situation"—what Charles Taylor calls a "social imaginary."[39] This tacit, unchallenged framework obscures the innate value of the natural world, and in doing so it warps our spontaneous intuitions about what kinds of actions are proper and licit within it. It is difficult to challenge these intuitions because doing so requires that individuals step out of their cultural context, where practices, languages, and symbols all conspire to reinforce the soundness of a particular view of the natural world and only that view. Christianity and other religious traditions, along with the humanities in general, go against the grain of contemporary instrumentalism by offering richly symbolic and non-reductionistic understandings of the natural world.[41] Nonscientific forms of thought (e.g., poetic, metaphysical, and religious) are better able to present the kind of holistic, multivalent, and inspiring imaginings of nature necessary for challenging default assumptions and awakening our moral instincts to the needs of creation. In addition, the Church's distinctive vision helpfully draws our attention to another dimension of the problem. The Church is attuned to the costs and hardships borne unevenly by the global community, with the Global South likely to bear the brunt of environmental problems, and its vision is morally informed by those concerns. Pope Francis's idea of an "integral ecology" highlights the complex and organic connections between economic, social, regional, and environmental issues and offers a critically needed challenge to approaches that view environmental and justice issues in isolation.[40]

For the Church to contribute effectively here, it must continue to denounce clearly the theological views of the human–nature relationship that were appropriated during the Renaissance and modern eras. For many Renaissance thinkers, humanity's likeness to God meant that it was to participate in God's mastery of the world. The Catholic priest and humanist philosopher Marsilio Ficino (d. 1499), for example, argued that humanity "acts as the vicar of God" and thus "not only uses animals but . . . rules them" and can "use [them] cruelly." Humanity "is the god without doubt of the animals."[42] In a similar vein, Enlightenment thinkers portrayed their quest to fashion a world hospitable to human flourishing as a new stage in the divinely mandated task of governing creation. Enthusiasm for that effort led scientific and philosophical advocates of human advancement to desacralize nature, instrumentalizing it and stripping it of any nonutilitarian value. Thus the devout Anglican Francis Bacon (d. 1626), sometimes called the father of the scientific method, saw science as a gift from God because it enabled us, finally, to bind nature to our "service" and make it our "slave," ultimately surmounting "the deplorably narrow" dominion over the world that had been humanity's lot until then.[43] His co-religionist Robert Boyle (d. 1691), another key figure in the development of Western science, condemned the "vulgarly received notion" that nature was imbued with its own purpose. Veneration of nature, he maintained, impeded the work of establishing "the empire of man over the inferior creatures of God."[44]

The theological foundation of these attitudes was cast aside in the succeeding centuries, but the resulting instrumentalizing worldview still shapes human attitudes, with consequences that are now increasingly taking their toll on human existence itself. In fashioning a technologized world, ostensibly to serve us, we have become enthralled in dependency on it. Human agency withers as our choices become constrained by the need for and reliance on the powers offered by our creations and contraptions.[45] Pope Francis has referred to this phenomenon as the "technocratic paradigm": "This paradigm exalts the concept of a subject who, using logical and rational procedures, progressively approaches and gains control over an external object. This subject makes every effort to establish the scientific and experimental method, which in itself is already a technique of possession, mastery and transformation. It is as if the subject were to find itself in the presence of something formless, completely open to manipulation."[46] He goes on to say that the paradigm diminishes our "capacity for making decisions"[47] and drives us toward a "compulsive consumerism."[48] At stake, then, are both the goods of creation and the healthiness of human living. Religiously inspired worldviews offer alternative images, symbols, and narratives of the natural world that can elicit new and better ways of "acting and living" in it.[49]

For Christianity, nature is intrinsically valuable because God has bestowed on it a transcendent goodness—one that does not depend on intraworld utility but is instead grounded in the goodness of the One who created it and draws it into a covenantal relationship. This view reconfigures the dominant understanding of the human–nonhuman relationship. The relational model of the technocratic paradigm, which is fundamentally uncovenantal, grants agency primarily to the human actor and eclipses both the active role of the creaturely other and the self-forming interrelationship that emerges within the mutual encounter. The result is manifest around us: a distortion of agency into a unidirectional assertion of will outward, devoid of trinitarian receptivity and directed to the creaturely other "as a mere 'given,' as an object of utility, as raw material to be hammered into useful shape."[50] In contrast, a Christian worldview keeps the human person embedded within creation, where he or she encounters nonhuman others as fellow creatures of the covenant.

Three components of the Christian worldview are particularly valuable for correcting the outlook of the technocratic paradigm: the innate creatureliness of both human and nonhuman existence, the sacramental quality of creation, and the covenantal relationship among all creatures. First, we are, like every other being on this planet, creatures. However distinctive we might be within the divine plan, we are, nonetheless, incomplete in ourselves, dependent on others, on the world around us, and ultimately on God. We are tempted to escape our creaturely poverty by grasping and controlling, but Christ offers a different possibility: to see our dependency on the other as good and our need for the other as gift. As the theologian Johannes B. Metz wrote, "We are all beggars. We are all members of a species that is not sufficient unto itself."[51] "The unending nature of our poverty as human beings is our only innate treasure."[52]

Second, the Catholic vision is committed to a sacramental universe; the world "discloses the Creator's presence."[53] Looking at the world sacramentally draws us into an attitude of "awe and wonder" and counters the temptation to act as "masters, consumers, [and] ruthless exploiters" of a world that we view as merely an object to be used.[54] The creatures that surround us are transformed in the light of Christ. They are never mere objects, because "the risen One is mysteriously holding them to himself and directing them towards fullness as their end." They are "now imbued with his radiant presence."[55]

Finally, the Church's understanding of the present is shaped by its vision of a covenantal future, that is, a world of creatures at peace with one another and drawn together in Christ. For the Christian, companionship with other creatures beckons as privileged moments of encounter with the God who labors for all creatures. The Christian vision, in stark contrast to any mere objectification of creation, looks out with hope onto a world abounding with the possibilities of grace-filled relationships. These three themes, mutually interpenetrating and codetermining, come together in the idea of solidarity: We perceive the nonhuman other as co-creature, are drawn by its sacramental goodness, and actively receive the gift of relationship offered therein.

These components are distinctively Christian but not uniquely so. Though their ethical implications will sometimes create tensions between the Christian community and the culture at large, they are also reflected in shared values that can form the basis of a broadly inclusive conversation about how to understand and treat the world around us. Christianity, for example, is not alone in encountering the sacred in nature, and many secular and religious worldviews acknowledge some form of creaturely solidarity. Inclusive dialogue can identify commitments like these that are shared across multiple ideologies and worldviews, thus becoming the foundation for what John Rawls calls an "overlapping consensus."[56] To emphasize again, however, the starting point cannot be that the Christian community has all the answers or that it has none. The Church can fruitfully dialogue with contemporary voices, discerning the good to be found there and challenging whatever falls short of its evangelical hopes.[57] There will be tensions and conflicts, both internal and external to the Christian community, but there will also be points of common cause and shared values.

My main point, however, is to suggest that determining specific norms about animal care will be particularly challenging in our time. We live at a historical juncture of cultural and theological shifts, where fundamental views of nature and animal life are in flux both within the Church and the mainstream community at large.

The Tension between the Universal Vocation of All Christians and a Personal Calling

Scripture portrays the Christian life as a radical interior and exterior transformation exemplified in the challenging counsels of Matthew's Sermon on the Mount. In the post-patristic era, Catholicism increasingly began to interpret the discipleship demanded by these hard sayings in line with the "two ways" approach of Eusebius of Caesarea (d. 339):

> Two ways of life were thus given by the law of Christ to His Church. The one is above nature, and beyond common human living, . . . wholly and permanently separate from the common customary life. . . . Such then is the perfect form of the Christian life. And the other more humble, more human way permits men to join in pure nuptials and to produce children, to undertake government, to give orders to soldiers fighting for right.[58]

It became part of the accepted Catholic view that some Christians were called to Gospel ideals of discipleship (e.g., priests and religious who lived the counsels of perfection), whereas others were called "only" to a life in keeping with the universal norms of natural law. During the past half century, the Church's moral theology has been renewed by more explicitly grounding it in evangelical values. The works of moralists like Fritz Tillmann (*The Master Calls: A Handbook of Christian Living*) and Gérard Gilleman (*The Primacy of Charity*), led to Vatican II's call that moral theology "draw more fully on the teaching of holy Scripture" and "throw light on the exalted vocation of the faithful in Christ."[59]

It had been assumed that the "two ways" model—that of the ordinary Christian life and that of the counsels of perfection—found support in Aquinas's moral theory; but recent scholarship has challenged that view, arguing that Aquinas believed *all* Christians are called to follow the new law of Christ and to live lives of Christian perfection.[60] Aquinas also recognized that the Christian's interior disposition toward the new law of Christ can be cultivated through other external practices than those associated with the counsels of perfection (i.e., celibacy, poverty, and obedience). Thus, the ways of following Christ will "differ and lead to distinct patterns of living."[61]

According to the moral theologian and Thomistic scholar Servais Pinckaers, at the heart of Aquinas's interpretation of the "New Law" is a summons to evangelical freedom, not a set of moral codes to be pursued.[62] My interpretation of the Christian vocation is similar in this sense: In keeping with the emphasis on the Spirit's creativity discussed in chapter 4, I understand the Christian moral life as both freeing and creative, and thus it takes diverse external forms. This variety is partly because we are limited creatures called to serve in a world wounded by sin but also because we are each unique and personally called. Given that no one individual's witness to the kingdom can fully express the eschatological life, the Christian vocation takes myriad forms: contemplative devotion (Thérèse of Lisieux), worker solidarity (Dorothy Day), martyrdom in the cause of justice (Óscar Romero), the rejection of violence (Martin of Tours), the communal embrace of the developmentally diverse (Jean Vanier), and, of course, evangelical care for nonhuman creatures (Francis of Assisi).

Similarly, the Christian's ethical task toward animals will, like other forms of moral action, be obedient to universal norms (e.g., animal abuse is to be rejected and care is to be encouraged), but it will also allow creative embodiment of these norms. Given the enormity of human suffering and the demands we face in responding to it, it is understandable that for many Christians their care for creation and the animals within it might consist of little more than a quotidian discipline, cultivating modest practices that avoid harm and provide support to animals and creation alike. But Christians are not utilitarians, calculating their vocational choices based on what will achieve the greatest reduction in the collective suffering of the world. God stirs up our energies and passions to labor for the kingdom, and Christian care for animals will appear in a complex variety of mundane and dramatic forms as individuals respond to God's distinctive call to them and in doing so represent the Church in its universal, redemptive mission.

My claim here requires that we rid ourselves of the idea that the Christian moral life is composed exclusively of universalizable norms. We do indeed have universal "duties which bind all of us," but, as Gilbert Meilaender puts it, we must reject the theoretical "imperialism" that requires all moral acts to fit in this mold.[63] In part, this is because, unlike God, our responsibilities are neither "unlimited" nor "universal in scope."[64] We choose certain acts—ones that are genuinely moral yet not universally required—because of the kind of person we want to be and how we perceive that these choices will affect our character.[65] Meilaender grounds these personally indexed moral acts in the vocational freedom of the Christian agent. Applying his views to our discussion, we can suggest that Christians will choose their own forms of care for creation in keeping with universal norms and with the particular kind of person they want to be. However, I believe that these personal choices also flow out of the Christian's dialogical encounter with God. In his or her relationship with Christ, each Christian experiences a personal call that is addressed to their particular identity and that finds expression in their moral acts.

Versions of this view can be found in the works of both Karl Rahner and Hans Urs von Balthasar (due in part, I suspect, to their common formation in Ignatius's *Spiritual Exercises*, with its teaching of the three times for making a choice).[66] For Rahner, the human person is sustained by God in a project of freedom in which the individual makes a choice regarding who he or she is before God. Through their ethical responses to God's call to love, each Christian's orientation becomes marked by a fundamental "yes" or "no" to God. However, because this life response is also the endeavor to realize *self*—that is, his or her unique, eternal identity—it is also an individuating response, not merely a universal, generic answer. For Rahner, the ground of this individualization of self must lie in God if this identity is to have eternal validity; it cannot be just a matter of an individual's choice for a particular vocation. Thus God leads the Christian into his or her unique and eternal personhood by calling them to follow particular ethical paths within the domain of universal laws and norms.[67] God's morally binding will for the individual, therefore, is directed not only to the "realization of the universal norm" but also "to the concrete and the individual."[68]

Balthasar, conversely, places this personalizing call in the context of his trinitarian theology. As we saw, just as the Father gives to the Son a specific task that defines his earthly existence, the Father similarly gives each Christian a particular, Christological, and person-defining mission wherein he or she shares in the one mission of Christ.[69]

The idea of a personalizing vocation does not require an eschatological horizon to make sense, of course. But the expansive openness of this horizon (the call to realize the kingdom utterly exceeds human capacity) intensifies the necessity that each Christian choose among the world's weighty needs (pursuing some, forgoing others), thus marking his or her vocation with distinctive and uniquely personal elements. Mere obedience to universal norms is too tepid a response, given the demands of the kingdom. Every Christian is required to do *something*—but not the *same* something. We are all required to work for the kingdom, but not in the same way. The Christian is drawn by the Spirit toward the ethically creative expansiveness of the kingdom's already / not yet; and there, before God, he or she discerns how their particular talents, dispositions, distinctive agency, and moral energies will be placed at the Father's will in Christ-like discipleship.

What I am eager to reject is the idea that once Christians have discerned the universal norms for animal care, the task of discerning their personal responsibilities is complete. Such an assumption has for too long inhibited our moral imagination about nonhuman creatures. Every Christian labors for the kingdom, and this task will take a multiplicity of forms. All Christians are bound by what they perceive as universal norms for animal care, and all should experience the kingdom's call to care for our fellow creatures. However, there are limits to our capacity to coordinate animal-specific ideals with other inspired forms of responding to the Gospel. The result is, concretely, that genuine care for animals and for the natural world should characterize the moral life of all Christians, but some will be invited in grace to more focused, devoted, and sometimes radically self-giving expressions of this care. Further complicating our discernment is the fact that because we live in a time of flux regarding environmental norms, the boundary between responses that are universally required of all Christians and those that arise out of the Christian's individual vocation will not be clear or certain.

PRINCIPLES FOR ANIMAL ETHICS

On the basis of the discussion above and the theory laid out in the preceding chapters, I offer the following ten principles to frame a Catholic approach to animal ethics. I group them in two categories: (1) a Christian understanding of animals and (2) the ethical response as formed by this understanding.

A Christian Understanding of Animals

Following Balthasar, I understand human action to be a response to the world as perceived by the agent, and thus an authentic vision of the world is a precondition for genuine Christian action. I developed this approach by suggesting that the Christian moral vision is an eschatological one. The Christian looks out onto a world in which God labors to realize creation's final destiny and experiences God's call to join in this labor.

I have appealed to two complementary themes to guide my understanding of this eschatological endpoint and explain its significance for the present: the covenant and the kingdom of God. The covenant underscores the central importance of relationality in God's hope for all creation, and the kingdom highlights the ideal of a just and harmonious order flourishing under God's reign. As Christians view the world in light of this approaching era, they give weighty consideration to the goods and values that are closely associated with it—that is, those attributes fundamental to covenantal relationships (e.g., agency, a subjectivity that endures across time, and the capacity for interrelationships and mutuality) and those ideals that characterize a flourishing and harmonious communal life (e.g., justice, peaceful relations, reconciliation, and freedom from suffering). The eschaton has begun in Christ, and thus Christians are to see the world in terms of its approach even while recognizing that its fullness is yet to come.

Scripture promises that God will draw *all* things together in the Son. Given this hope, Pope Francis is right to maintain that the ultimate end and purpose of creatures is not found in human want and need. I further argue that our hope for an inclusive redemption is particularly warranted for those animals with fairly advanced cognitive abilities and capacity for agency (e.g., dolphins, elephants, dogs, cats, great apes, lions, and magpies). The triune God of the covenant will, we can hope, show a redemptive tenderness toward each and every such creature. Consequently, our theology of animals must be informed by a Christian vision of the eschaton insofar as they will be co-sharers in it.

With these reflections in mind, I offer five principles for a Christian theological understanding of animals:

1. We have good theological grounds for hoping that animals will be redeemed and welcomed into the covenant.
2. The ultimate purpose and value of animals is not that of serving human need.
3. Each animal has a distinctive dignity as lovingly created by God and living in a web of relationships, not only with us and other creatures of the world but ultimately with God.
4. The values of the kingdom and the qualities associated with covenantal potential are essential goods in a Christian vision and offer a prima facie starting point for understanding our relationships with other creatures, both human and nonhuman.
5. Because the kingdom is yet to be realized in its fullness, the Christian vision of the world and of the animals in it will reflect an eschatological reserve—an awareness that important goods and values are regularly entangled with the world's brokenness and sin.

The Christian Ethical Response

I understand the Christian response to animals within the context of this eschatological vision. The Church has been given the task of continuing Christ's work by exercising his servant leadership and making the kingdom real in the midst of a broken world. Because animals are to be part of this kingdom, the Church should include them as objects of its redemptive labor. However, because the kingdom has not yet arrived in its fullness, important goods will come into conflict as the Christian endeavors to witness to the kingdom, leading to situations wherein Christians must sacrifice some goods (e.g., those related to animal well-being) in order to achieve others. Although such acts (e.g., setting mouse traps, eating animal flesh, and using animals for experiments) are sometimes justified, they are not activities originally intended by God in giving humanity dominion over other creatures; nor do they reflect God's ultimate hope for nonhuman creatures.

Because what is at stake is an embodied and spiritual reality, Christian labors have both practical and liturgical dimensions. Christians are to effect the kingdom through concrete actions, and they are also to lift up in prayerful, doxological petition their hope for God's saving intervention. The liturgical dimension of the Christian life will more clearly express the Church's eschatological hope, while its praxis will often be marked by the divided complexity of the kingdom's already / not yet.[70] For three reasons, generating specific norms for the concrete care of animals is difficult. First, both scientific and theological understandings of animal life are still developing. Second, although the age to come will, I argue, reflect a "transformed continuity" with this world, the work for the kingdom cannot be conceived as a linear progression from our world to the next, especially as it relates to animals. Third and finally, because the needs are many and pressing, the opportunities for serving the kingdom and the forms such service can take are virtually limitless. Though the Christian will sometimes allow utilitarian considerations to inform his or her labors, ultimately their service is a matter of grace and God's personal call to the person.

On the basis of these reflections, I suggest five principles for understanding the Christian ethical response to animals:

6. The Church is to be the agent of the kingdom, reflecting the servant model of Christ's ministry as it continues his redemptive work and stewards his creation. In this work, the Christian is to strive to

cultivate a relationship with nonhuman creation that is covenantal and reflects the ideals of the kingdom.

7. As with all its labors, the Church's care for animals must take a liturgical form. The Church should pray for animals' flourishing and express its hope for their redemption.

8. All Christians are called to labor for creation, but God will call each Christian to do so in distinctive ways.

9. Acts that, with moral justification, inflict suffering on animals or compromise their flourishing should be seen as consequent to the kingdom's status as yet unrealized.

10. Achieving full clarity about norms for the treatment of animals is not possible. The values and goods associated with the covenant and the kingdom are weighty considerations that must inform our discernment, but their precise implications for animal care do not easily translate into exacting and concrete norms.

TWO ILLUSTRATIVE CASES: EATING MEAT FROM FACTORY FARMS AND USING ANIMALS FOR EXPERIMENTS

These ten principles provide a context for discerning the ethical treatment of animals. Given the complexities and tensions noted above, it is to be expected that they do not establish neat boundaries between good and bad treatments of animals: "True 'moral clarity' doesn't make things clearer, but rather more vividly ambiguous and complicated."[71] In order to provide examples of ethical discernment informed by these principles, I examine two cases. Due to space considerations, these reflections are neither exhaustive nor comprehensive.[72] My goal is not to defend specific conclusions on the issues but rather to show how the ten principles highlight important values at play and prompt particular avenues of investigation.

Eating Meat from Factory Farms

The term "factory farming" is used to refer loosely to large-scale operations that are driven by the goal of maximizing meat production with little regard for animal welfare.[73] Common estimates are that 95 percent or more of the meat we eat comes from such operations. I know of no ethicist who defends factory farming. Simply, the suffering that it inflicts on animals in order to deliver cheap meat is appalling and horrific.[74] This is not a matter of sentimentalizing animal lives. One could argue, as the philosopher Christopher Belshaw does, that "killing animals is very often permitted" and "very often required," and still recognize, as Belshaw also does, that supporting factory meat production is a matter of "defending the indefensible."[75] The industrial practice is all the more abhorrent when one considers that farmed animals are fairly developed creatures, both socially and cognitively, features that in a Christian, covenantal context should be aggressively protected.[76] My focus, then, is not on arguing the ethics of factory farming itself; I assume that the practice is morally indefensible. The question I address here is whether Christians can, given the cruelty of factory farms and the covenantal status of the animals within them, choose to eat food produced in such an unethical fashion.

I believe that it is acceptable for Christians to eat meat.[77] Though Christianity has long valued the practice of abstaining from meat, that choice was typically driven more by ascetic interests and a desire to discipline the body than by concern for the animals themselves.[78] It is true that compassion for animals was often seen as a sign of saintliness and sometimes a precondition of it,[79] but even the patron saint of animals, Francis of Assisi, renowned for his devotion to creation and its animals, "was emphatically not a vegetarian."[80] I recognize, then, the possibility that Christians can genuinely care for animals and still eat meat. The question, however, is whether a caring Christian can eat meat from factory farming operations.

An illuminating discussion of the issue appears in an exchange between the Catholic ethicists John Berkman and Julie Hanlon Rubio. They approach the topic in terms of the Catholic distinction between material and formal cooperation with evil. The distinction is one way that the Catholic tradition has tried to negotiate the challenge of being faithful to moral norms within an imperfect world dominated by structures and systems that are flawed and often sinful. Our good acts will be limited both by finitude and by the world's woundedness, and thus our intent to achieve certain goods will sometimes require that we compromise, choosing acts that do good but also promote states of affairs that we consider evil. Such acts can still be considered good, and not sinful, depending on the agent's intent and the proximity to and the gravity of the resulting evil. A common example is that of a politician voting for a bill that has moral flaws but also advances an important social good. Such an act cooperates with evil (by supporting the "moral flaws"), but it is not, presumably, the desire of the politician to do so. Acts such as these are often matters of "material" cooperation and thus are not sinful choices by politicians.

Berkman argues, however, that eating meat from factory farms is a case of *formal*, not material, cooperation with evil—and thus it is sinful. In factory farming, "cruelty is an essential and necessary part" of its goal. Factory farms are *intentionally* producing—and we are *intentionally* choosing to purchase—meat that is cheap, and the cheapness of this meat depends essentially on it being produced in a way that disregards concerns for animal well-being and prioritizes brutal efficiency. Thus, "cruelty is not a mere evil side effect or by-product."[81] The suffering inflicted upon animals and the quest for cheap meat are, in the operations of factory farms, bound together, so that in choosing one, we are effectively choosing the other.

Rubio agrees that the treatment of animals on factory farms is unethical and thus we must try to eschew their products. However, she argues that eating food from such operations is not always sinful but, in some cases, is an instance of material cooperation. The weakness in Berkman's argument, she suggests, is that it examines the issue exclusively in terms of a solitary individual making choices about his or her own food. If that were the only case that Christians confronted, Berkman would be right to condemn eating factory-farmed meat. Rubio, however, highlights cases in which the choice to eat meat takes place in social contexts tied to important social goods—for example, when "you cook for a family with children, host holiday gatherings for relatives, contribute food for church and school social functions, entertain your children's friends, and host neighborhood parties." Such cases show how concern for animals can conflict "with duties of hospitality."[82] Because of the important value of relationships and the role that food plays in them, a decision to use meat from factory farms can be an unwanted and unintended choice in a circumstance of limited options; in such cases, the choice is a matter of material cooperation. She argues, then, for an approach that accepts an "in principle" rejection of factory farming and its products while also recognizing that commitments to critical human values are sometimes tied to food choices that are not easily or entirely under the agent's control. Our choices in these social contexts are analogous to other, non-sinful acts where the goodness intended and supported by those acts is marred because of its entanglement in sinful structures (e.g., purchasing clothing that might be produced in sweatshops).

One could agree with Rubio's flexitarian position yet differ with her regarding how exceptional cases would need to be to justify using factory-farmed meat. The social practices to which she refers (preparing food for children, hosting events for family and friends, supporting social gatherings that are jointly organized, etc.) are common, and so, presumably, will be the circumstances that justify eating factory-farmed meat. The issue is perplexing, as Rubio shows, but one might raise cautions about her conclusions, on three grounds. First, because factory-farmed animals are, typically, fairly advanced creatures (both socially and cognitively), and because the cruelty inflicted on them is significant, a high bar is required to justify using their products, something perhaps more momentous than the everyday good of social relationships. Second, unlike many of the classic examples of material cooperation, where the evil-cooperating act is an occasional exception to what is otherwise a licit occupation (e.g., the nurse who is asked to participate in an illicit operation or the taxi driver who is asked to drive a customer to a known house of prostitution), eating and socializing in an American context *routinely* involves food gained through what virtually all ethicists agree is a morally abhorrent process. Third and finally, in using factory-farmed meat, we are dealing with a state of affairs that, unlike the intricate complexities of politics and the economy, has at its heart an evil reality that can be more easily and institutionally demarcated than the structural evils of, for example, a flawed economic system. Factory farming is a bounded, localized form of evil, and as such it can and should be resisted. Nonetheless, I agree with Rubio that there are exceptions to a prima facie rejection of factory-farmed meat (e.g., a struggling family receiving meat items from a local food bank) and that sometimes these exceptions will entail preserving important social goods (e.g., a small dinner hosted, at some personal cost, by a socially vulnerable individual). A comprehensive study of the ethics of eating factory-farmed meat would require a more detailed analysis of these exceptional cases and the values at stake in them.

Placing factory-farmed animals within an eschatological horizon introduces additional concerns for Christian consideration. Rubio argues for flexitarianism based on an evaluation of competing intraworldly goods viewed from a broadly human vantage. She sees Christian vegetarianism, in contrast, as a Christian moral ideal similar to Christian pacifism, a practice that is not required but commended.[83] However, reflecting on animals within an eschatological context encourages us to evaluate our treatment of them in terms of the distinctively Christian responsibility to the values of the kingdom (i.e., as more than an issue of intraworldly goods). Typical practices in meat production reflect neither the way God values creation nor the Christian's task of bringing God's creatures into the liberation of the kingdom.[84] Not all Christians are required to embody the eschatological values of harmony and friendship with animals by abstaining from meat, but it does seem important to avoid when possible practices that are so pointedly antithetical to those values.

There is another reason why Christians might feel moved to practice some form of meat renunciation, whether selective or absolute: Such actions can encourage increased animal sensitivity in others. Christianity's treatment of animals (including meat eating) should, like all its practices, witness to the kingdom. The duty of the entire Christian community, not just the spiritual elite, is to act before others in ways that edify and build up, even when and perhaps especially when these practices upend and destabilize socially ingrained expectations about how we are to relate to nonhuman creatures. Given how entrenched factory-farmed meat has become in our eating practices over the last several decades, these destabilizing witnesses are acutely needed. Such witnesses disclose possibilities that would otherwise be obscured by the fallenness of the world.[85] It is understandable, then, that the manualist Gerald Kelly allowed that a nurse could cooperate with an evil act but only after first expressing his or her disapproval of the act to those involved.[86]

My argument is not that all Christians should be vegetarians because such will be the norm in God's reign. But the evil of factory farming presents distinctive opportunities for Christians to embody and witness to the kingdom. In addition, some Christians will, I believe, be called to offer more generous and even self-sacrificing care toward animals. I understand this possibility not in terms of a distinction between the ordinary life and the call to perfection but as a personal vocation, in which God calls the individual to embrace a distinctive task as part of his or her unique and personal way of following Christ. Such a personal calling might involve eschewing *any* violence against animals or abstaining from eating any flesh (even if "humanely" prepared). Perhaps, as in the case of Saint Robert Bellarmine, such a calling could go so far as a refusal to disturb even the fleas residing in one's beard.

Using Animals in Experiments

The difficulty of assessing the ethics of animal experimentation is that unlike the case of factory farming, which is universally denounced by ethicists, the basic moral facts of animal experiments—most important, whether these experiments are actually beneficial and necessary—are more contested. Some laud "the undeniable achievements of research with animals" and "the promises of current and projected research."[87] Others argue that the conclusions drawn from animal research are not "sufficiently reliable as a basis for predicting the effects of drugs, products, and other materials on human beings."[88] Space does not permit me to adjudicate these differing claims, but I think most who are familiar with animal experiments would agree that there are a number of critical ethical questions that can be raised about these practices. How successful does animal testing need to be to justify its continuation? Some drug toxicity studies done on animals, for example, have no more than a 50 percent success rate in predicting human toxicity; is that sufficient? Are the safeguards and ethical protocols for protecting animals adequately enforced? Are there forms of institutional inertia—caused by funding structures, investment preferences, pressures on faculty performance, bio-industrial interests (e.g., marketing engineered mice)—that encourage tacit and uncritical support for experimental practices? Are the "3Rs" of animal research—*replace* animals with alternatives, *reduce* the number of animals used, and *refine* methods so as to alleviate pain and distress—pursued aggressively enough? New experiments involving species transgressions (e.g., engineering mice so as to better mimic human diseases) are raising new ethical concerns. Underlying all these questions is the most basic one: Can any experiment on an animal be justified, given the regard that sentient creatures should receive?

It is this last, basic question that I explore briefly here. As with the previous case, I will not attempt to analyze this issue comprehensively. My goal here is to note some of the values and concerns that the ten principles highlight and not to arrive at particular conclusions.

Because of the scope and severity of the harm caused to animals by experiments on them (e.g., suffering, mutilation, genetic modifications, and behavioral manipulation), an ethical analysis of experiments on animals, perhaps more than any other use of animals, requires that we first clarify our understanding of what exactly we believe animal life to be, including its status as an object of moral concern. Answering this fundamental question will ultimately depend on some kind of theological or metaphysical interpretive framework, as Charles Camosy and Susan Kopp argue in a recent essay.[89] They look at the growing practice of bioengineering animals, sometimes in grossly deforming ways, in order to increase their usefulness in advancing human medicine. The moral abhorrence that many of us feel at the idea of such creaturely mutilations cannot be adequately explained, they argue, by moral principles abstracted from any deeper metaphysical assumptions. We need a "thick" description of animals, theological or metaphysical, in order to understand why such an intentional mutilation violates something fundamental about that animal and thus evokes our moral repugnance. The example of bioengineering new animal lifeforms only highlights more vibrantly what is the case for all animal experimentation: To address the ethics of the practice from a Christian perspective, we need to start with a clear understanding of animals, i.e., a theological vision of them.

Camosy and Kopp answer this question by reflecting on the natural teleology of animal life. The particular health and flourishing associated with an animal, its natural "end," indicates to us the distinctive nature of that particular animal. Experiments on animals, especially ones that profoundly and grotesquely alter the animal's physiology, violate that identity. My approach is similar; but whereas Camosy and Kopp focus on the *natural* end of the creature as the key to understanding its nature, my reflections specifically incorporate the creature's *eschatological* destiny, what I have referred to above as a stereoscopic vision—that is, viewing a nonhuman creature in terms of both its natural existence and its supernatural end.

Traditionally, Catholic thought assumed that the use of animals in experiments is, like other uses of animals, permitted as a natural consequence of God's anthropocentric design for them. The purpose of these creatures, it was generally believed, is to serve the needs of humanity; even when this service entails their suffering and death, it posed no conflict with their divinely intended purpose. The animal's "end" was being respected, given the starting assumption about its purpose in existing. This exclusively anthropocentric view is increasingly criticized in contemporary Christian thought. Framing experiments within an eschatological perspective introduces an even more ambivalent view. The initial starting assumption, as instructed by the values of the kingdom to which Christians are to witness, is that animal experiments are to be avoided; they do not reflect what God ultimately intends for that creature, that is, its eschatological end. There might be exceptions, given the unrealized, not-yet nature of the kingdom, but such practices are to be mourned as postlapsarian, interim responses to a world subjected to the fall. In addition, an eschatological perspective encourages a standard for these exceptions that is stricter than what the *Catechism* calls "reasonable limits."[90] Pressing human need and the well-founded expectation of redressing that need, assessed within the context of an empathetic concern for the well-being of the animal, seem more appropriate as standards in light of the covenantal end that has been established for all creatures in Christ.

Though space constraints do not permit a thorough examination of contemporary practices, it is, I believe, fairly uncontroversial to assert that at least some present practices fail with regard to both secular and Christian norms. However, unlike the case of factory farming, for which Christians can as individuals refuse their support, resistance to unethical forms of animal research requires a public, collective challenge. Short of forgoing all medical treatment, individual Christians cannot realistically make the unilateral choice to refuse the benefits of animal experiments. Medical care depends on an interconnected web of historical experiments and contemporary investigations that cannot be untangled so as to allow even the most committed activist to choose only those medical procedures, therapies, and drugs that result from ethical research. It is, then, hard to imagine—unlike what we saw in the case of using animals for food—how the individual Christian could witness to kingdom values in the choices he or she makes about health care.

The *communal* witness of the Church, however, is particularly important because the attitudes and assumptions underlying support for animal experiments (attitudes and assumptions to which Christian beliefs have historically contributed) are socially legitimatized and not merely the punctuated expression of individual sin. Challenging what I referred to above as the technocratic paradigm and its instrumentalization of animal life needs to rise to an institutional and symbolic level because of its social and communal entrenchment. The collective "No's" of society's institutions can play a vital part in raising social awareness about the untested and unreflected assumptions operating within our moral instincts and re-forming them to be more critically conscious of the needs of animal well-being.

This ecclesial witness will be a matter of teaching and public discourse, in which the Christian community (collectively and as individuals) shares with the world its distinctive vision of animal life. I noted above that this vision is shaped by several commitments: the innate creatureliness common to all beings, the sacramental dimension appearing in each creature, and the good of relationality. Each of these commitments can be used to illuminate some value at stake in animal experimentation, but I focus here on one aspect of the third. As noted in chapter 2, we have become aware of the rich interior lives of animals and the complexity of their social relationships; and we can imagine, given God's covenantal plans, that these qualities are highly valued and desired by God. Animals can be in relation with us because they are "subjects," agents that can respond. Animal "subject-hood" merits particular Christian consideration because of its value in the Christian narrative and the fact that it is severely threatened by the technocratic instrumentalization characteristic of our age.

Animals share with us in the capacity to be subjects with distinctive experiences of agency and selfhood.[91] In line with the dignity that Christianity attributes to the individual human person as a unique agent and a uniquely valued participant in God's covenant, it is arguable that we should also value, even if not absolutely so, the individual subjectivity of each animal, and with this the goodness of its desire to live a life free of pain, fear, and desperate need. Although all forms of animal use (whether as food sources, beasts of burden, or objects of enjoyment and sports) include an element of animal objectification and a corresponding muddying of their subjectivity, the use of animals in experiments is distinctively instrumentalizing in that it effectively eliminates any other frame of reference for engaging the animal beyond that of tool for human need. This totalizing instrumentalization is evidenced in the deprivations, genetic modifications, and bodily mutilations inflicted upon the animals and also, with disquieting irony, in the fact that even their subjectivity is made an object of study. The erasure of subjectivity is intentional in animal research. The natural empathy one might experience for animals as sentient subjects must be suppressed so that they can be made into engines of data to be collected. Any sense of the animal's individuality and distinctive subjectivity is expunged; it is a mere tool, some "thing" to be ordered from suppliers.[92]

Christianity's keen interest in opposing this purging of creaturely subject-hood is grounded in what it sees as the teleology of creation and the task it has been given to serve that end. The biologically odd appearance of subjectivity in evolutionary history—odd in that we still understand so little about how and why it emerged—is a revolutionary event for God's goal of establishing a covenantal relationship with creation. It was with this covenantal intent in mind that I underscored in chapter 1 the importance of perceiving that animals are, like us, subjects. We do not genuinely "see" animals—see what God has made them to be—when we treat them merely as objects for our use. Their identity as agential creatures with rich interior lives is erased, transformed into an "absent referent," to use Carol Adams's disturbing term, a feature of animal life now "absorbed into a human-centered hierarchy."[93] In response, feminists and other critics have emphasized the need to revitalize nature by cultivating a renewed sense of the agency of its creatures and of their status as living "others" worthy of care and compassion.[94]

As a way of helping us recalibrate how we think about the animal subjects used in experimentation, we can consider the thought experiment offered by the Christian ethicist Donna Yarri. She proposes prohibiting "any kind of pain and suffering to experimental animals to which a pet owner would be unwilling to expose her own pet."[95] Imagining such a scenario elicits in us moral passions attuned to the distinctive subjectivity of nonhuman animals more readily than abstract thinking about them. The care we show for companion animals becomes a kind of casuist standard, reminding us that laboratory animals are, in every morally relevant way, similar to the animals that share our homes; in both cases, we are dealing with nonhuman, creaturely subjects with individual personalities, developed cognition, and the desire for their own distinctive forms of flourishing. As the casuist tradition rightly assumed, similar cases should be treated similarly.

The value that Christian thought ascribes to animal subjectivity because of its covenantal hopes is not, however, a uniquely Christian concern. The basis for valuing nonhuman subjectivity may differ across ideological lines, but the value itself is often shared and thus can become part of an overlapping consensus among people with diverse worldviews. An important voice in this regard has been that of the late philosopher Tom Regan. In his groundbreaking *The Case for Animal Rights*, he argued that some animals are, like humans, "subjects-of-a-life"—that is, they have memory, an experience of agency, an ability to anticipate a future, some sense of selfhood, and, most important, a keen interest in and desire for their own life existence. Before most Christian thinkers had even recognized the need for an ethics of animal care, Regan, as a secular philosopher, began exploring religious traditions in order to uncover their resources for animal advocacy, and he enjoined their believers to attend to the often-unrecognized, subterranean riches of their respective worldviews.[96] His defense of animal rights has its critics,[97] and Christians advocating for animals can understandably question whether the language of "rights" best suits the value commitments at stake in a Christian worldview.[98] Nonetheless, by situating the discussion in terms of animals as "subjects-of-a-life," Regan offers a possible common ground for secular and Christian animal advocates. Drawing moral attention to the subjectivity and selfhood of each animal reminds us that practices using animals merely as objects in the service of human advancement depend on a fundamental falsehood: Sentient animals are never *only* objects but are always also subject-agents.

Though one might understandably conclude from these arguments that animal experiments should always be opposed by Christians as inherently wrong, I am not ready to argue that here. My hesitation is due in part to the incompleteness of this analysis (e.g., I have not examined in any depth the key question of whether or how animal experiments are beneficial to humans); but in addition, I believe that the "not yet" of the kingdom means that we will sometimes be forced to choose between the good of human persons and that of animals. The advancement of science and medicine is a general good to be praised; it serves the worthy endeavor of liberating our world from the natural evils that plague it. Nonetheless, efforts to overcome disease and suffering that depend on inflicting pain on animals should be resisted when possible and mourned as symptoms of our world's fallenness when not. Even granting, however, the possibility that there are licit forms of animal experimentation, most agree that at least some contemporary practices do not meet basic ethical standards, Christian or secular.[99]

CONCLUSION: RESPONDING TO THE WORLD
"HIS HUMAN EYES CONTEMPLATED AND ADMIRED"

My argument has been that the Christian's eschatological view transforms our way of seeing the world and the goods at stake in it. I have focused on animals, but the claim applies broadly to all creatures: "The very flowers of the field and the birds which his human eyes contemplated and admired are now imbued with his radiant presence."[100] The Christian is called to "see" this world and respond to it. This vision will sometimes lead Christians to perform actions that will appear absurd and nonsensical, actions that make sense *only* to those who share in their view of the world. What Cardinal Suhard famously said about Christian witness and God's existence—to witness is "to live in such a way that one's life would not make sense if God did not exist"—applies equally well to the Christian belief that in Christ a new era in human history has begun.[101] The kingdom has been inaugurated, and because of the hope it offers, those who follow Christ are to live in ways that will sometimes appear odd, impractical, and imprudent. In Christ, the Christian looks out at a different world and sees it stereoscopically, colored by the already and the not yet.

Acting for the kingdom requires a conversion, the embrace of a new set of beliefs, valuations, and dispositions without which the kingdom remains existentially inconsequential. In our contemporary context, the metanoia required will often entail a change in attitudes toward both creation and the creatures within it. Thus Pope John Paul II, known for his aggressive defense of *human* life, called for an "ecological conversion" that would lead

Christians to protect not only human life but also "the fundamental good of life in all its manifestations." Such a labor for life in *all* its creaturely forms is necessary for fashioning "an environment more in conformity with the Creator's plan."[102] Also keenly aware of the urgent need for fundamental changes in how we treat nonhuman creation, Pope Francis similarly "summons" Christians to a "profound interior conversion." Christians must allow "the effects of their encounter with Jesus Christ [to] become evident in their relationship with the world around them." Refusing "to change [one's] habits" about the environment is to "become inconsistent."[103]

Yet, perhaps such inconsistency is also part of being a Christian. To be a Christian is to be a hypocrite, albeit one who recognizes the fact and publicly acknowledges as much. It is to profess that one follows Christ while recognizing one's repeated failure to do so. The liberation offered by the kingdom as proclaimed by Jesus includes liberation from past sins. Each person, in the Spirit, humbly confesses sinful failure and receives God's promise of mercy. The liberation from sin is one of the tidings of the good news proclaimed by Christ and preached by the Church. In light of its historical neglect of God's creatures, the Church has an opportunity to give tangible witness to this emancipating message by embodying it. The Christian community's confession before Christ and the world of its failure to act as a protector of God's handiwork can be transformed, through grace, into an instrument of the Spirit's labor. Its humbled and inviting testimony of past failings can provide a space for others to do the same and can provoke self-scrutiny in those yet unconvinced of society's pernicious treatment of animals and the natural world. Such a witness can fruitfully enter the contemporary dialogue in a new mode, transforming itself into a voice that speaks not of triumphal truth but of a repentance for past wrongs and a newly energized freedom to do good. Humbly embraced, the narrative of a sinful past can become a prophetic and potent address that speaks with hope of a different future, not from a stance of "superiority" but one "of solidarity in sin and redemption."[104]

Given the present environmental crisis, conversion to a creation-caring attitude is a challenge that confronts all people. However, the particular valence that care for creation takes in the Christian context is marked by God's covenantal hopes and the in-breaking of the kingdom. Creatures are created for the eschatological covenant. Faithful to the relational and redemptive care that God has for our fellow creatures, Christians will similarly relate to nonhuman creatures in ways that embody and further God's covenantal plans. Animal care is one aspect of the task that has been

given to all Christians individually and the Church corporately: to participate in Christ's proclamation of the kingdom by witnessing to the kingdom and fostering its presence. Our fidelity to that task includes giving
attentive care to individual creatures, laboring for the well-being of creation as a whole, participating in the Church's liturgical mimesis of the
new covenant, and praying with the people of God for the redemption of
all creation.

I developed Balthasar's theology into a case for the restoration of animals existing in the present age (or, at the very least, some of them) in
order to argue that they are fellow creatures of the covenant and should be
treated as such. However, the claim for covenantal inclusion does not
depend on the success of Balthasar's theological approach or that of any
other theological system. The resources at hand for defending a more
inclusive redemption are numerous, and their consequences have yet to
be fully integrated into the Church's theology and ethics. Among the
resources we examined are the Old Testament's portrayal of the solidarity
of all creation, the cosmic Christ theme, creation-friendly voices in the
tradition, the compassionate witnesses of the saints, the revised interpretations of the Genesis mandates in contemporary biblical studies, and the
affirmation of God's eschatological plans for *all* creation in the teachings
of Vatican II and popes John Paul II, Benedict XVI, and Francis. The
contemporary case for an animal eschatology with its corresponding
moral claims is broader than any particular theological system. Moreover,
developments beyond the Church, both secular and scientific, amplify the
demand that we rethink our theology of animals: the doubts raised by
evolution about some Christian doctrines, the challenge raised by genetics
to the claim of human uniqueness in biological history, the startling ethological discoveries of the cognitive sophistication and social complexities
of animals, the environmental crisis and its connection to modern Christian attitudes toward nature, and philosophical critiques of instrumentalist
attitudes and technological hubris.

In part because of such signs, both internal and external to the Church,
a revolutionary shift in the Church's views of nonhuman creatures is
already underway, even if the Christian community has yet to fully recognize its repercussions. The early step in that transformation was taken
when participants at the Second Vatican Council made the decision to
move from an individualistic understanding of eschatology to an ecclesial
and cosmic one. Thus, *Lumen Gentium* states that in the eschaton "the
human race as well as the entire world, which is intimately related to man
and attains to its end through him, will be perfectly reestablished in

Christ,"[105] and *Gaudium et Spes* hopes for a time when all creation will be "unchained from the bondage of vanity."[106] This was a profound change, casting doubts as it did on the scholastic commitment to an animal-free eschaton. Unsurprisingly, some of the council fathers resisted this departure from the tradition. Preferring a biotically impoverished view of redemption, Abbot Prou, for example, argued that "only a spiritual creature, and on earth only the human soul can be elevated to the supernatural order."[107] The council rejected such arguments, and subsequent magisterial teaching has shown that the council's decision to embrace a cosmic, inclusive understanding of the eschaton was no theological fad. "The Holy Spirit," stated John Paul II, "will enter into human *and cosmic* suffering with a new outpouring of love, which will redeem the world" (emphasis added).[108] Benedict XVI repeatedly maintained that Jesus's mission is universal; "its scope is the whole of creation, the world in its entirety." With the participation of those who follow Christ, "the world as a whole is to be torn free from its alienation, it is to rediscover unity with God."[109] "Revelation affirms," the *Catechism of the Catholic Church* notes in its reflection on the Apostles' Creed, "the profound common destiny of the material world and man."[110] Pope Francis insistently supports these teachings and affirms their authority for the Catholic tradition.[111] He further develops them on two points. First, he explicitly rejects the view that the ultimate purpose of creatures is found in human need.[112] And second, he suggests (even if not as clearly as one might want) that God's love and redemptive care are directed toward creatures in their individuality, and not merely as part of a collective creation; "each creature," he writes, will be "resplendently transfigured."[113]

Given the cumulative weight of these teachings, the more urgent task confronting Catholicism is not developing Church teaching but rather discerning their ethical implications and acting in accord with them. Recognizing the problem, Pope Francis lamented that too many "committed and prayerful" Christians do not act as "protectors of God's handiwork." Some, he said, use "the excuse of realism and pragmatism" in order to "ridicule expressions of concern for the environment."[114] We can hope that such attitudes will change. As the Church's response to the signs of our time matures, the question confronting the Catholic community is becoming less whether animals go to heaven but rather how should we treat them, given our belief that they do. If God's ultimate hope and desire for the individual animals of our present age are that they come to enjoy a world where they will know only the harmony and compassion of the covenant, it seems reasonable to suppose that God would want those whom he has appointed "stewards" to begin fashioning such a world. It is, of course, beyond human ability to liberate creation from its present travails. But the Christian community can, nonetheless, without "the excuse of realism and pragmatism," strive to embody God's eschatological hope whenever and however grace allows it to do so.

NOTES

Epigraph: Francis, "Angelus."

1. Middleton, *New Heaven*, 245. The Synoptics' emphasis on the kingdom of God is not found in John's Gospel, where the term appears only twice (Jn 3:3 and 3:5). Regarding the translation of the phrase *"basileia tou theou,"* many scholars prefer to use the term God's "reign" instead of God's "kingdom," because the images and parables used by Jesus suggest that the kingdom is not so much a place as a relationship in which creation submits to God's rule.

2. A helpful history of the development of eschatology during the twentieth century is given by Schwöbel, "Last Things First."

3. *"Eschatology has already begun with the coming of Christ."* John Paul II, *Crossing the Threshold*, 184; emphasis in the original.

4. Moltmann, *Ethics*, 9. Also: "Ethics is lived eschatology." Middleton, *New Heaven*, 24. For a discussion of eschatology and ethics, see Cahill, "The Kingdom Come?" in *Love Your Enemies*, 15–38.

5. Thiel, "For What May We Hope?" 539. Similarly, David Gushee and Glen Stassen argue that "rebuilding community" is one of the seven marks of the kingdom. Gushee and Stassen, *Kingdom Ethics*, 8–10.

6. Dunn, *Jesus' Call*, 85.

7. Bauckham, *Bible*, 168. Also see Edwards, *God*, loc. 1123 of 1462, Kindle: "Reconciliation in Christ must lead to reconciliation with all God's creatures."

8. Benedict XVI, *Jesus of Nazareth: From the Baptism*, 81.

9. Vatican Council II, *Lumen Gentium*, no. 5.

10. This ecclesiology is not idiosyncratic to Catholicism. E.g., the Methodist minister Kenneth Wilson states that "the earthly and earthy church is the embodiment in the world of the work effected by God in Christ." Wilson, "World," 39. Similarly, in its statement on the kingdom of God, the United Methodist Church describes "the church as a sign of the Kingdom. Imperfect as it is, the community of believers nevertheless provides the best clue we have to God's vision." As Christians "witness and serve," they "take part in the Kingdom's dawning." United Methodist Church, "Our Christian Roots."

11. "The harmony which man must establish, or restore, in the whole of creation includes his relationship to the animals." International Theological Commission, "Communion," no. 79.

12. Ratzinger, *Spirit of the Liturgy*, 27.

13. United States Conference of Catholic Bishops, *Book of Blessings*, 415. To pray for nonhuman creatures does not, to stress again, imply that we regard animals as equal in dignity and value to the human person. Nor does it deny that circumstances in our broken world will require that the goods and interests of animals be harmed in order to preserve those of human persons (perhaps regularly so). The compassion that we feel for both human and nonhuman creatures is not zero-sum, even if our capacity to act on that compassion often is.

14. Wenham, "Genesis," 33.

15. Westermann, *Genesis 1–11*, 159.

16. A helpful set of essays discussing stewardship and its critics is given by Berry, *Environmental Stewardship*. Richard Bauckham reviews the debate in Bauckham, "Stewardship in Question," in *Bible*, 1–36.

17. See, e.g., Johnson, "Discerning Kinship with Earth," in *Women, Earth, and Creator Spirit*, 29–40.

18. Patrick McLaughlin gives a helpful overview of biblical and theological opinion on this role and its tie to the *imago Dei*. McLaughlin, "Noblesse Oblige," 134–37.

19. Bauckham, "Modern Domination," 46.

20. "There is another kind of subjection which is called economic or civil, whereby the superior makes use of his subjects for their own benefit and good; and this kind of subjection existed even before sin." Aquinas, *ST* I.92.1 *ad*. 2. "But a man is the master of a free subject, by directing him either towards his proper welfare, or to the common good. Such a kind of mastership would have existed in the state of innocence between man and man . . . because man is naturally a social being." *ST* I.96.4.

21. Camosy, "Other Animals," 274.

22. Catholic Church, Compendium [no. 473], 207.

23. Catholic Church [no. 460], 201. It cites John Paul II, "Address of Pope John Paul II to the 35th General Assembly."

24. Catholic Church, *Catechism*, no. 2415.

25. Catholic Church, no. 2417.

26. John Paul II, *Evangelium Vitae*, no. 52. He cites Paul VI, *Humanae Vitae*, no. 13.

27. Francis, *Laudato Si'*, no. 217.

28. Murdoch, *Sovereignty*, 37.

29. Williams, "Creation," 28–29.

30. Webb, *On God*, 10.

31. McDaniel, "Practicing the Presence," 133.

32. Webb, *On God*, 177.

33. Webb, "Ecology," 245.

34. Wennberg acknowledges the value of preventing predation were we able to do so wisely; however, he believes that because of human limits "there is very little, perhaps nothing, that we can do to improve on nature's working." Wennberg, *God*,

50–51. Another ambivalent view of ecological intervention is given by Thornhill and Morris, "Animal Liberationist Responses."

35. It is a "work of grace in eschatological hope rather than in an expectation for present reality." Deane-Drummond, *Wisdom*, 307.

36. Linzey, *Creatures*, 43.

37. Hayward and Somers, *Reintroduction*.

38. Farley, "Grace," 167–68.

39. Taylor, *Modern Social Imaginaries*, 25.

40. For a helpful discussion of this theme's appearance in *Laudato Si'*, see Miller, "Integral Ecology," 24: We live within a system that "trains us to think that everything *is not* connected" (emphasis in the original).

41. Gardner, *Inspiring Progress*; Swearer and McGarry, *Ecology*.

42. Cited by Trinkhaus, *In Our Image*, 483–84. The passage is from book II of Ficino, *Theologia Platonica de immortalitate animorum*.

43. Farrington, "Masculine Birth of Time," in *Philosophy*, 62. Carolyn Merchant's *The Death of Nature* was influential in making the case that Bacon and his successors in science fostered the objectification and domination of nature. In a 2006 essay, she provides an update on her thesis and a helpful overview of the debates that have ensued during the twenty-five years since the publication of her book. Merchant, "Scientific Revolution."

44. Boyle, *Vulgarly Received Notion*, 18–19. For a helpful overview of this historical development, see Bauckham, "Dominion Interpreted: A Historical Account," in *Living*, 14–62.

45. The German philosopher Hans Jonas, building on the work of Martin Heidegger, raised this concern in his *Phenomenon*, 193: "Control, by making ever more things available for more kinds of uses, enmeshes the user's life in ever more dependences on external objects."

46. Francis, *Laudato Si'*, no. 106.

47. Francis, no. 108.

48. Francis, no. 203.

49. Swearer and McGarry, *Ecology*, 10.

50. Francis, *Laudato Si'*, no. 115. Pope Francis here cites Guardini, *End*, 55.

51. Metz, *Poverty*, 27.

52. Metz, 29.

53. United States Conference of Catholic Bishops, *Renewing the Earth*, no. III.A

54. Francis, *Laudato Si'*, no. 11.

55. Francis, no. 100. Cf., "Creation as a whole has become a monstrance of God's real presence." Balthasar, *Glory*, vol. 1, 420. Recent works that explore how a sacramental worldview can be a resource for ecology include O'Brien, "The Sacramental Value of the Variety of Life," chap. 3 in *Ethics*, 58–75; Eggemeier, "Sacramental Vision"; and McCormick, "Tending Eden's Beauty," in *God's Beauty*, 113–49.

56. Rawls, *Political Liberalism*, 150–54.

57. A helpful theoretical analysis of the various forms that the Church's advocacy for animals might take in the public arena can be found in Heyer, "Catholic Public Theology for the Twenty-First Century," chap. 5 in *Prophetic*, 177–214.

58. Eusebius of Caesarea, *Proof* [book I.8], 48–49.

59. Vatican Council II, *Optatam Totius* [no. 16], 720.

60. Pinckaers, *Sources*, 168–90.

61. Pinckaers, 187.

62. Pinckaers, 185–88.

63. Meilaender, "What Is Right," 128, 129.

64. Meilaender, 132.

65. Meilaender, 130.

66. Ignatius, *Spiritual Exercises* [nos. 175–88], 76–79. The emphasis in the first two "times" is God's movement of the person's soul, whereas in the third time, the soul "uses its natural faculties" to make a decision. Rahner briefly connects his idea of a personal vocation to Ignatius's three times for making a choice; Rahner, "Formal Existential Ethics," 231–32. Balthasar does the same; Balthasar, *Christian State*, 451–52.

67. "Christian life is not merely satisfying universal norms which are proclaimed by the official church. Rather in these norms and beyond them it is the always unique call of God which is mediated in a concrete and loving encounter with Jesus in a mysticism of love." Rahner, *Foundations*, 311.

68. Rahner, "Formal Existential Ethics," 227.

69. The "word which God addresses to man is always, in addition, the gift of a sharing in God's nature, the individual who receives the word acquires a new quality: he becomes a *unique person*." Balthasar, *Theo-Drama*, vol. 2, 402 (emphasis in the original). Balthasar's development of this view can be found in two sections: "Theological Persons" in *Theo-Drama*, vol. 3, esp. 456–61; and Balthasar, "Nature of the Call," in *Christian State*, 391–461.

70. I explore this tension between the liturgical and the ethical in "Graced Encounters."

71. Mathewes, *Republic*, loc. 1538 of 3693, Kindle.

72. A comprehensive ethical analysis of these two cases from a Christian theological perspective is given by Clough, *On Animals: Volume Two*.

73. A related term, CAFO (concentrated animal feeding operations), sometimes used interchangeably with factory farming, is a technical designation assigned by the US Department of Agriculture based on factors like the overall weight of the animals involved, the degree of confinement, and the endpoint of the resulting animal waste.

74. For those unfamiliar with the perversity of factory farming, there are abundant resources covering the issue. A thorough overview of the facts and issues is given in Imhoff, *CAFO Reader*. See also Eisnitz, *Slaughterhouse*. Undercover videos and numerous descriptive accounts can be found online. The only way to make sense of the fact that these horrendous practices continue in a culture like ours, one that is otherwise adamantly opposed to animal cruelty, is that most are unaware of the practices. Perhaps, some choose to remain so. Nancy Williams argues that the latter is often at

work: "The lack of extensive public debate about factory farming and, its corollary, extreme animal suffering, is probably due, in part, to affected ignorance." Williams, "Affected Ignorance," 371. There are also human health issues at stake: Anomaly, "What's Wrong with Factory Farming?"

75. Belshaw, "Meat," 10, 12.

76. Barry Estabrook offers an accessible and balanced account of the cognitive qualities of pigs and the suffering they endure in factory farming. Pigs are, he shows, extremely social and playful creatures with an intelligence and conscious awareness at least as developed as that of dogs. Estabrook, *Pig Tales*.

77. For a discussion of Jesus's meat-eating practices, see Webb, "Didn't Jesus Eat Lamb?" and Alexis-Baker, "Didn't Jesus Eat Fish?"

78. See, Bazell, "Strife."

79. E.g., the fourth-century bishop John Chrysostom writes that saints are those who extend their gentleness "even to the unreasoning creatures." Chrysostom, *Chrysostom: Homilies*, 546. Also, as noted in chapter 1, the *Acta Sanctorum* of the Bollandists is filled with stories of saints displaying kindness toward animals; English translations of some of these stories can be found in *Church and Kindness* (the author is anonymous).

80. Thompson, *Francis*, 56.

81. Berkman, "Addicted," 135.

82. Rubio, "Animals," 38.

83. Rubio, 52.

84. Berkman examines how the theme of recreating the Edenic state by meat renunciation appears in the writings of early Christian thinkers, among them Basil of Caesarea, John Chrysostom, and Jerome. Berkman, "Consumption," 179–81.

85. "The power" of an individual's moral example "to activate and channel behavior has been abundantly documented." Bandura, *Social Foundations*, 206, cited by Oman and Thoresen, "Spiritual Modeling," 151. See also Zagzebski, *Exemplarist Moral Theory*.

86. Nurses "must do more than internally disapprove; they must show in some way that they do not approve of these operations." Kelly, *Medico-Moral Problems*, 333.

87. Gori, "Animals," 576. A more nuanced and qualified case for animal experiments can be found in the helpful review of the literature given by Cheluvappa, Scowen, and Eri, "Ethics."

88. DeGrazia and Beauchamp, "Reassessing," 385.

89. Camosy and Kopp, "Use."

90. "Medical and scientific experimentation on animals is a morally acceptable practice if it remains within *reasonable limits* and contributes to caring for or saving human lives" Catholic Church, *Catechism*, no. 2417 (emphasis added).

91. For a discussion of animal personhood, see Camosy, "Other Animals."

92. Birke, Arluke, and Michael, *Sacrifice*, 13.

93. Adams, *Sexual Politics*, 67.

94. See Clifford, "Feminist Perspectives."

95. Yarri, *Ethics*, 102.

96. Later, Regan would coedit a volume with the Christian theologian Andrew Linzey. Linzey and Regan, *Animals*.

97. See, e.g., Cohen, "Do Animals Have Rights?"

98. Hauerwas and Berkman, "Chief End," 200–201. Also ambivalent about an animal rights approach is Carol Adams. She believes that animal rights theory pays insufficient attention to care as both a motivating factor in our response to animal suffering and an obligation owed to the creature that suffers. Adams, "Caring," 201–2.

99. I see this claim as uncontroversial. A comprehensive critique of animal experiments can be found in the volume edited by Linzey and Linzey, *Ethical Case*.

100. Francis, *Laudato Si'*, no. 100.

101. Suhard, *Priests*, 50.

102. John Paul II, "General Audience (January 17, 2001)," no. 4.

103. Francis, *Laudato Si'*, no. 217.

104. McBride, *Church*, 214.

105. Vatican Council II, *Lumen Gentium*, no. 48.

106. Vatican Council II, *Gaudium et Spes*, no. 39.

107. Reported by Xavier Rynne, pseud., *Letters*, 137, cited by O'Halloran, "Each Creature," 387.

108. John Paul II, *Dominum*, no. 39.

109. Benedict XVI, *Jesus of Nazareth: Part Two*, 100.

110. Catholic Church, *Catechism*, no. 1046.

111. Toward the beginning of *Laudato Si'*, Pope Francis states his intention that the teachings of the encyclical, which reflect and develop the cosmic eschatology reintroduced as formal Catholic teaching at Vatican II, are to be "added to the body of the Church's social teaching." Francis, *Laudato Si'*, no. 15.

112. "The ultimate purpose of other creatures is not to be found in us." Francis, no. 83.

113. Francis, no. 243.

114. Francis, no. 217.

BIBLIOGRAPHY

The Church and Kindness to Animals. London: Burns & Oates, 1906.

Accattoli, Luigi. *When a Pope Asks Forgiveness: The Mea Culpa's of John Paul II.* Boston: Pauline Books & Media, 1998.

Adams, Carol J. "Caring about Suffering: A Feminist Exploration." In *The Feminist Care Tradition in Animal Ethics: A Reader,* edited by Josephine Donovan and Carol J. Adams, 198–226. New York: Columbia University Press, 2007.

———. *The Sexual Politics of Meat: A Feminist-Vegetarian Critical Theory.* 20th anniversary edition. New York: Continuum, 2010.

———. "'a very rare and difficult thing': Ecofeminism, Attention to Animal Suffering, and the Disappearance of the Subject." In *A Communion of Subjects: Animals in Religion, Science, and Ethics,* edited by Paul Waldau and Kimberley C. Patton, 591–604. New York: Columbia University Press, 2006.

Alexis-Baker, Andy. "Didn't Jesus Eat Fish?" In *A Faith Embracing All Creatures: Addressing Commonly Asked Questions about Christian Care for Animals,* edited by Tripp York and Andy Alexis-Baker, 64–74. Eugene, OR: Cascade Books, 2012.

Allers, Rudolf. "Microcosmus: From Anaximandros to Paracelsus." *Traditio: Studies in Ancient and Medieval History, Thought, and Religion* 2 (January 1944): 319–407.

Anatolios, Khaled, ed. *Athanasius.* The Early Church Fathers. New York: Routledge, 2004.

Anderson, Ray S. "On Being Human: The Spiritual Saga of a Creaturely Soul." In *Whatever Happened to the Soul? Scientific and Theological Portraits of Human Nature,* edited by Warren S. Brown, Nancey C. Murphy, and H. Newton Malony, 175–94. Minneapolis: Fortress Press, 1998.

Anomaly, J. 2015. "What's Wrong with Factory Farming?" *Public Health Ethics* 8, no. 3 (November 2015): 246–54.

Aquinas, Thomas. *Commentary on the Letter of Saint Paul to the Romans.* Edited by Fabian R. Larcher, John Mortensen, and Enrique Alarcón. Lander, WY: Aquinas Institute for the Study of Sacred Doctrine, 2012.

———. *On the Power of God (Quæstiones Disputatæ De Potentia Dei).* Translated by English Dominican Fathers. London: Burns, Oates & Washbourne, 1932.

———. *Summa Contra Gentiles.* Translated by James F. Anderson. Notre Dame, IN: University of Notre Dame Press, 1975.

———. *Summa Theologica*. Translated by Dominican Fathers of the English Province. London: R. & T. Washbourne; Benziger, 1912.

Ariely, Dan. *Predictably Irrational: The Hidden Forces That Shape Our Decisions*. New York: Harper, 2008.

Augustine. *The City of God*. Translated by Henry Bettenson. New York: Penguin Books, 1985.

Austin, Richard Cartwright. *Beauty of the Lord: Awakening the Senses*. Atlanta: John Knox Press, 1988.

Balcombe, Jonathan P. *What a Fish Knows: The Inner Lives of Our Underwater Cousins*. New York: Scientific American and Farrar, Straus & Giroux, 2016.

Balthasar, Hans Urs von. *The Christian State of Life*. Translated by Mary Frances McCarthy. San Francisco: Ignatius Press, 1983.

———. *Cosmic Liturgy: The Universe according to Maximus the Confessor*. Translated by Brian Daley. San Francisco: Ignatius Press, 2003.

———. "The Counsel of the Holy Spirit." In *Explorations in Theology: Creator Spirit*. Vol. 3, 245–68. Translated by Brian McNeil. San Francisco: Ignatius Press, 1993.

———. *Epilogue*. Translated by Edward Oakes. San Francisco: Ignatius Press, 2004.

———. "Finite Time within Eternal Time." In *Explorations in Theology: Man Is Created*. Translated by Edward T. Oakes. Vol. 5, 47–65. San Francisco: Ignatius Press, 1995.

———. *The Glory of the Lord: A Theological Aesthetics*. Vol. 1, *Seeing the Form*. Translated by Andrew Louth, Francis McDonagh, and Brian McNeil. San Francisco: Ignatius Press, 1982.

———. *The Glory of the Lord: A Theological Aesthetics*, Vol. 2, *Studies in Theological Style, Clerical Styles*. Translated by Andrew Louth, Francis McDonagh, and Brian McNeil. San Francisco: Ignatius Press, 1984.

———. "The Holy Spirit as Love." In *Explorations in Theology: Creator Spirit*. Translated by Brian McNeil. Vol. 3, 117–34. San Francisco: Ignatius Press, 1993.

———. "Improvisation on Future and Spirit." In *Explorations in Theology: Creator Spirit*. Translated by Brian McNeil. Vol. 3, 135–72. San Francisco: Ignatius Press, 1993.

———. "Some Points of Eschatology." In *Explorations in Theology: Spirit and Institution*. Translated by A. V. Littledale. Vol. I, 255–77. San Francisco: Ignatius Press, 1989.

———. *Sponsa Verbi: Skizzen Zur Theologie*. Vol. 2. Einsiedeln, Germany: Johannes Verlag, 1971.

———. *Theo-Drama: Theological Dramatic Theory*, Vol. 1, *Prolegomena*. Translated by Graham Harrison. San Francisco: Ignatius Press, 1988.

———. *Theo-Drama: Theological Dramatic Theory*, Vol. 2, *The Dramatis Personae, Man in God*. Translated by Graham Harrison. San Francisco: Ignatius Press, 1990.

———. *Theo-Drama: Theological Dramatic Theory*, Vol. 3, *The Dramatis Personae, The Person in Christ*. Translated by Graham Harrison. San Francisco: Ignatius Press, 1992.

————. *Theo-Drama: Theological Dramatic Theory*, Vol. 4, *The Action*. Translated by Graham Harrison. San Francisco: Ignatius Press, 1994.

————. *Theo-Drama: Theological Dramatic Theory*, Vol. 5, *The Last Act*. Translated by Graham Harrison. San Francisco: Ignatius Press, 1998.

————. *Theo-Logic: Theological Logical Theory*, Vol. 1, *Truth of the World*. Translated by Adrian J. Walker. San Francisco: Ignatius Press, 2001.

————. *Theo-Logic: Theological Logical Theory*, Vol. 2, *Truth of God*. Translated by Adrian J. Walker. San Francisco: Ignatius Press, 2004.

————. *Theo-Logic: Theological Logical Theory*, Vol. 3, *The Spirit of Truth*. Translated by Graham Harrison. San Francisco: Ignatius Press, 2005.

————. *A Theological Anthropology*. New York: Sheed & Ward, 1967.

————. *The Theology of Karl Barth*. Translated by Edward J. Oakes. San Francisco: Ignatius Press, 1992.

————. *Two Say Why*. Translated by John Griffiths. London: Search Press and Franciscan Herald Press, 1973.

————. "The Unknown Lying beyond the Word." In *Explorations in Theology: Creator Spirit*. Translated by Brian McNeil. Vol. 3, 105–16. San Francisco: Ignatius Press, 1993.

Banaji, Mahzarin R., and Anthony G. Greenwald. *Blindspot: Hidden Biases of Good People*. New York: Delacorte Press, 2013.

Bandura, Albert. *Social Foundations of Thought and Action: A Social Cognitive Theory*. Englewood Cliffs, NJ: Prentice-Hall, 1986.

Barth, Karl. *Church Dogmatics: The Doctrine of Creation*. Translated by Geoffrey William Bromiley and Thomas F. Torrance. Vol. III.2. Edinburgh: T&T Clark, 1960.

————. *Church Dogmatics: The Doctrine of God*. Translated by Geoffrey William Bromiley. Edited by G. W. Bromiley and Thomas F. Torrance. Vol. II.2. New York: Scribner, 1957.

Bauckham, Richard. *Bible and Ecology: Rediscovering the Community of Creation*. London: Darton, Longman & Todd, 2010.

————. "Jesus and Animals I: What Did He Teach?" In *Animals on the Agenda: Questions about Animals for Theology and Ethics*, edited by Andrew Linzey and Dorothy Yamamoto, 33–48. Urbana: University of Illinois Press, 1998.

————. "Jesus and Animals II: What Did He Practice?" In *Animals on the Agenda: Questions about Animals for Theology and Ethics*, edited by Andrew Linzey and Dorothy Yamamoto, 49–60. Urbana: University of Illinois Press, 1998.

————. *Living with Other Creatures: Green Exegesis and Theology*. Waco, TX: Baylor University Press, 2011.

————. "Modern Domination of Nature: Historical Origins and Biblical Critique." In *Environmental Stewardship: Critical Perspectives, Past and Present*, edited by R. J. Berry, 32–50. London: T&T Clark, 2006.

Bazell, Dianne M. "Strife among the Table-Fellows: Conflicting Attitudes of Early and Medieval Christians toward the Eating of Meat." *Journal of the American Academy of Religion* 65, no. 1 (Spring 1997): 73–99.

Bekoff, Marc. *Why Dogs Hump and Bees Get Depressed: The Fascinating Science of Animal Intelligence, Emotions, Friendship, and Conservation.* Novato, CA: New World Library, 2013.

Bekoff, Marc, and Jessica Pierce. *Wild Justice: The Moral Lives of Animals.* Chicago: University of Chicago Press, 2009.

Belshaw, Christopher. "Meat." In *The Moral Complexities of Eating Meat,* edited by Ben Bramble and Bob Fischer, 9–29. New York: Oxford University Press, 2015.

Benedict XVI. *The Garden of God: Toward a Human Ecology.* Translated by Maria Milvia Morciano. Washington, DC: Catholic University of America Press, 2014.

———. "Homily: Baptism of the Lord (January 13, 2008)." http://w2.vatican.va/content /benedict-xvi/en/homilies/2008/documents/hf_ben-xvi_hom_20080113_batte simo.html.

———. "Homily: Sacred Body and Blood of Christ (June 15, 2006)." https://w2.vatican .va/content/benedict-xvi/en/homilies/2006/documents/hf_ben-xvi _hom_20060615_corpus-christi.html.

———. "Homily: Solemnity of Pentecost, Vigil (June 3, 2006)." http://w2.vatican.va /content/benedict-xvi/en/homilies/2006/documents/hf_ben-xvi_hom_200 60603_veglia-pentecoste.html.

———. *Jesus of Nazareth: From the Baptism in the Jordan to the Transfiguration.* New York: Doubleday, 2007.

———. *Jesus of Nazareth: Part Two, Holy Week: From the Entrance into Jerusalem to the Resurrection.* San Francisco: Ignatius Press, 2011.

———. "Message: World Day of Peace (January 1, 2010)." http://w2.vatican.va/content /benedict-xvi/en/messages/peace/documents/hf_ben-xvi_mes_20091208_xliii -world-day-peace.html#_edn25.

———. *Spe Salvi.* 2007. http://w2.vatican.va/content/benedict-xvi/en/encyclicals /documents/hf_ben-xvi_enc_20071130_spe-salvi.html.

Bentham, Jeremy. *An Introduction to the Principles of Morals and Legislation.* Oxford: Clarendon Press, 1879.

Benzoni, Francisco. "Thomas Aquinas and Environmental Ethics: A Reconsideration of Providence and Salvation." *Journal of Religion* 85, no. 3 (July 2005): 446–76.

Berkman, John. "Are We Addicted to the Suffering of Animals? Animal Cruelty and the Catholic Moral Tradition." In *A Faith Embracing All Creatures: Addressing Commonly Asked Questions about Christian Care for Animals,* edited by Tripp York and Andy Alexis-Baker, 124–38. Eugene, OR: Cascade Books, 2012.

———. "The Consumption of Animals and the Catholic Tradition." *Logos: A Journal of Catholic Thought and Culture* 7, no. 1 (Winter 2004): 174–90.

———. "Towards a Thomistic Theology of Animality." In *Creaturely Theology: On God, Humans, and Other Animals,* edited by David Clough and Celia Deane-Drummond, 21–40. London: SCM Press, 2009.

Berry, R. J. *Environmental Stewardship: Critical Perspectives, Past and Present*. London: T&T Clark, 2006.

Berry, Thomas. "The Dream of the Earth." *Cross Currents* 37, no. 2 (Summer 1987): 200–215.

Birke, Lynda I. A., Arnold Arluke, and Mike Michael. *The Sacrifice: How Scientific Experiments Transform Animals and People*. West Lafayette, IN: Purdue University Press, 2007.

Blenkinsopp, Joseph. *Isaiah: A New Translation with Introduction and Commentary*. Vol. 19. New York: Doubleday, 2000.

Blowers, Paul M. *Drama of the Divine Economy: Creator and Creation in Early Christian Theology and Piety*. Oxford: Oxford University Press, 2012.

———. "Unfinished Creative Business: Maximus the Confessor, Evolutionary Theodicy, and Human Stewardship in Creation." In *On Earth as It Is in Heaven: Cultivating a Contemporary Theology of Creation*, edited by David Vincent Meconi, 142–54. Grand Rapids: Wm. B. Eerdmans, 2016.

Bonaventure. *The Journey of the Mind to God*. Translated by Philotheus Boehner. Edited by Stephen Brown. Indianapolis: Hackett, 1993.

Bougeant, Guillaume-Hyacinthe. *A Philosophical Amusement upon the Language of Beasts*. London: Printed for T. Cooper, at the Globe in Pater-Noster Row; Gale: Ecco, 1739.

Boylan, Patrick. *St. Paul's Epistle to the Romans: Translation and Commentary*. Dublin: M. H. Gill, 1934.

Boyle, Robert. *A Free Enquiry into the Vulgarly Received Notion of Nature*. London: Printed by H. Clark for John Taylor. Early English Books, 1686.

Bräuer, Juliane, Juliane Kaminski, Julia Riedel, Joseph Call, and Michael Tomasello. "Making Inferences about the Location of Hidden Food: Social Dog, Causal Ape." *Journal of Comparative Psychology* 120, no. 1 (February 2006): 38–47.

Brody, Baruch A. *The Ethics of Biomedical Research: An International Perspective*. New York: Oxford University Press, 1998.

Bromander, Lennart. "The Vivisection Debate in Sweden in the 1880s." In *Vivisection in Historical Perspective*, edited by Nicolaas A. Rupke, 214–35. New York: Croom Helm, 1987.

Burrell, David B. "Creation as Original Grace." In *God, Grace, and Creation*, edited by Philip J. Rossi, 97–106. Maryknoll, NY: Orbis Books, 2010.

———. "Does Process Theology Rest on a Mistake?" *Theological Studies* 43, no. 1 (March 1982): 125–35.

Burrell, David, and Stanley Hauerwas. "Self-Deception and Autobiography: Theological and Ethical Reflections on Speer's 'Inside the Third Reich.'" *Journal of Religious Ethics* 2, no. 1 (Spring 1974): 99–117.

Butler, Joseph. *Fifteen Sermons Preached at the Rolls Chapel: To Which Are Added Six Sermons Preached on Public Occasions*. New correct. ed. Vol. 1. Glasgow: Printed for R. Urie; Gale: Ecco, 1769.

———. *The Whole Works of Joseph Butler*. Rev. ed. London: T. Tegg, 1839.

Byrne, Brendan. "Creation Groaning: An Earth Bible Reading of Romans 8.18–22." In *Readings from the Perspective of Earth*, edited by Norman C. Habel. Sheffield, UK: Pilgrim Press, 2000, vol. 1, 193–203.

———. *Romans*. Vol. 6. Collegeville, MN: Liturgical Press, 1996.

Cahill, Lisa Sowle. "The Atonement Paradigm: Does It Still Have Explanatory Value?" *Theological Studies* 68, no. 2 (June 2007): 418–32.

———. *Love Your Enemies: Discipleship, Pacifism, and Just War Theory*. Minneapolis: Fortress Press, 1994.

Calhoun, John C. *Speeches of John C. Calhoun: Delivered in the House of Representatives and in the Senate of the United States*. In *The Works of John C. Calhoun*, vol. 2, edited by Richard Kenner Crallé. New York: D. Appleton; Gale: Sabine Americana: 1500–1926, 1853.

Camosy, Charles C. "Other Animals as Persons? A Roman Catholic Inquiry." In *Animals as Religious Subjects: Transdisciplinary Perspectives*, edited by Celia Deane-Drummond, Rebecca Artinian-Kaiser, and David Clough, 259–77. New York: Bloomsbury, 2013.

Camosy, Charles C., and Susan Kopp. "The Use of Non-Human Animals in Biomedical Research: Can Moral Theology Fill the Gap?" *Journal of Moral Theology* 3, no. 2 (June 2014): 54–71.

Canadian Conference of Catholic Bishops. "'You Love All That Exists . . . All Things Are Yours, God, Lover of Life . . .': A Pastoral Letter on the Christian Ecological Imperative." *Catholic Education: A Journal of Inquiry and Practice* 8, no. 1 (September 2004): 34–43.

Carere, Claudio, and Dario Maestripieri. *Animal Personalities: Behavior, Physiology, and Evolution*. Chicago: University of Chicago Press, 2013.

Catholic Church. *Catechism of the Catholic Church*. 2nd ed. New York: Doubleday, 1997.

———. *Compendium of the Social Doctrine of the Church*. Vatican City: Libreria Editrice Vaticana, 2004.

Chalmers, David John. *The Conscious Mind: In Search of a Fundamental Theory*. New York: Oxford University Press, 1996.

Cheluvappa, Rajkumar, Paul Scowen, and Rajaraman Eri. "Ethics of Animal Research in Human Disease Remediation, Its Institutional Teaching; and Alternatives to Animal Experimentation." *Pharmacology Research & Perspectives* 5, no. 4 (August 2017). doi:10.1002/prp2.332.

Chrysostom, John. *Chrysostom: Homilies on the Acts of the Apostles and the Epistle to the Romans: Nicene and Post-Nicene Fathers, Volume 11*, 2nd ed., edited by Philip Schaff. Peabody, MA: Hendrickson, 1995.

Clifford, Anne M. "Feminist Perspectives on Science: Implications for an Ecological Theology of Creation." In *Readings in Ecology and Feminist Theology*, edited by Mary Heather MacKinnon and Moni McIntyre, 334–60. Kansas City: Sheed & Ward, 1995.

Clough, David. *On Animals: Vol. 1, Systematic Theology*. New York: T&T Clark, 2012.

———. *On Animals:* Vol. 2, *Theological Ethics*. New York: T&T Clark, 2018.

Cobbe, Frances Power. *Life of Frances Power Cobbe*. Vol. 2. Boston: Houghton, Mifflin; Internet Archive, 1894.

Cohen, Carl. "Do Animals Have Rights?" *Ethics & Behavior* 7, no. 2 (June 1997): 91–102.

Cole-Turner, Ronald. "Toward a Theology for the Age of Biotechnology." In *Beyond Cloning: Religion and the Remaking of Humanity*, edited by Ronald Cole-Turner, 137–50. Harrisburg, PA: Trinity Press International, 2001.

Congregation for the Doctrine of the Faith. "Letter on Certain Questions Concerning Eschatology." Rome, 1979. www.vatican.va/roman_curia/congregations/cfaith /documents/rc_con_cfaith_doc_19790517_escatologia_en.html.

Coppens, Charles. *Moral Principles and Medical Practice, the Basis of Medical Jurisprudence*. New York: Benziger Brothers; Internet Archive, 1897.

Cornell, Heather N., John M. Marzluff, and Shannon Pecoraro. "Social Learning Spreads Knowledge about Dangerous Humans among American Crows." *Proceedings: Biological Sciences* 279, no. 1728 (February 2012): 499–508.

Cullmann, Oscar. *Christ and Time: The Primitive Christian Conception of Time and History*. Rev. ed. Philadelphia: Westminster Press, 1964.

Curtis, E. M. "Man as the Image of God in Genesis in the Light of Ancient Near Eastern Parallels." PhD diss., University of Pennsylvania, 1984.

Dagg, Anne Innis. *Animal Friendships*. New York: Cambridge University Press, 2011.

Daley, Brian. "A Hope for Worms: Early Christian Hope." In *Resurrection: Theological and Scientific Assessments*, edited by Ted Peters, Robert J. Russell, and Michael Welker, 136–64. Grand Rapids: Wm. B. Eerdmans, 2002.

———. *Gregory of Nazianzus*. New York: Routledge, 2006.

Darwin, Charles. "To Asa Gray, 22 May [1860]." Darwin Correspondence Project, "Letter No. 2814." University of Cambridge. www.darwinproject.ac.uk/DCP -LETT-2814.

Davis, Henry. *Moral and Pastoral Theology*, 2nd ed. Vol. 2. London: Sheed & Ward, 1935.

Davy, Barbara Jane. "An Other Face of Ethics in Levinas." *Ethics and the Environment* 12, no. 1 (April 2007): 39–65.

de Waal, Frans. *Are We Smart Enough to Know How Smart Animals Are?* New York: W. W. Norton, 2016.

Dean, Richard. *An Essay on the Future Life of Brutes*. Vol. I. Manchester: Printed by J. Harrop; Gale: Ecco, 1768.

Deane-Drummond, Celia. "Are Animals Moral? Taking Soundings through Vice, Virtue, Imago Dei, and Conscience." In *Creaturely Theology: On God, Humans, and Other Animals*, edited by David Clough and Celia Deane-Drummond, 190–210. London: SCM Press, 2009.

———. "The Breadth of Glory: A Trinitarian Eschatology for the Earth through Critical Engagement with Hans Urs Von Balthasar." *International Journal of Systematic Theology* 12, no. 1 (January 2010): 46–64.

———. *Christ and Evolution: Wonder and Wisdom*. Minneapolis: Fortress Press, 2009.

———. "*Laudato Si'* and the Natural Sciences: An Assessment of Possibilities and Limits." *Theological Studies* 77, no. 2 (June 2016): 392–415.

———. *The Wisdom of the Liminal: Evolution and Other Animals in Human Becoming.* Grand Rapids: Wm. B. Eerdmans, 2014.

DeGrazia, David, and Tom L. Beauchamp. "Guest Editorial: Reassessing Animal Research Ethics." *Cambridge Quarterly of Healthcare Ethics* 24, no. 4 (October 2015): 385–89.

Delio, Ilia. *Christ in Evolution.* Maryknoll, NY: Orbis Books, 2008.

Dell, Katharine J. "Covenant and Creation in Relationship." In *Covenant as Context: Essays in Honour of E. W. Nicholson*, edited by A. D. H. Mayes and R. B. Salters, 111–33. New York: Oxford University Press, 2003.

Descartes, René. *The Philosophical Writings of Descartes: The Correspondence.* Translated by John Cottingham. Vol. 3. Cambridge: Cambridge University Press, 1991.

Devenish, Philip E. "Postliberal Process Theology: A Rejoinder to Burrell." *Theological Studies* 43, no. 3 (September 1982): 504–13.

Dickey, James. *Self-Interviews.* Garden City, NY: Doubleday, 1970.

Duffy, Stephen. *The Graced Horizon: Nature and Grace in Modern Catholic Thought.* Vol. 37. Collegeville, MN: Liturgical Press, 1992.

Duncan, Ian J. H. "The Changing Concept of Animal Sentience." *Applied Animal Behaviour Science* 100, no. 1 (October 2006): 11–19.

Dunn, James D. G. *Jesus' Call to Discipleship.* Cambridge: Cambridge University Press, 1992.

———. "The New Perspective on Paul (1983)." In *The New Perspective on Paul: Collected Essays*, 89–110. Tübingen, Germany: Mohr Siebeck, 2005.

———. "The New Perspective on Paul: When, What, and Wither?" In *The New Perspective on Paul: Collected Essays*, 1–88. Tübingen: Mohr Siebeck, 2005.

Dych, William V. *Thy Kingdom Come: Jesus and the Reign of God.* New York: Crossroad, 1999.

Edwards, Denis. *The God of Evolution: A Trinitarian Theology.* New York: Paulist Press, 1999.

———. "Every Sparrow That Falls to the Ground: The Cost of Evolution and the Christ-Event." *Ecotheology* 11, no. 1 (March 2006): 103–23.

———. *Partaking of God: Trinity, Evolution and Ecology.* Collegeville, MN: Michael Glazier, 2014.

———. "'Sublime Communion': The Theology of the Natural World in *Laudato Si'*." *Theological Studies* 77, no. 2 (June 2016): 377–91.

Eggemeier, Matthew T. "A Sacramental Vision: Environmental Degradation and the Aesthetics of Creation." *Modern Theology* 29, no. 3 (July 2013): 338–60.

Eisnitz, Gail A. *Slaughterhouse: The Shocking Story of Greed, Neglect, and Inhumane Treatment inside the U.S. Meat Industry.* Amherst, NY: Prometheus Books, 2007.

Ephrem the Syrian. *Hymns on Paradise.* Translated by Sebastian P. Brock. Crestwood, NY: St. Vladimir's Seminary Press, 1990.

Erigena, Johannes Scotus. *Periphyseon.* Edited by Edouard Jeauneau. Turnhout, Belgium: Brepols, 1996.

Estabrook, Barry. *Pig Tales: An Omnivore's Quest for Sustainable Meat*. New York: W. W. Norton, 2015.

Eusebius of Caesarea. *The Proof of the Gospel: Being the Demonstratio Evangelica of Eusebius of Cæsarea*. Translated by William John Ferrar. London: SPCK. HathiTrust, 1920.

EWTN. "JPII Said Animals Do Have Souls. . . . Question from Anonymous on 3/15/2011." March 15, 2011. www.ewtn.com/v/experts/showmessage.asp?num ber=604934.

Farley, Margaret A. "Ethics, Ecclesiology, and the Grace of Self-Doubt." In *Changing the Questions: Explorations in Christian Ethics*, edited by Jamie L. Manson, 161–81. Maryknoll, NY: Orbis Books, 2015.

———. "Fragments for an Ethic of Commitment in Thomas Aquinas." In *Changing the Questions: Explorations in Christian Ethics*, edited by Jamie L. Manson, 24–46. Maryknoll, NY: Orbis Books, 2015.

———. "Moral Discourse in the Public Arena." In *Changing the Questions: Explorations in Christian Ethics*, edited by Jamie L. Manson, 69–87. Maryknoll, NY: Orbis Books, 2015.

Farrington, Benjamin. *The Philosophy of Francis Bacon: An Essay on Its Development from 1603 to 1609*. Liverpool: Liverpool University Press, 1964.

Fingarette, Herbert. *Self-Deception*. New York: Humanities Press, 1969.

Fitzgerald, Amy J., Linda Kalof, and Thomas Dietz. "Slaughterhouses and Increased Crime Rates: An Empirical Analysis of the Spillover from *The Jungle* into the Surrounding Community." *Organization & Environment* 22, no. 2 (June 2009): 158–84.

Fitzmyer, Joseph A. "The Letter to the Romans." In *The New Jerome Biblical Commentary*, edited by Raymond Edward Brown, Joseph A. Fitzmyer, and Roland E. Murphy, 830–68. Englewood Cliffs, NJ: Prentice-Hall, 1990.

———. *Romans: A New Translation with Introduction and Commentary*. New York: Doubleday, 1993.

Fox, Matthew, and Jonathon Porritt. "Green Spirituality [Interview]." *Creation Spirituality* 7, no. 3 (May–June 1991): 14–15.

Francis, Pope. "Angelus (September 24, 2017)." http://w2.vatican.va/content/fran cesco/en/angelus/2017/documents/papa-francesco_angelus_20170924.html.

———. *Evangelii Gaudium*. New York: Image, 2014.

———. *Laudato Si'*. Mahwah, NJ: Paulist, 2015.

Francis, Pope, and Bartholomew, Ecumenical Patriarch. "Joint Message: World Day of Prayer for Creation (September 1, 2017)." https://w2.vatican.va/content/fran cesco/en/messages/pont-messages/2017/documents/papa-francesco_2017 0901_messaggio-giornata-cura-creato.html.

Francis Crick Memorial Conference. "The Cambridge Declaration on Consciousness." 2012. http://fcmconference.org/img/CambridgeDeclarationOnConsciousness .pdf.

French, William C. "Beast Machines and the Technocratic Reduction of Life: A Creation-Centered Perspective." In *Good News for Animals? Christian Approaches* to *Animal Well-Being*, edited by Charles Pinches and Jay B. McDaniel, 24–33. New York: Orbis Books, 1993.

Gaffney, James. "Can Catholic Morality Make Room for Animals?" In *Animals on the Agenda: Questions about Animals for Theology and Ethics*, edited by Andrew Linzey and Dorothy Yamamoto, 100–112. Urbana: University of Illinois Press, 1998.

———. "The Relevance of Animal Experimentation to Roman Catholic Ethical Methodology." In *Animal Sacrifices: Religious Perspectives on the Use of Animals in Science*, edited by Tom Regan, 149–70. Philadelphia: Temple University Press, 1986.

Galloway, Allan Douglas. *The Cosmic Christ*. London: Nisbet, 1951.

Gardner, Gary T. *Inspiring Progress: Religions' Contributions to Sustainable Development*. New York: W. W. Norton, 2006.

Gavrilyuk, Paul L. *The Suffering of the Impassible God: The Dialectics of Patristic Thought*. Oxford: Oxford University Press, 2004.

Gilleman, Gérard. *The Primacy of Charity in Moral Theology*. Westminster, MD: Newman Press, 1959.

Gladstone, Rick. "Dogs in Heaven? Pope Leaves Pearly Gate Open." *New York Times*, December 12, 2014.

Godet, Frédéric Louis. *Commentary on St. Paul's Epistle to the Romans*. Edinburgh: T&T Clark, 1880.

Godzieba, Anthony. "Bodies and Persons, Resurrected and Postmodern: Toward a Relational Eschatology." In *Theology and Conversation: Towards a Relational Theology*, edited by Jacques Haers and Peter de Mey, 211–25. Leuven: Peeters, 2003.

Gori, Gio Batta. "Animals and Ethical Research." *Regulatory Toxicology and Pharmacology* 70, no. 3 (December 2014): 575–76.

Gosling, Samuel D. "Personality in Non-Human Animals." *Social and Personality Psychology Compass* 2, no. 2 (March 2008): 985–1001.

Gowan, Donald E. *Eschatology in the Old Testament*. Edinburgh: T&T Clark, 2000.

Granger, James. *An Apology for the Brute Creation, or Abuse of Animals Censured; in a Sermon on Proverbs XII.10*. London: T. Davies. Google Books, 1772.

Green, Joel B. *Body, Soul, and Human Life: The Nature of Humanity in the Bible*. Grand Rapids: Paternoster, 2008.

Gregersen, Niels Henrik, ed. *Incarnation: On the Scope and Depth of Christology*. Minneapolis: Fortress, 2015.

Gregory of Nyssa. "The Making of Man." In *Gregory of Nyssa: Dogmatic Treatises— Nicene and Post-Nicene Fathers*, edited by Philip Schaff. Vol. 5. Peabody, MA: Hendrickson, 1994.

Grenz, Stanley J. *The Social God and the Relational Self: A Trinitarian Theology of the Imago Dei*. Louisville: Westminster John Knox Press, 2001.

Griffin, Donald. "From Cognition to Consciousness." In *A Communion of Subjects: Animals in Religion, Science, and Ethics*, edited by Paul Waldau and Kimberley C. Patton, 481–504. New York: Columbia University Press, 2006.

Guardini, Romano. *The End of the Modern World: A Search for Orientation.* Translated by Joseph Theman and Herbert Burke. Edited by Frederick D. Wilhelmsen. New York: Sheed & Ward, 1956.

Guarnieri, Patrizia. "Moritz Schiff (1823–96): Experimental Physiology and Noble Sentiment in Florence." In *Vivisection in Historical Perspective*, edited by Nicolaas A. Rupke, 105–24. New York: Croom Helm, 1987.

Gushee, David P., and Glen Harold Stassen. *Kingdom Ethics: Following Jesus in Contemporary Context.* 2nd ed. Grand Rapids: Wm. B. Eerdmans, 2016.

Hadley, Christopher. "The All-Embracing Frame: Distance in the Trinitarian Theology of Hans Urs von Balthasar." PhD diss., Marquette University, 2009. https://epublications.marquette.edu/dissertations_mu/547/.

Harrington, Daniel J. *The Gospel of Matthew.* Vol. 1. Collegeville, MN: Liturgical Press, 1991.

Harris, Murray J. *Raised Immortal: Resurrection and Immortality in the New Testament.* Grand Rapids: Wm. B. Eerdmans, 1985.

Hatkoff, Amy, and Jane Goodall. *The Inner World of Farm Animals: Their Amazing Social, Emotional, and Intellectual Capacities.* New York: Stewart, Tabori, and Chang, 2009.

Hauerwas, Stanley, and John Berkman. "The Chief End of All Flesh: Christian Theology regarding Animal Rights." *Theology Today* 49, no. 2 (July 1992): 196–208.

Haught, John F. *God after Darwin: A Theology of Evolution.* 2nd ed. Boulder, CO: Westview Press, 2008.

———. *Making Sense of Evolution: Darwin, God, and the Drama of Life.* 1st ed. Louisville: Westminster John Knox Press, 2010.

———. *Resting on the Future: Catholic Theology for an Unfinished Universe.* New York: Bloomsbury Academic, 2015.

Hauser, Marc. "Are Animals Moral Agents? Evolutionary Building Blocks of Morality." In *A Communion of Subjects: Animals in Religion, Science, and Ethics*, edited by Paul Waldau and Kimberley C. Patton, 505–18. New York: Columbia University Press, 2006.

Hayward, Matt, and Michael J. Somers. *Reintroduction of Top-Order Predators.* 1st ed. Vol. 5. Chichester, UK: Wiley-Blackwell. Ebook Central-Academic Complete, 2009.

Healy, Nicholas, and David L. Schindler. "For the Life of the World: Hans Urs von Balthasar on the Church as Eucharist." In *The Cambridge Companion to Hans Urs von Balthasar*, edited by Edward T. Oakes and David Moss, 51–63. Cambridge: Cambridge University Press, 2004.

Herzog, Hal. *Some We Love, Some We Hate, Some We Eat: Why It's So Hard to Think Straight about Animals.* New York: Harper, 2010.

Heyer, Kristin E. *Prophetic and Public: The Social Witness of U.S. Catholicism.* Washington, DC: Georgetown University Press, 2006.

Hiuser, K., and M. Barton. "A Promise Is a Promise: God's Covenantal Relationship with Animals." *Scottish Journal of Theology* 67, no. 3 (August 2014): 340–56.

Hiuser, Kris. "Maximizing Animal Theology: Maximus the Confessor on the Value of Non-Human Animals and the Human Calling." *Toronto Journal of Theology* 30, no. 2 (Fall 2014): 247–56.

Hogenboom, Melissa. "The 'Lucy' Rewrote the Story of Humanity." 2017. www.bbc .com/earth/story/20141127-lucy-fossil-revealed-our-origins.

Hopkins, Gerard Manley. *Gerard Manley Hopkins: A Selection of His Finest Poems*. Edited by Catherine Phillips. Oxford: Oxford University Press, 1995.

Horowitz, Alexandra. *Inside of a Dog: What Dogs See, Smell, and Know*. New York: Scribner, 2009.

Hughes, Gerard J. *Is God to Blame? The Problem of Evil Revisited*. Dublin: Veritas, 2007.

Hunt, Cherryl, David G. Horrell, and Christopher Southgate. "An Environmental Mantra? Ecological Interest in Romans 8:19–23 and a Modest Proposal for Its Narrative Interpretation." *Journal of Theological Studies* 59, no. 2 (October 2008): 546–79.

Ignatius of Loyola. *The Spiritual Exercises of Saint Ignatius: A Translation and Commentary*. Edited by George E. Ganss. Saint Louis: Institute of Jesuit Sources, 1992.

Imhoff, Dan. *The CAFO Reader: The Tragedy of Industrial Animal Factories*. Healdsburg, CA: Watershed Media, 2010.

Inoue, Sana, and Tetsuro Matsuzawa. "Working Memory of Numerals in Chimpanzees." *Current Biology* 17, no. 23 (December 2007). doi:10.1016/j.cub.2007 .10.027.

International Theological Commission. "Communion and Stewardship: Human Persons Created in the Image of God." 2002. www.vatican.va/roman_curia/congre gations/cfaith/cti_documents/rc_con_cfaith_doc_20040723_communion -stewardship_en.html.

———. "Some Current Questions in Eschatology." 1992. www.vatican.va/roman _curia/congregations/cfaith/cti_documents/rc_cti_1990_problemi-attuali -escatologia_en.html.

Irenaeus, Lyon, Saint. *St. Irenaeus of Lyons against Heresies: The Complete English Translation from the First Volume of the Ante-Nicene Fathers*, edited by Alexander Roberts and James Donaldson. South Bend, IN: Ex Fontibus, 2010.

Jasper, Ronald, Claud Dudley, and G. J. Cuming. *Prayers of the Eucharist: Early and Reformed*. 3rd ed. Collegeville, MN: Liturgical Press, 1990.

Jenkins, Willis. "Biodiversity and Salvation: Thomistic Roots for Environmental Ethics." *Journal of Religion* 83, no. 3 (July 2003): 401–20.

———. *Ecologies of Grace: Environmental Ethics and Christian Theology*. Oxford: Oxford University Press, 2008.

John Paul II, Pope. "Address of Pope John Paul II to Members of the Agency of the United Nations (Kenya)." 1985. https://w2.vatican.va/content/john-paul-ii/en /speeches/1985/august/documents/hf_jp-ii_spe_19850818_centro-nazioni -unite.html.

———. "Address of Pope John Paul II to the 35th General Assembly of the World Medical Association (1983)." https://w2.vatican.va/content/john-paul-ii/en/speeches /1983/october/documents/hf_jp-ii_spe_19831029_ass-medica-mondiale.html.

————. "Correspondence to Reverend George V. Coyne, SJ (June 1, 1988)." https://
w2.vatican.va/content/john-paul-ii/en/letters/1988/documents/hf_jp-ii_let
_19880601_padre-coyne.html.

————. *Crossing the Threshold of Hope*. Translated by Jenny McPhee and Martha
McPhee. Edited by Vittorio Messori. New York: Alfred A. Knopf, 1994.

————. *Dominum et Vivificantem*. Vol. 103. Washington, DC: United States Catholic
Conference, 1986.

————. *Ecclesia De Eucharistia*. Vol. 5–559. Washington, DC: United States Conference of Catholic Bishops, 2003.

————. *Evangelium Vitae*. Vol. 316–17. Washington, DC: United States Catholic Conference, 1995.

————. "General Audience (January 10, 1990)." http://w2.vatican.va/content/john
-paul-ii/it/audiences/1990/documents/hf_jp-ii_aud_19900110.html.

————. "General Audience (January 17, 2001)." https://w2.vatican.va/content/john
-paul-ii/en/audiences/2001/documents/hf_jp-ii_aud_20010117.html.

————. *Laborem Exercens*. Washington, DC: United States Catholic Conference, 1981.

————. *Redemptor Hominis*. London: Catholic Truth Society, 1979.

————. *Sollicitudo Rei Socialis*. Vol. 205–5. Washington, DC: United States Catholic
Conference, 1988.

Johnson, Elizabeth A. *Ask the Beasts: Darwin and the God of Love*. London: Bloomsbury,
2014.

————. *She Who Is: The Mystery of God in Feminist Theological Discourse*. New York:
Crossroad, 1992.

————. *Women, Earth, and Creator Spirit*. New York: Paulist Press, 1993.

Jonas, Hans. *The Phenomenon of Life: Toward a Philosophical Biology*. New York: Dell,
1966.

Jone, Heribert. *Moral Theology*. Westminster, MD: Newman, 1945.

Jones, Deborah M. *A School of Compassion: A Roman Catholic Theology of Animals*. Here-
fordshire, UK: Gracewing, 2009.

Joy, Melanie. *Why We Love Dogs, Eat Pigs, and Wear Cows: An Introduction to Carnism—
The Belief System That Enables Us to Eat Some Animals and Not Others*. San Francisco: Conari Press, 2010.

Kaplan, Jonas T., Sarah I. Gimbel, and Sam Harris. "Neural Correlates of Maintaining
One's Political Beliefs in the Face of Counterevidence." *Scientific Reports (Nature
Publisher Group)* 6, no. 39589 (December 2016). doi:10.1038/srep39589.

Kärkkäinen, Veli-Matti. *Creation and Humanity*. Vol. 3. Grand Rapids: Wm. B. Eerdmans, 2015.

Kasper, Walter. *The God of Jesus Christ*. New York: Crossroad, 1994.

Kelle, Brad E. *Hosea 2: Metaphor and Rhetoric in Historical Perspective*. Vol. 20. Atlanta:
Society of Biblical Literature, 2005.

Kelley, Bennet. *Saint Joseph Baltimore Catechism: The Truths of Our Catholic Faith
Clearly Explained and Illustrated*. Rev. ed. Vol. 1. New York: Catholic Book Pub.
Co., 1966.

Kelly, Gerald. *Medico-Moral Problems*. Saint Louis: Catholic Hospital Association, 1958.

Kingsford, Anna Bonus, and Edward Maitland. *The Credo of Christendom: And Other Addresses and Essays on Esoteric Christianity*. London: J. M. Watkins. HathiTrust, 1916.

Korsgaard, Christine M., and Onora O'Neill. *The Sources of Normativity*. Cambridge: Cambridge University Press, 1996.

LaCugna, Catherine Mowry. *God for Us: The Trinity and Christian Life*. New York: HarperSanFrancisco, 1993.

LaVerdiere, Eugene. *The Eucharist in the New Testament and the Early Church*. Collegeville, MN: Liturgical Press, 1996.

Lecky, William Edward Hartpole. *History of European Morals from Augustus to Charlemagne*. Vol. 2. London: Longmans, Green; Gutenberg EBook, 1902.

Leo XIII, Pope. "*Aeterni Patris*, Encyclical of Pope Leo XIII: On the Restoration of Christian Philosophy." *Logos: A Journal of Catholic Thought and Culture* 12, no. 1 (Winter 2009): 169–92.

LeVasseur, Todd, and Anna Peterson. *Religion and Ecological Crisis: The 'Lynn White Thesis' at Fifty*. New York: Routledge, 2017.

Levering, Matthew. *Jesus and the Demise of Death: Resurrection, Afterlife, and the Fate of the Christian*. Waco, TX: Baylor University Press, 2012.

Lewis, C. S. *The Problem of Pain*. New York: Touchstone, 1996.

Linzey, Andrew. *Animal Theology*. Urbana: University of Illinois Press, 1995.

———. *Creatures of the Same God: Explorations in Animal Theology*. New York: Lantern Books, 2009.

———. "Unfinished Creation: The Moral and Theological Significance of the Fall." *Ecotheology: Journal of Religion, Nature & the Environment* 5, no. 4 (January 1998): 20–26.

Linzey, Andrew, and Clair Linzey. *The Ethical Case against Animal Experiments*. Urbana: University of Illinois Press, 2018.

Linzey, Andrew, and Tom Regan. *Animals and Christianity: A Book of Readings*. New York: Crossroad, 1988.

Lloyd, Michael. "Are Animals Fallen?" In *Animals on the Agenda: Questions about Animals for Theology and Ethics*, edited by Andrew Linzey and Dorothy Yamamoto, 147–60. London: SCM Press, 1998.

Lohfink, Gerhard. *Is This All There Is? On Resurrection and Eternal Life*. Collegeville, MN: Liturgical Press, 2018.

Lohse, Eduard. *Colossians and Philemon: A Commentary on the Epistles to the Colossians and to Philemon*. Philadelphia: Fortress Press, 1975.

Louth, Andrew. "Between Creation and Transfiguration: The Environment in the Eastern Orthodox Tradition." In *Ecological Hermeneutics: Biblical, Historical and Theological Perspectives*, edited by David G. Horrell, 211–22. London: T&T Clark, 2010.

———. "The Six Days of Creation according to the Greek Fathers." In *Reading Genesis after Darwin*, edited by Stephen C. Barton and David Wilkinson, 40–55. Oxford: Oxford University Press, 2009.

Mahoney, Jack. *Christianity in Evolution: An Exploration.* Washington, DC: Georgetown University Press, 2011.

Mann, Janet, Margaret A. Stanton, Eric M. Patterson, Elisa J. Bienenstock, and Lisa Singh. "Social Networks Reveal Cultural Behaviour in Tool-Using Dolphins." *Nature Communications* 3 (December 2012). doi:10.1038/ncomms1983.

Mansini, Guy. "Henri De Lubac, the Natural Desire to See God, and Pure Nature." *Gregorianum* 83, no. 1 (January 2002): 89–109.

Mathewes, Charles T. *The Republic of Grace: Augustinian Thoughts for Dark Times.* Grand Rapids: Wm. B. Eerdmans, 2010.

Maximus Confessor. *Maximus the Confessor*, edited by Andrew Louth. New York: Routledge, 1996.

———. *On Difficulties in the Church Fathers: The Ambigua.* Edited and translated by Nicholas Constas. Cambridge, MA: Harvard University Press, 2014.

———. *On the Cosmic Mystery of Jesus Christ: Selected Writings from St. Maximus the Confessor*, edited by Paul M. Blowers and Robert Louis Wilken. Crestwood, NY: St. Vladimir's Seminary Press, 2003.

Maxwell, John Francis. *Slavery and the Catholic Church: The History of Catholic Teaching concerning the Moral Legitimacy of the Institution of Slavery.* Chichester, UK: Barry Rose Publisher, 1975.

McBride, Jennifer M. *The Church for the World: A Theology of Public Witness.* New York: Oxford University Press, 2012.

McCarthy, Dennis J., and Roland E. Murphy. "Hosea." In *The New Jerome Biblical Commentary*, edited by Raymond Edward Brown, Joseph A. Fitzmyer, and Roland E. Murphy, 217–28. Englewood Cliffs, NJ: Prentice Hall, 1990.

McClelland, V. A. *Cardinal Manning, His Public Life and Influence, 1865–1892.* London: Oxford University Press, 1962.

McCormick, Patrick T. *God's Beauty: A Call to Justice.* Collegeville, MN: Liturgical Press, 2012.

McDaniel, Jay B. *Of God and Pelicans: A Theology of Reverence for Life.* Louisville, KY: Westminster John Knox Press, 1989.

———. "Practicing the Presence of God: A Christian Approach to Animals." In *A Communion of Subjects: Animals in Religion, Science, and Ethics*, edited by Paul Waldau and Kimberley C. Patton, 132–45. New York: Columbia University Press, 2006.

McFadyen, Alistair I. *The Call to Personhood: A Christian Theory of the Individual in Social Relationships.* Cambridge: Cambridge University Press, 1990.

McLaughlin, Ryan Patrick. *Christian Theology and the Status of Animals: The Dominant Tradition and Its Alternatives.* London: Palgrave Macmillan, 2014.

———. "Noblesse Oblige: Theological Differences between Humans and Animals and What They Imply Morally." *Journal of Animal Ethics* 1, no. 2 (October 2011): 132–49.

———. *Preservation and Protest: Theological Foundations for Eco-Eschatological Ethics.* Minneapolis: Fortress Press, 2014.

Meconi, David Vincent. "Establishing I/Thou Relationship between Creator and Creature." In *On Earth As It Is in Heaven: Cultivating a Contemporary Theology of Creation*, edited by David Vincent Meconi, 219–36. Grand Rapids: Wm. B. Eerdmans, 2016.

Meilaender, Gilbert. "Is What Is Right for Me Right for All Persons Similarly Situated?" *Journal of Religious Ethics* 8, no. 1 (Spring 1980): 125–34.

Mendenhall, George E. "Covenant Forms in Israelite Tradition." *Biblical Archaeologist* 17, no. 3 (September 1954): 49–76.

Merchant, Carolyn. *The Death of Nature: Women, Ecology, and the Scientific Revolution*. San Francisco: Harper & Row, 1980.

———. "The Scientific Revolution and the Death of Nature." *Isis* 97, no. 3 (September 2006): 513–33.

Messer, Neil. "Natural Evil after Darwin." In *Theology after Darwin*, edited by Michael S. Northcott and R. J. Berry, 139–54. Colorado Springs: Paternoster, 2009.

Metz, Johannes Baptist. *Poverty of Spirit*. Glen Rock, NJ: Newman Press, 1968.

Meyer, Eric D. *Inner Animalities: Theology and the End of the Human*. New York: Fordham University Press, 2018.

Middleton, J. Richard. *The Liberating Image: The Imago Dei in Genesis 1*. Grand Rapids: Brazos Press, 2005.

———. *A New Heaven and a New Earth: Reclaiming Biblical Eschatology*. Grand Rapids: Baker Academic, 2014.

Miller, Patrick D. "Creation and Covenant." In *Biblical Theology: Problems and Perspectives: In Honor of J. Christiaan Beker*, edited by Johan Christiaan Beker, Steven John Kraftchick, Charles Davison Myers, and Ben C. Ollenburger, 155–68. Nashville: Abingdon Press, 1995.

Miller, Vincent J. "Integral Ecology: Francis's Spiritual and Moral Vision of Interconnectedness." In *The Theological and Ecological Vision of Laudato Si': Everything Is Connected*, edited by Vincent J. Miller, 11–28. London: Bloomsbury, 2017.

Moltmann, Jürgen. *Ethics of Hope*. Minneapolis: Fortress Press, 2012.

———. *The Way of Jesus Christ: Christology in Messianic Dimensions*. Minneapolis: Fortress Press, 1993.

Mongrain, Kevin. *The Systematic Thought of Hans Urs Von Balthasar: An Irenaean Retrieval*. New York: Crossroad, 2002.

Montgomery, Sy. *The Soul of an Octopus: A Surprising Exploration into the Wonder of Consciousness*. New York: Atria Books, 2015.

Murdoch, Iris. *Metaphysics as a Guide to Morals*. New York: Allen Lane, the Penguin Press, 1993.

———. *The Sovereignty of Good*. London: Routledge and Kegan Paul, 1970.

Murphy, Nancey C. *Bodies and Souls, or Spirited Bodies?* Cambridge: Cambridge University Press, 2006.

Murray, Robert. "The Cosmic Covenant." *Ecologist* 30, no. 1 (January 2000): 25–29.

Nagel, Thomas. "What Is It Like to Be a Bat?" *Philosophical Review* 83 (October 1974): 435–50.

Newman, John Henry. *Meditations and Devotions of the Late Cardinal Newman.* New York: Longmans, Green; HathiTrust, 1893.

———. *Parochial and Plain Sermons.* New ed. Vol. 7. London: Longmans, Green; Internet Archive, 1908.

———. *Sermons Preached on Various Occasions.* 2nd ed. London: Burns and Lambert; Internet Archive, 1874.

Nichols, Aidan. *Say It Is Pentecost: A Guide through Balthasar's Logic.* Vol. 3. Washington, DC: Catholic University of America Press, 2001.

Noonan, John. *A Church That Can and Cannot Change: The Development of Catholic Moral Teaching.* Notre Dame, IN: University of Notre Dame Press, 2005.

Northcott, Michael S. "Planetary Moral Economy and Creaturely Redemption in *Laudato Si'*." *Theological Studies* 77, no. 4 (December 2016): 886–904.

O'Brien, Kevin J. *An Ethics of Biodiversity: Christianity, Ecology, and the Variety of Life.* Washington, DC: Georgetown University Press, 2010.

O'Halloran, Nathan W. "Cosmic Alienation and the Origin of Evil: Rejecting the 'Only Way' Option." *Theology and Science* 13, no. 1 (January 2015): 43–63.

———. "'Each Creature, Resplendently Transfigured': Development of Teaching in *Laudato Si'*." *Theological Studies* 79, no. 2 (June 2018): 376–98.

O'Hanlon, Gerard F. *The Immutability of God in the Theology of Hans Urs von Balthasar.* Cambridge: Cambridge University Press, 1990.

Oman, Doug, and Carl E. Thoresen. "Spiritual Modeling: A Key to Spiritual and Religious Growth?" *International Journal for the Psychology of Religion* 13, no. 3 (July 2003): 149–65.

Pacifici, Mimmo. "The Pope Has Said: 'Animals Too Have Souls, Just like Men.'" *Genre Magazine,* January 1990. Translated by Piera Smith. www.dreamshore.net /rococo/pope.html.

Paul VI, Pope. *Humanae Vitae.* 1968. http://w2.vatican.va/content/paul-vi/en/encycli cals/documents/hf_p-vi_enc_25071968_humanae-vitae.html.

———. *Octogesima Adveniens.* Washington, DC: United States Catholic Conference, 1971.

———. *Populorum Progressio.* Vol. 6–60. Washington, DC: United States Catholic Conference, 1967.

Peacocke, Arthur R. *Theology for a Scientific Age: Being and Becoming—Natural, Divine, and Human.* Minneapolis: Fortress Press, 1993.

People for the Ethical Treatment of Animals. "John Paul II: A Saint to Animals." May 3, 2011. www.peta.org/blog/pope-saint-animals.

Philippi, Friedrich Adolph. *Commentary on St. Paul's Epistle to the Romans.* Vols. 60 and 61. Edinburgh: T&T Clark, 1878.

Pico della Mirandola, Giovanni. *Oration on the Dignity of Man.* Chicago: Henry Regnery, 1956.

Pinckaers, Servais. *The Sources of Christian Ethics.* Washington, DC: Catholic University of America Press, 1995.

Plumer, William S. *Commentary on Romans.* Grand Rapids: Kregel, 1971.

Poisson, Nicolas. *Commentaire ou remarques sur la Méthode de Mr. Descartes: Où on établit plusieurs principles généraux necessaries pour entendre ses oeuvres.* Paris, 1670.

Polkinghorne, John C. *Exploring Reality: The Intertwining of Science and Religion.* New Haven, CT: Yale University Press, 2005.

———. *Reason and Reality: The Relationship between Science and Theology.* Philadelphia: Trinity Press International, 1991.

Pope, Stephen J. "Darwinism and Moral Theology." In *Darwinism and Catholicism: The Past and Present Dynamics of a Cultural Encounter*, edited by Louis Caruana, 190–206. London: Continuum, 2009.

———. *Human Evolution and Christian Ethics.* Cambridge: Cambridge University Press, 2007.

Porter, Jean. "Moral Passions: A Thomistic Argument of Moral Emotions in Non-Human and Human Animals." *Journal of Moral Theology* 3, no. 2 (June 2014): 93–108.

Preece, Rod. *Brute Souls, Happy Beasts, and Evolution: The Historical Status of Animals.* Vancouver: University of British Columbia Press, 2006.

Primatt, Humphrey. *The Duty of Mercy and the Sin of Cruelty to Brute Animals.* Fontwell, UK: Centaur, 1992; orig. pub. 1776.

Prümmer, Dominic M. *Handbook of Moral Theology.* New York: P. J. Kennedy, 1957.

Rahner, Karl. "Christology within an Evolutionary View of the World." In *Theological Investigations: Later Writings*, vol. 5, 157–92. Translated by Karl Kruger. Baltimore: Helicon Press, 1966.

———. "The Eternal Significance of the Humanity of Jesus for Our Relationship with God." In *Theological Investigations: The Theology of the Spiritual Life*, vol. 3, 35–46. Translated by Karl-H Kruger. Baltimore: Helicon Press, 1967.

———. *Foundations of Christian Faith: An Introduction to the Idea of Christianity.* Translated by William V. Dych. New York: Crossroad, 1996.

———. "The Historicity of Theology." In *Theological Investigations: Writings of 1965–67*, vol. 9, 64–82. Translated by Graham Harrison. Baltimore: Darton, Longman, & Todd, 1972.

———. *Im Gespräch.* Edited by Paul Imhof and Hubert Biallowons. Vol. 1. Munich: Kösel, 1982.

———. "On the Question of a Formal Existential Ethics." In *Theological Investigations: Man in the Church*, vol. 2, 217–34. Translated by Karl-H Kruger. Baltimore: Helicon Press, 1963.

———. *On the Theology of Death.* New York: Herder & Herder, 1961.

———. *The Trinity.* New York: Crossroad, 1997.

Ratzinger, Joseph. "Kardinal Frings über das Konzil und Die Gedankenwelt." *Herder-Korrespondenz* 16 (1961–62): 168–74.

———. *The Spirit of the Liturgy.* San Francisco: Ignatius Press, 2000.

Rawls, John. *Political Liberalism.* New York: Columbia University Press, 1993.

Regalado, Antonio. "Rewriting Life: First Gene-Edited Dogs Reported in China." *MIT Technology Review*, October 19, 2015. www.technologyreview.com/s/542616/first-gene-edited-dogs-reported-in-china/.

Regan, Tom. *The Case for Animal Rights*. Berkeley: University of California Press, 1983.

Richard, Lucien. *Christ: The Self-Emptying of God*. New York: Paulist Press, 1997.

Rickaby, Joseph. *Moral Philosophy: Or, Ethics and Natural Law*. 2nd ed. London: Longmans, Green; Internet Archive, 1888.

Rolnick, Philip A. *Origins: God, Evolution, and the Question of the Cosmos*. Waco, TX: Baylor University Press, 2015.

Rolston, Holmes. "Does Nature Need to Be Redeemed?" *Zygon* 29, no. 2 (June 1994): 205–29.

———. *Science and Religion: A Critical Survey*. Philadelphia: Temple University Press, 1987.

Rosenfield, Leonora Cohen. *From Beast-Machine to Man-Machine: Animal Soul in French Letters from Descartes to La Mettrie*. New York: Octagon Books, 1968.

Rubio, Julie Hanlon. "Animals, Evil, and Family Meals." *Journal of Moral Theology* 3, no. 2 (June 2014): 35–53.

Ruland, Ludwig. *Foundation of Morality: God; Man; Lower Creatures*. Translated by Tarcisius Anthony Rattler and Newton Wayland Thompson. Saint Louis: B. Herder, 1936.

Ryder, Richard D. *Animal Revolution: Changing Attitudes towards Speciesism*. Rev. ed. New York: Berg, 2000.

Rynne, Xavier, pseud. *Letters from Vatican City: Vatican Council II, First Session: Background and Debates*. New York: Farrar, Straus & Giroux, 1963.

Sachs, John R. "Current Eschatology: Universal Salvation and the Problem of Hell." *Theological Studies* 52, no. 2 (June 1991): 227–54.

Safina, Carl. *Beyond Words: What Animals Think and Feel*. New York: Picador, 2016.

Salt, Henry Stephens. *Animals' Rights Considered in Relation to Social Progress*. New York: Macmillan; Internet Archive, 1894.

Sanders, E. P. *Paul and Palestinian Judaism: A Comparison of Patterns of Religion*. Philadelphia: Fortress Press, 1977.

Santmire, H. Paul. *The Travail of Nature: The Ambiguous Ecological Promise of Christian Theology*. Philadelphia: Fortress Press, 1985.

Schaab, Gloria. *Trinity in Relation: Creation, Incarnation, and Grace in an Evolving Cosmos*. Winona, MN: Anselm Academic, 2012.

Schloss, Jeffrey P. "From Evolution to Eschatology." In *Resurrection: Theological and Scientific Assessments*. Edited by Ted Peters, Robert J. Russell, and Michael Welker. Grand Rapids: W.B. Eerdmans, 2002.

Schwager, Raymund. *Banished from Eden: Original Sin and Evolutionary Theory in the Drama of Salvation*. Translated by James G. Williams. Leominster, UK: Gracewing, 2006.

Schwöbel, Christoph. "Last Things First: The Century of Eschatology in Retrospect." In *The Future as God's Gift: Explorations in Christian Eschatology*, edited by Marcel Sarot and David Fergusson, 217–41. Edinburgh: T&T Clark, 2000.

Scott, Peter A. "The Technology Factor: Redemption, Nature, and the Image of God." *Zygon* 35, no. 2 (June 2000): 371–84.

Shanor, Karen, and Jagmeet S. Kanwal. *Bats Sing, Mice Giggle: The Surprising Science of Animals' Inner Lives*. London: Icon Books, 2010.

Sideris, Lisa H. "Censuring Nature and Critiquing God." In *Diversity and Dominion: Dialogues in Ecology, Ethics, and Theology*, edited by Kyle Van Houtan and Michael S. Northcott, 25–41. Eugene, OR: Cascade Books, 2010.

———. *Environmental Ethics, Ecological Theology, and Natural Selection*. New York: Columbia University Press, 2003.

Singer, Peter. *Animal Liberation: The Definitive Classic of the Animal Movement*. Rev. ed. New York: Open Road Media, 2015.

Smith, George Duncan. *The Teaching of the Catholic Church: A Summary of Catholic Doctrine*. New York: Macmillan, 1948.

Southgate, Christopher. *The Groaning of Creation: God, Evolution, and the Problem of Evil*. Louisville: Westminster John Knox Press, 2008.

Stackhouse, Max L. "The Moral Meanings of Covenant." *Annual of the Society of Christian Ethics* 16 (January 1996): 249–64.

Stamps, Judy, and Ton G. G. Groothuis. 2010. "The Development of Animal Personality: Relevance, Concepts and Perspectives." *Biological Reviews* 85, no. 2 (2010): 301–25.

Stead, Julian. *The Church, the Liturgy, and the Soul of Man: The Mystagogia of St. Maximus the Confessor*. Still River, MA: St. Bede's, 1982.

Steck, Christopher W. *The Ethical Thought of Hans Urs von Balthasar*. New York: Crossroad, 2001.

———. "Graced Encounters: Liturgy and Ethics from a Balthasarian Perspective." *Horizons* 30, no. 2 (Fall 2003): 255–79.

Stegman, Thomas D. "'Run That You May Obtain the Prize': Using St. Paul as a Resource for the Spiritual Exercises." *Studies in the Spirituality of Jesuits* 44, no. 4 (Winter 2012): 1–43.

Stillman, J. W. "The Jesuits and Cruelty to Animals." *Spectator*, February 12, 1898, 235.

Strickland, Lloyd. "God's Creatures? Divine Nature and the Status of Animals in the Early Modern Beast-Machine Controversy." *International Journal of Philosophy and Theology* 74, no. 4 (December 2013): 291–309.

Suhard, Emmanuel-Célestin. *Priests among Men*. Chicago: Fides, 1949.

Swearer, Donald K., and Susan Lloyd McGarry. *Ecology and the Environment: Perspectives from the Humanities*. Cambridge, MA: Center for the Study of World Religions at Harvard Divinity School, 2009.

Taylor, Charles. *Modern Social Imaginaries*. Durham, NC: Duke University Press, 2004.

Teilhard de Chardin, Pierre. *Christianity and Evolution*. New York: Harcourt Brace Jovanovich, 1971.

———. *The Human Phenomenon*. Brighton, UK: Sussex Academic Press, 1999.

Thiel, John E. "For What May We Hope? Thoughts on the Eschatological Imagination." *Theological Studies* 67, no. 3 (September 2006): 517–41.

Thigpen, Paul. "Do Animals Go to Heaven?" *Our Sunday Visitor*, December 22, 2014. www.osv.com/OSVNewsweekly/Story/TabId/2672/ArtMID/13567/ArticleID /16633/Do-animals-go-to-heaven.aspx.

Thomas, Keith. *Man and the Natural World: A History of the Modern Sensibility*. New York: Pantheon Books, 1983.

Thompson, Augustine. *Francis of Assisi: A New Biography*. Ithaca, NY: Cornell University Press, 2012.

Thornhill, Richard, and Michael Morris. "Animal Liberationist Responses to Nonanthropogenic Animal Suffering." *Worldviews: Global Religions, Culture, and Ecology* 10, no. 3 (January 2006): 355–79.

Thunberg, Lars. *Microcosm and Mediator: The Theological Anthropology of Maximus the Confessor*. 2nd ed. Chicago: Open Court, 1995.

Tillich, Paul. *Systematic Theology*. Vol. 2. Chicago: University of Chicago Press, 1967.

Tillmann, Fritz. *The Master Calls: A Handbook of Christian Living*. Baltimore: Helicon Press, 1961.

Timm, Simon Christopher. "Moral Intuition or Moral Disengagement? Cognitive Science Weighs in on the Animal Ethics Debate." *Neuroethics* 9, no. 3 (December 2016): 225–34.

Torrance, Thomas F. *Divine and Contingent Order*. Oxford: Oxford University Press, 1981.

Trickett, Rachel. "Imagination and Belief." In *God Incarnate: Story and Belief*, edited by Anthony Ernest Harvey, 34–41. London: SPCK, 1981.

Trinkhaus, Charles E. *In Our Image and Likeness, Humanity and Divinity in Italian Humanist Thought*, Vol. 2. Notre Dame, IN: University of Notre Dame Press, 1970; ACLS Humanities eBook.

Tröhler, Ulrich, and Andreas-Holger Maehle. "Animal Experimentation from Antiquity to the End of the Eighteenth Century: Attitudes and Arguments." In *Vivisection in Historical Perspective*, edited by Nicolaas A. Rupke, 14–47. New York: Croom Helm, 1987.

———. "Anti-Vivisection in Nineteenth-Century Germany and Switzerland: Motives and Methods." In *Vivisection in Historical Perspective*, edited by Nicolaas A. Rupke, 149–87. New York: Croom Helm, 1987.

Turner, E. S. *All Heaven in a Rage*. New York: St. Martin's Press, 1965.

United Methodist Church. "Our Christian Roots: God's Reign," 2018. www.umc.org /what-we-believe/our-christian-roots-gods-reign.

United States Conference of Catholic Bishops. *Book of Blessings: Approved for Use in the Dioceses of the United States of America by the National Conference of Catholic Bishops and Confirmed by the Apostolic See*. Collegeville, MN: Liturgical Press, 1989.

———. *Renewing the Earth: An Invitation to Reflection and Action on Environment in Light of Catholic Social Teaching*. Washington, DC: Office of Publishing Services, United States Catholic Conference, 1991.

———. *The Roman Missal.* Totawa, New Jersey: Catholic Book Publishing Corporation, 2011.

Vallery, Jeremiah. "Pope Benedict XVI's Cosmic Soteriology and the Advancement of Catechesis on the Environment." In *Environmental Justice and Climate Change: Assessing Pope Benedict XVI's Ecological Vision for the Catholic Church in the United States,* edited by Jame Schaefer and Tobias L. Winright, 173–93. Lanham, MD: Lexington Books, 2013.

van Driel, Edwin Christiaan. *Incarnation Anyway: Arguments for Supralapsarian Christology.* Oxford: Oxford University Press, 2008.

Vatican Council II. *Gaudium et Spes.* 1965. www.vatican.va/archive/hist_councils/ii _vatican_council/documents/vat-ii_const_19651207_gaudium-et-spes_en.html.

———. *Lumen Gentium.* 1964. www.vatican.va/archive/hist_councils/ii_vatican_council /documents/vat-ii_const_19641121_lumen-gentium_en.html.

———. *Optatam Totius.* In *Vatican Council II: The Conciliar and Post Conciliar Documents,* vol. 1, 707–24. Rev. ed., edited by Austin Flannery. Collegeville, MN: Liturgical Press, 1984.

Vaughan, John. "The Ethics of Animal Suffering." *Dublin Review* 19, no. 1 (January 1888): 166–79.

Vischer, Lukas. "Listening to Creation Groaning: A Survey of Main Themes of Creation Theology." In *Listening to Creation Groaning: Report and Papers from a Consultation on Creation Theology,* edited by Lukas Vischer, 11–31. Geneva: Centre International Reforme John Knox, 2004.

Wahlberg, Mats. "Was Evolution the Only Possible Way for God to Make Autonomous Creatures? Examination of an Argument in Evolutionary Theodicy." *International Journal for Philosophy of Religion* 77, no. 1 (February 2015): 37–51.

Walsh, Bryan. "New Natural Selection: How Scientists Are Altering DNA to Genetically Engineer New Forms of Life." *Newsweek,* June 29, 2017. www.newsweek .com/2017/07/07/natural-selection-new-forms-life-scientists-altering-dna -629771.html.

Ward, Keith. *Christ and the Cosmos: A Reformulation of Trinitarian Doctrine.* Cambridge: Cambridge University Press, 2015.

Webb, Stephen H. "Didn't Jesus Eat Lamb?" In *A Faith Embracing All Creatures: Addressing Commonly Asked Questions about Christian Care for Animals,* edited by Tripp York and Andy Alexis-Baker, 53–63. Eugene, OR: Cascade Books, 2012.

———. "Ecology vs. the Peaceable Kingdom: Toward a Better Theology of Nature." *Soundings: An Interdisciplinary Journal* 79, no. 1/2 (April 1996): 239–52.

———. *On God and Dogs: A Christian Theology of Compassion for Animals.* New York: Oxford University Press, 1998.

Wenham, Gordon J. "Genesis." In *Word Biblical Commentary,* edited by David A. Hubbard. Vol. 1.1. Waco, TX: Word Books, 1987.

Wennberg, Robert N. *God, Humans, and Animals: An Invitation to Enlarge Our Moral Universe.* Grand Rapids: Wm. B. Eerdmans, 2003.

Wesley, John. *Sermons on Several Occasions.* Vol. 5. New York: Ezekiel Cooper and John Wilson; Christian Classics Ethereal Library, 1806.

Westermann, Claus. *Genesis 1–11: A Commentary*. Minneapolis: Augsburg, 1984.

White, Lynn. "The Historical Roots of Our Ecologic Crisis." *Science* 155, no. 3767 (March 1967): 1203–7.

Widener, Michael. "A Papal Bull against Bullfighting." Yale Law School, December 17, 2014. https://library.law.yale.edu/news/papal-bull-against-bullfighting.

Williams, Nancy M. "Affected Ignorance and Animal Suffering: Why Our Failure to Debate Factory Farming Puts Us at Moral Risk." *Journal of Agricultural and Environmental Ethics* 21, no. 4 (2008): 371–84.

Williams, Rowan. "Afterword: Making Differences." In *Balthasar at the End of Modernity*, edited by Lucy Gardner, David Moss, Ben Quash, and Graham Ward, 173–80. Edinburgh: T&T Clark, 1999.

———. "Creation, Creativity, and Creatureliness: The Wisdom of Finite Existence." In *Being-in-Creation: Human Responsibility in an Endangered World*, edited by Brian Treanor, Ellis Benson, and Norman Wirzba, 23–36. New York: Fordham University Press, 2015.

Williams, Ruth. "Effects of Neanderthal DNA on Modern Humans." *The Scientist*, October 5, 2017. www.the-scientist.com/?articles.view/articleNo/50571/title/Effects-of-Neanderthal-DNA-on-Modern-Humans/.

Wilson, Kenneth. "The World as Creation: The God-Given Context of God's Glory." In *Christian Community Now: Ecclesiological Investigations*, vol. 2, 21–42, edited by Paul M. Collins, Gerard Mannion, Gareth Powell, and Kenneth Wilson. London: T&T Clark, 2008.

Wollaston, William. *The Religion of Nature Delineated*. 7th ed. London: Printed for J. and P. Knapton; HathiTrust, 1750.

Wright, N. T. *Pauline Perspectives: Essays on Paul, 1978–2013*. London: SPCK, 2013.

———. *Surprised by Hope: Rethinking Heaven, the Resurrection, and the Mission of the Church*. New York: HarperOne, 2008.

Yarri, Donna. *The Ethics of Animal Experimentation: A Critical Analysis and Constructive Christian Proposal*. New York: Oxford University Press, 2005.

Yeago, David S. "Literature in the Drama of Nature and Grace: Hans Urs von Balthasar's Paradigm for a Theology of Culture." *Renascence-Essays on Values in Literature* 48, no. 2 (Winter 1996): 95–109.

Zagzebski, Linda Trinkaus. *Exemplarist Moral Theory*. New York: Oxford University Press, 2017.

Zizioulas, John. *Being as Communion: Studies in Personhood and the Church*. Vol. 4. Crestwood, NJ: St. Vladimir's Seminary Press, 1985.

———. "Priest of Creation." In *Environmental Stewardship: Critical Perspectives, Past and Present*, edited by R. J. Berry, 273–90. London: T&T Clark, 2006.

———. "Proprietors or Priests of Creation?" 1990. www.orthodoxytoday.org/articles2/MetJohnCreation.php.

Życiński, Józef. *God and Evolution: Fundamental Questions of Christian Evolutionism*. Washington, DC: Catholic University of America Press, 2006.

INDEX

Abrahamic covenant, 78, 93n120
Acta Sanctorum, 23, 51n91, 211n79
activism, 16, 17, 19–23, 202
Adams, Carol, 201, 212n96
agency: of animals, 109–11, 129n73,
    146–47, 157, 166n60, 201–2;
    Balthasar on, 116–17, 159; Christian
    vision and, 190–91; in evolutionary
    theodicies, 60–61, 88n4; of Holy
    Spirit, 141–44; human distinctiveness
    through, 74, 82; morality and, 73–74,
    92n97; in technocratic paradigm, 185
Albert the Great, 127n7
Alexander of Hales, 127n7
Allers, Rudolf, 168n94
"already / not yet" perspective on the
    kingdom, 1, 2, 172–73, 178–82, 191–
    93, 199, 203
Anderson, Ray S., 52n120
Anglicans and Anglicanism, 16, 37
animal abuse, 34, 37–38, 44, 188
animals: agency of, 109–11, 129n73,
    146–47, 157, 166n60, 201–2; cogni-
    tive and social capabilities of, 11–12,
    57, 68–76, 83, 86–87, 91n70, 91n82,
    91n91, 205; covenant with, 80–85,
    102, 109, 111, 124, 140, 191, 194,
    206–7; definitions of, 2–3, 6, 68–69;
    divine *magis* and, 3, 113, 120; genetic
    engineering of, 62, 198–99, 201;
    goodness of, 27, 77, 87, 108, 111, 113,
    116–17, 147; Holy Spirit and, 4, 123,
    145–47, 154–55, 157, 159–63; human
    distinctiveness from, 68–77, 184–85,
    208n13; identity/particularity of, 32,
    107–13, 116–20, 131n108, 158,

201–2; moral awareness of, 6, 8,
    15–16, 25, 68, 86, 179, 198–99;
    morality of, 73–74, 91n91, 124,
    166n60; norms for treatment of, 1–2,
    5, 182–87, 190, 192, 199–200; solidar-
    ity with humans, 65, 90–91n67, 145,
    146, 155–58, 163–64, 186, 205; suf-
    fering and, 38–39, 44–46, 57–58,
    70–71, 84, 100, 108, 152, 181–82,
    193. *See also* experiments on animals;
    factory farms; meat and meat con-
    sumption; predation and prey;
    redemption (animals); *specific types*
animal welfare movement, 16, 17, 19–23,
    202
Anomaly, J., 211n74
Anselm of Canterbury, 136
Anthony of Padua, 23
anthropocentrism: in animal studies, 70;
    anthropomonism vs., 94n139; Aqui-
    nas on, 12, 48n34; covenantal, 3,
    85–87; dominion mandate and, 177–
    78; environmentalism vs., 68, 85; epic
    eschatology and, 110; experiments on
    animals and, 199; *imago Dei* and, 68;
    in Romans 8:19–23, 104; stewardship
    and, 175; Teilhard and, 60; theocen-
    trism vs., 85–86, 94n138
anthropomonism, 86, 94n139
apes, 69, 72, 109, 191
Apollinarianism, 93n129
Apologists, 29
Apostolic Constitutions, 160, 161
Aquinas, Thomas: on animals as divine
    expression, 68, 83, 90n54, 90n65,
    147, 167n63; Balthasar on, 119, 121;

Aquinas, Thomas *(continued)*
   De potentia, 12; on the eschaton, 9–15,
      33–34, 48n32, 108–9, 126; first prac-
      tical precept, 34–35; on governance,
      177; infralapsarian approach and,
      127n7; on instrumentalization,
      208n20; on moral object, 76; on natu-
      ral evil, 87–88n3, 88n7; nature/grace
      distinction and, 96, 126; on passions,
      92n100; on Romans 8, 40; on the
      soul, 9–13, 31, 33, 52n124. See also
      Summa Theologica
Ariely, Dan, 53n140
Aristotle: *De Anima*, 10
Arnauld, Antoine, 38
Athanasius of Alexandria, 100, 127n16,
   159
Augustine of Hippo, 10, 101, 128n18
Austin, Richard Cartwright, 151
autonomy. *See* agency

Bacon, Francis, 184, 209n43
Balthasar, Hans Urs von: aesthetic fittingness and, 64, 167n75; animal
   redemption and, 3–4, 123–25; on
   Aquinas, 119, 121; on Christ, 116,
   121–23, 131n111, 131n115, 143–44,
   147–49; creation theology of, 115–20,
   130nn96–98, 132n121, 169n113,
   169n115, 209n55; on eucharistic celebration, 161–62; on the fall, 90n48; on
   Father/Son theo-drama, 121–23,
   137–39, 141–45; on Holy Spirit, 122,
   131n118, 140–45, 165n38, 165nn33–
   35, 166n40, 166n56; on human/
   creation solidarity, 158–59; human
   redemption and, 120–23, 136; on
   predation, 153–54; soteriology of,
   135–38, 141, 158–59, 163; theo-drama
   of, 4, 119–23, 125–26, 130n93, 147–
   50, 166n42, 167n67; Trinity and, 110,
   117–18, 121–23, 131n99, 131n113,
   131n118, 137–39, 165nn33–35; on
   vocation and personhood, 189; working method of, 165n16
Baltimore Catechism, 87
Banaji, Mahzarin, 53n140

Bandura, Albert, 211n85
Barth, Karl, 66, 115, 127n5, 157
Bartholomew I, 8, 34
Basil of Caesarea, 156, 211n84
bats, 73
Bauckham, Richard, 89n35, 94n138, 157,
   159, 208n16
beatific vision, 13, 14, 47
beauty, 117, 147, 181
Bekoff, Marc, 46, 73–74, 84, 92n97
Bell, Ernest, 20, 21
Bellarmine, Robert, 23, 197
Belshaw, Christopher, 194
Benedict XIV, 36
Benedict XV, 25, 46
Benedict XVI: on animals and the last
   judgment, 52–53n129; on covenant
   with environment, 83, 162; on cre-
   ation in the eschaton, 155, 205, 206;
   environmentalism of, 168n91; on
   kingdom of God, 173; on Maximus
   the Confessor, 101; on nature/grace
   distinction, 32
Bentham, Jeremy, 71
Benzoni, Francisco, 48n34
Berdoe, Edward, 19–21
Berkman, John, 52n126, 194–95, 211n84
Berry, Thomas, 92n107, 208n16
Blowers, Paul, 128n21
bodies: Aquinas on, 10–11, 13; Aristotle's
   hylomorphic theory of, 10; Augustine
   on, 128n18; in the eschaton, 14, 152;
   Rahner on, 157–58; souls' immortal-
   ity and, 28–30
Bonaventure, 27, 166n59
bonobos, 68, 72, 75
A Book of Blessings, 174
Bougeant, Guillaume-Hyacinthe, 39,
   54n162
Boullier, David, 39
Boylan, Patrick, 41
Boyle, Robert, 184
brokenness. *See* sin and sinfulness
Broome, Donald, 42
bullfighting, 24
Butler, Joseph, 35
Byrne, Brendan, 156, 168n98

CAFO (concentrated animal feeding operations), 210n73
Cahill, Lisa Sowle, 1, 136
Calhoun, John, 35
Camosy, Charles, 198–99
Canciani, Mario, 53n132
Catechism of the Catholic Church: on animal care, 24; on animals as divine expression, 113; on experiments on animals, 199, 211n90; on human dominion, 177–78; on human soul, 33, 52n125; on interdependence of creatures, 98; on revelation, 170n139, 206
Catholics and Catholicism: animal redemption and, 99–100; animal welfare movement and, 17, 22–23; Church's mission in, 5, 172–78, 183, 184, 186, 192–93, 204, 210n57; creation theology in, 125, 155; creaturely natures in, 4, 98, 124; on environmental exploitation, 177–78; ethical response to animals, 4–5, 192–93, 206–7; on evolution and morality, 74; *imago Dei* and, 65–68; post-Vatican II doctrines of, 104–6; sacramental vision of, 27, 186; sinfulness and, 35–37, 46; on slavery, 35–36; souls' immortality in, 9, 27–32; supralapsarian thought in, 97, 127n6, 127n7; Thomas's teachings interpreted in, 27–28. See also *Catechism of the Catholic Church*
cats, 109, 191
CDF (Congregation for the Doctrine of the Faith), 30, 31
Chalcedon, Council of, 81–82, 93n133, 123
charity: for animals, 15–16, 22; Aquinas on, 15, 49n37, 49n39; Newman on, 24
chimpanzees, 32, 69, 70, 72, 73
Christ and Christology: on animals, 102–3; Balthasar on, 116, 121–23, 131n111, 131n115, 143–44, 147–49; divine *magis* and, 97–98; God and creation aligned in, 4, 77, 81–84, 93n133, 163–64; humanity/

physicality of, 13–14, 47n30, 81–83, 93n129, 93n130, 123; *imago Christi* and, 77, 83–85, 98; in *Laudato Si'*, 114; predation and, 155; soteriology and, 134–36, 157; vocation and, 189
Christians and Christianity: "already / not" yet perspective in, 1; animal suffering and, 39, 44–45; animal welfare movement and, 16–17, 25–26, 34; art and literature's role in, 63, 183–84; biases against animals in, 85, 86, 91n67, 99–100, 184; covenant and, 78–79, 185; environmental responsibilities of, 174, 183–86; ethical response to animals, 4–5, 192–93, 206–7; experiments on animals and, 199–203; inconsistency in, 204; meat consumption and, 194–97, 200; principles for understanding animals, 190–91; sinfulness and, 35–37, 41; vocation and, 5, 26, 177, 187–90, 197, 210n66. See also Catholics and Catholicism
Chrysostom, John, 100, 211n79, 211n84
Church: in kingdom of God, 173–78; mission of, 5, 172–78, 183, 184, 186, 192–93, 204, 210n57; slavery and, 36–37; on the soul, 30–31; theological inertia in, 45–46. See also *Catechism of the Catholic Church*; Catholics and Catholicism; Protestants and Protestantism
Clough, David, 63, 90n44, 90n47, 93n133, 94n138, 151–52, 166n60
Cobbe, Frances Power, 17–19, 51n90
cockfighting, 42–43
communion: Balthasar on, 158–59; Edwards on, 107, 137, 144–45; *imago Dei* and, 67, 84, 85; *Laudato Si'* on, 111–12; the Trinity and, 118, 131n101; worship and, 162, 174; Zizioulas on, 157
community of creation, 175
companion animals, 9, 42, 98, 109, 181, 202
concentrated animal feeding operations (CAFO), 210n73

Congregation for the Doctrine of the Faith (CDF), 30, 31
consciousness in animals, 71–72. *See also* agency; identity/particularity
consumerism, 111, 185
cooperation, material vs. formal, 194–96
Coppens, Charles, 50n60; *Moral Principles and Medical Practice*, 18
corporeality. *See* bodies
cosmic fall, 57–59, 62–63, 65
covenant: animals and, 80–85, 102, 109, 111, 124, 140, 191, 194, 206–7; anthropocentrism and, 3, 85–87; Balthasar on creation's receptivity to, 117, 136, 148; Bible and, 76–81, 92n114; Church's labor for, 192–93; creation and, 79–83, 93n123, 117–19, 204–5; defined, 6, 78; eschaton and, 89n27, 92n111, 109; evolution of subjectivity and, 201; human capacity for, 77–85; kinship model and, 175–76; in *Laudato Si'*, 114; technocratic paradigm vs., 185; theo-drama and, 144; theological perspectives on, 78–80, 92n111, 93n120, 97, 125, 185, 191
creation: Aquinas on, 40–41; autonomy of, 59–61, 89n30, 116, 125, 166n53; Balthasar's theology of, 115–20, 130nn96–98, 132n121, 169n113, 169n115, 209n55; Catholic doctrine on, 104–5, 111; Christ's fulfillment of, 4, 77, 81–84, 93n133, 163–64; Church's responsibility to, 174–78; covenant and, 79–82, 93n123, 117–19; divine *magis* and, 97–99, 127n2, 127n5; evolution and, 61–63; John Paul II on, 32–33; *Laudato Si'* on, 111–12; love and, 59, 64, 75, 83; redemption/elevation of, 96, 100–106, 109–11, 152, 155, 159–64; Spirit's reach through, 145–46; suffering/imperfection in, 57–60, 64–65, 89n25
creaturely bipolarity, 110, 117
creatures. *See* animals
Crousaz, Jean-Pierre de, 39
Cullmann, Oscar: *Christ and Time*, 172

Dagg, Anne: *Animal Friendships*, 72
Daley, Brian, 28–29
Darwin, Charles, 150
Davidic covenant, 78
Davis, Henry, 50n60; *Moral and Pastoral Theology*, 17
Day, Dorothy, 188
Dean, Richard: *An Essay on the Future Life of Brutes*, 100
Deane-Drummond, Celia: on animals' moral agency, 166n60; on Balthasar, 137, 148–50, 167n75; on evolutionary theodicies, 61, 209n35; on *Laudato Si'*, 113, 114, 130n85; on theocentrism, 94n138; on theo-drama, 167n67
deep incarnationalism, 82, 123
Delio, Ilia, 62
Dell, Katharine, 93n123
De Lubac, Henri, 97, 127n2
Descartes, René, 38, 39
De Waal, Frans, 91n70, 91n76
Dickey, James, 153
Didache, 159
Dilly, Antoine, 38
divine *magis*, 3, 96–99, 113, 120, 125–26, 127n2, 127n5
Docetism, 93n129
dogs, 32, 69, 72, 73, 109, 191
dolphins, 32, 70, 72, 109, 191
domesticated animals, 180–82
dominion mandate, 3, 56, 105–6, 111, 175–78, 183–85, 192, 209n43
Domville, Margaret, 19–21
Dunn, James, 79, 92n118, 173

Easter, 122, 153–55
eating animals. *See* meat and meat consumption; predation and prey
ecocentrism, 76–77
economy. *See* salvific economy
ecotheology and ecotheologians: Bauckham on, 89n35; defined, 7; evolution and, 62; Holy Spirit in, 133; on predation, 151–52; Ruland as, 26; soteriology of, 134–35; stewardship and, 175–78; theocentrism in, 85–86

Edwards, Denis: on animal redemption, 100, 107; on Balthasar, 137; on Holy Spirit, 144–45; on human nature, 127n8; on Kasper, 166n48; on *Laudato Si'*, 111, 114; on reconciliation, 207n7; theocentrism of, 94n138

Eggemeier, Matthew, 209n55

elephants, 72, 73, 91n83, 109, 191

environment: Benedict XVI on, 83, 162, 168n91; Church's responsibility to, 174; covenant with, 83, 162, 204–5; ecocentric approaches to, 76–77; Francis on, 6, 184, 205; John Paul II on, 42, 105, 203–4; *Laudato Si'* on, 111, 113; theocentrism and, 85; theo-dramatic approach to, 149; unclear understanding of ecosystems and, 176–77

environmentalism: anthropocentrism vs., 68, 85–86; Aquinas and, 48n34; of Benedict XVI, 168n91; Catholic doctrine on, 105–6, 177, 183; cultural norms vs., 182–87, 190; Romans 8:19–23 and, 104; Sideris on, 107

Ephrem the Syrian: *Hymns on Paradise*, 100

epic eschatology, 101, 106–11, 114–15

Erigena, John Scotus, 63, 90n50

eschatology and the eschaton: animals redemption and, 99–106, 108–9, 114–15, 191; Aquinas on, 12–15, 48n32, 108–9, 126; Balthasar on, 148; Christian calling and, 203–7; contemporary significance of, 99; continuities in, 14–15, 48n33, 97–98, 124, 130n83, 152, 192; covenant and, 89n27, 92n111, 109; "epic," 101, 106–11, 114–15; ethics and, 5, 173, 199, 207n4; evolution and, 60–62; individualistic vs. cosmic, 205–6; John Paul II on, 207n3; kingdom of God and, 99, 171–72, 191; "not yet" of kingdom and, 179–82; predation and natural evils in, 89n27, 151–53; speculation about, 14, 153

Estabrook, Barry, 211n76

ethical norms vs. values of the kingdom, 1–2, 182–87, 190, 192, 199–200

ethics: animal diversity and, 76–77; Aquinas and, 43; brokenness and, 85; creativity in, 188; eschatology and, 5, 173, 199, 207n4; of experimentation on animals, 197–203; *imago Dei* and, 67; of meat from factory farms, 193–97, 200; "not yet" of kingdom and, 1–2, 171–72, 179–82; principles for, 190–93; theocentrism and, 85–86; theology required for, 4–5, 56; Thomistic framework for, 15–16

ethologists and ethology, 69, 72–74, 205

Eucharist: Balthasar on, 161–62; 1 Corinthians on, 79; Eucharistic Prayers of the Roman Missal, 161; human/animal solidarity in, 146, 162–63; prayers of, 159–61; redemption and, 4, 157, 159–63, 174; Zizioulas on, 157. *See also* communion

Eusebius of Caesarea, 159, 187

evil and natural evils: Aquinas on, 34–35, 87–88n3, 88n7; creation and, 58, 64, 89n25; cruelty to animals as, 18, 33–34; experiments on animals and, 203; factory-farming industry and, 43, 44, 194–97; the fall and, 63; free will and, 60; in *Laudato Si'*, 114; modern attempts to explain, 37–39

evolution and evolutionary biology: animal/human distinction in, 8, 68, 74–76, 82–83; eschatology and, 60–62; the fall and, 56–60; intelligence development in, 69; in *Laudato Si'*, 114; moral behavior in, 74; salvation history distinct from, 133, 134; social dynamics in, 72–73; subjectivity in, 201; technology and, 62; theodicies of, 3, 58–65, 205

experiments on animals: *Catechism* on, 178, 211n90; ethics of, 197–203; Manning and, 51n99; Newman on, 24; Ruland on, 25–27; vivisection, 16, 17

Exsultet, 95–96, 99

Ezekiel, 102, 156

factory farms, 42–44, 172, 193–97, 200, 210nn73–74
the fall: cosmic, 57–59, 62–63, 65, 90n44; divine *magis* and, 95–96; in evolutionary theodicies, 57–65, 88n4; historical, 57, 58, 61–63, 65; Jenkins on, 87–88n3; kingdom's ideals tempered by, 171–72, 182; love's redemptive capacity after, 83–84; predation and, 150–51; sin and, 57, 58, 63–65, 85, 87–88n3, 88n4, 95; vocation and, 188
Farley, Margaret, 45, 165n29, 183
Ficino, Marsilio, 184
Fitzmyer, Joseph, 41, 80
flexitarianism, 195–96
floating peanut task, 91n70
forgiveness and reconciliation, 173
Fountaine, Nicholas, 49n41
Fox, George, 16
Fox, Matthew, 89n35, 151
Francis: on animal redemption, 191, 205; on Church's mission, 178; on God's plan for animals, 206, 212n112; on integrated ecology, 6, 184, 204; on kingdom of God, 171; *Laudato Si'*, 34, 61, 93n135, 111–15, 212n111; pets' souls and, 9; on prayer, 8, 34; on sanctification of creation, 162
Francis Crick Memorial Conference, 91n82
Francis of Assisi, 23, 188, 194
free process argument, 59–60, 89n27, 166n53
free will, 60, 61
French, William C., 48n34

Gaffney, James, 23, 40
Galloway, Allan, 103
Gasparri, Pietro, 46
Gaudium et Spes, 129n44, 129n55, 206, 212n106
Gavrilyuk, Paul, 138
genetic engineering, 62, 198–99, 201
Gilleman, Gérard, 187
Godet, Frédéric, 54n173

Good Friday, 121, 122, 153, 154
goodness: of animals, 27, 77, 87, 108, 111, 113, 116–17, 147; animal suffering and, 38–39; Aquinas on, 34–35, 43; Balthasar on, 115; of the body, 13; in broken world, 194–95; convenience vs., 35, 37; of creaturely diversity, 10, 12, 15, 47n17, 48n34, 83, 98, 167–68n80, 181–82; in evolutionary theodicies, 58–64; of nature, 185; Spirit's generation of, 145
gorillas, 68, 72
grace. *See* nature/grace distinction
Granger, James, 16
Gray, Asa, 150, 167n76
Greenwald, Anthony, 53n140
Gregory of Nazianzus, 159
Gregory of Nyssa, 63, 90nn48–49
Gregory XVI, 36
Grenz, Stanley, 66
Griffin, Donald, 91n91
Guarnieri, Patrizia, 49n40, 50n84
Gushee, David, 207n5

Hadley, Christopher, 131n120
Harris, Murray, 28
Haught, John: on evolutionary heritage, 75–76; evolutionary theodicy of, 59, 62, 89n30, 110, 130n79; on meaningfulness from Christ, 154; on process theology, 129n59; soteriology and, 134
Hauser, Marc, 91n91
Hegel, Georg Wilhelm Friedrich, 119
Heidegger, Martin, 209n45
Herzog, Hal, 42–43
Heyer, Kristin, 210n57
Holy Spirit: agency of, 141–44; animal sanctification and, 4, 123, 145–47, 154–55, 157, 159–63; Athanasius on, 127n16; in Balthasar's theo-drama, 122, 131n118, 140–45, 165n38, 165nn33–35, 166n40, 166n56; in eco-theologies, 133–35; in evolutionary theodicies, 59, 61; John Paul II on, 206; soteriology and, 136; soul's immortality and, 28, 31; stewardship

and, 67; Trinity and, 122, 123, 141–46, 163, 165nn33–35, 172–73
Hopkins, Gerard Manley, 27
Horrell, David, 104
horses, 72
humans: animal conflict with, 175–76, 181, 192; in Balthasar's theo-drama, 122–23; covenantal capacity of, 77–85; distinctiveness from animals, 68–77, 184–85, 208n13; divine *magis* and responsibility of, 85, 86, 105, 106, 188–89; *imago Christi* and, 83–85; *imago Dei* and, 65–68, 74–77, 104, 156; interconnectivity and, 112, 129n71, 130n83, 185; as microcosmos, 155–60, 162, 163–64; ministerial role of, 162, 164, 173, 177, 178, 180; nature/grace distinction in, 96–97; self-awareness and consciousness in, 71, 88n4; solidarity with animals, 65, 90–91n67, 145, 146, 155–58, 163–64, 186, 205. *See also* anthropocentrism
Hunt, Cherryl, 104
hunting, 16, 182
hypocrisy, 204

identity/particularity: of animals, 32, 107–13, 116–20, 131n108, 158, 201–2; Balthasar on, 116–20, 122–23, 125–26, 159, 210n69; *Laudato Si'* on, 112; resurrection and, 29–31
Ignatius of Loyola, 44, 189, 210n66
imago Christi, 77, 83–85, 98
imago Dei: Aquinas on, 90n54; Basil on, 156; Catholic doctrine on, 104; covenant and, 82–85; dominion mandate and, 176, 208n18; human uniqueness and, 65–68, 74–75, 77, 104; John Paul II on, 56, 82; *Laudato Si'* on, 112–13; stewardship and, 176
Imhoff, Dan, 210n74
immortal souls. *See* souls
infralapsarian views, 96, 125, 127n7
instrumentalization of nature and animals, 5, 9, 48n34, 68, 111, 178, 183–86, 200–201, 205

intellect and intellectual capabilities: of animals, 32, 37, 38, 69–70, 75; Aquinas on, 10–13, 31, 47n15, 47n29, 90n54; *imago Dei* and, 66, 67, 73
International Theological Commission (ITC), 30–32, 52n122, 66–67, 77, 118, 131n101, 207n11
Irenaeus of Lyon, 59, 100, 159–60
Italian Society for the Protection of Animals, 46
ITC (International Theological Commission), 30–32, 52n122, 66–67, 77, 118, 131n101, 207n11

Jaquelot, Isaac, 38
Jenkins, Willis, 48n34, 87–88n3, 135, 151
Jerome, 211n84
Jesus. *See* Christ and Christology
John Paul II: on animals' souls, 32, 33, 53n132; on environment, 42, 105, 203–4; on eschatology, 207n3; on God's love for creation, 140, 205; on *imago Dei*, 56, 82; on ministering creation, 178; on original sin, 65; on sanctification of creation, 133, 162, 206; slavery and, 36; on soul's immortality, 31
Johnson, Elizabeth, 61, 145, 164n1
Jonas, Hans, 209n45
Jone, Heribert, 17–18, 50n60

Kärkkäinen, Veli-Matti, 118
Kasper, Walter, 118, 164n1
Kelly, Gerald, 197, 211n86
kenosis, 59, 123, 136, 153, 179
kingdom of God: "already / not yet" perspective on, 1, 2, 172–73, 178–82, 191–93, 199, 203; Christian calling and, 203–7; Church's role in, 173–78; covenant and, 6, 78–79; cultural norms and, 1–2, 5, 182–87, 190, 192, 199–200; eschatology and, 99, 171–72, 191; ethical principles for animals and, 191–93; Methodists on, 207n10; stewardship of, 67, 175–76; translation of, 207n1; vocation and, 189–90

Kingsford, Anna, 22
kinship model of creation, 175–76
Koko (gorilla), 68
Kopp, Susan, 198–99

LaCugna, Catherine Mowry, 118, 164n1
Lecky, William Edward Hartpole, 22
Leo XIII, 36
Levering, Matthew, 48n32, 52n124
Lewis, C. S., 124
Linzey, Andrew, 62–64, 157, 212n96
lions, 191
Liturgy of Saint Basil, 160, 161
Lloyd, Michael, 90n44
logoi, 101, 128n21, 160
Lohfink, Gerhard, 109–10, 129n72, 130n78
Louth, Andrew, 168n90
love: creation as act of, 59, 64, 75, 83; divine *magis* and, 95, 97, 98, 125; *imago Christi* and, 83; particularity of, 108, 111, 112; triune manifestation of, 4, 48n32, 121–22, 137–43
Lucy (fossil discovery), 75
Lumen Gentium, 129n52, 170n147, 205–6, 207n9, 212n105

magpies, 72, 91n76, 191
Mahoney, Jack, 88n6, 134, 135
Malebranche, Nicolas, 38
Manning, Henry Edward, 24–25, 36–37, 51n99
manuals and Catholic moral thought, 17, 25
Martin, André, 38
Martin of Tours, 188
Maximus the Confessor, 63, 90n53, 101, 119, 130n79, 156, 160
McCormick, Patrick, 209n55
McDaniel, Jay, 44, 124, 179
McFadyen, Alistair, 129n71
McLaughlin, Ryan Patrick, 48n34, 59–60, 208n18
meat and meat consumption, 5–6, 42–44, 172, 175, 178, 192–97, 211n77, 211n84
Meconi, David, 129n73
Meilaender, Gilbert, 188–89

Merchant, Carolyn, 209n43
Messer, Neil, 90n44
Methodists, 16, 28, 36, 207n10
Metz, Johannes B., 185
Meyer, Eric Daryl, 90–91n67
Miller, Patrick, 80, 209n40
mirror test, 71–72
Moltmann, Jürgen, 60, 89n28, 157, 173
Monophysitism, 93n129
morality and moral awareness: agency and, 73–74, 92n97; of animals, 73–74, 91n91, 124, 166n60; claims of animals on humans and, 6, 8, 15–16, 25, 68, 86, 179, 198–99; creativity in, 188; difficulty of changing, 34–35, 44–45; eschatological vision for, 190–91; experimentation on animals and, 197–203; factory farming and, 193–97; *imago Dei* and, 67, 73–76; individual example and, 211n85; intentionality in, 92n97, 194–95, 198–99, 201; suffering of animals and, 44–46; theology and, 56. *See also* ethics; Thomistic framework
Morris, Michael, 209n34
Mosaic covenant, 78
mousetraps, 192
Murdoch, Iris, 44, 46n1, 179

natural evils. *See* evil and natural evils
nature. *See* creation; environment
nature/grace distinction, 32, 96–99, 118, 125–26, 152
Neanderthals, 75
Neri, Philip, 24
Nestorianism, 93n129
Newman, John Henry, 20, 24, 50n70
New Testament, 78–81, 92n114, 103. *See also* scriptural citations (New Testament)
niche construction, 149
Noahic covenant, 79–81, 93n123, 101–2, 112
nonhuman creatures. *See* animals
Noonan, John, 36
Norris, John, 38
Northcott, Michael, 114

O'Brien, Kevin, 167–68n80, 209n55
O'Halloran, Nathan, 89n25
O'Hanlon, Gerard, 131n117
Old Testament, 78, 79, 92n114, 102, 110, 156, 157. *See also* scriptural citations (Old Testament)
orangutans, 69, 72
Origen, 29
otherness and the other, 98, 117–19, 121, 124, 140–41, 201

paschal mystery, 31, 79, 97, 124, 125, 135, 144, 159
Paul III, 36
Pauline theology, 79–80, 92n118, 100, 156, 162
Peacocke, Arthur, 58
People for the Ethical Treatment of Animals (PETA), 33
pets, 9, 42, 98, 109, 180–81, 202
Philippi, Friedrich Adolph, 54n173
Pico della Mirandola, Giovanni, 129n69
Pierce, Jessica, 73–74, 84, 92n97
pigs, 211n76
Pinckaers, Servais, 188
Pius V: *De Salute Gregis Dominici*, 24
Pius IX, 17, 23, 24, 53n132
Pius X, 25
Pius XII, 127n2
Plato: *Timaeus*, 155–56
Plumer, William S., 54n173
pneumatology, 136, 141, 144–45, 163. *See also* Holy Spirit
Poisson, Nicholas, 38
Polignac, Melchior de, 38–39
Polkinghorne, John, 59, 88n4
Pope, Stephen, 74
Porter, Jean, 92n100
prayer, 174, 193, 208n13
predation and prey, 4, 58, 63, 84, 150–55, 163, 180, 181, 208–9n34
Preece, Rod, 127n11
Primatt, Humphrey: *The Duty of Mercy and the Sin of Cruelty to Brute Animals*, 16
process theology, 58, 88n5, 89n30, 129n59

Protestants and Protestantism: on animal redemption, 41, 100; animal welfare movement and, 23; *imago Dei* and, 66; slavery and, 36; supralapsarian views in, 97. *See also* Christians and Christianity; Methodists; Quakers and Quakerism
Prou, Jean, 206
Prümmer, Dominic, 50n60; *Handbook of Moral Theology*, 17, 18

Quakers and Quakerism, 16, 36

Rahner, Karl: on Balthasar, 137; on beatific vision, 47n30; on Catholic doctrine, 45; on Christian life, 210n67; on Christ's humanity, 13–14; on cosmic solidarity, 157–58, 169n110, 169n112; on creation, 125, 127n5; on human nature, 82, 93n130, 169n109; Moltmann on, 89n28; on transcendence, 169n108; on vocation and personhood, 189, 210n66
rationality and reason: animal capacity for, 11–12; emotion's influence on, 74; instrumentalization and, 184–85. *See also* agency; self-deception and morality
Ratzinger, Joseph, 1, 66, 174
Rawls, John, 186
reconciliation and forgiveness, 173
redemption (general): anthropocentrism and, 94n139; Balthasar on, 120–23, 136; covenant and, 92n111; of creation, 96, 100–106, 109–11, 152, 155, 159–64; deep incarnationalism and, 82; evolution and, 62; *Exsultet* and, 95; love and, 83. *See also* Christ and Christology; eschatology and the eschaton
redemption (animals): Aquinas on, 9–13, 33–34, 126; Balthasar on, 3–4, 123–25; Catholic views on, 27–28; Church's responsibilities to, 174–75; eschatology and, 14–15, 41, 99–106, 108–9, 114–15, 191; ethical principles for, 191–93; the fall and, 57, 65; for individual creatures, 147–55, 163–64;

redemption (animals) *(continued)*
    Laudato Si' on, 114–15; Lohfink on,
    109–10, 130n78; Ruland on, 26; in
    solidarity with humans and creation,
    155–63, 205–7; souls' continuity and,
    31–33, 40; through suffering, 39–40;
    Trinity and, 123–24, 145–46
Regan, Tom, 212n96; *The Case for
    Animal Rights*, 202
resurrection: body/soul dualism and,
    28–30; intermediate state preceding,
    52n117, 52n122; sacrifice and, 152
Rickaby, Joseph, 18, 49–50n60
Robinson, Thomas, 37
Rolnick, Philip A., 89n30
Rolston, Holmes, 58, 107, 151–52, 154
Romero, Óscar, 188
Rubio, Julie Hanlon, 194–96
Ruland, Ludwig: *Die allgemeinen Grund-
    lagen des sittlichen Handelns*, 25–27,
    44–45

sacramental tradition, 27, 48, 86, 113,
    164, 168n80, 185–86, 209n55; Aquinas
    on animals as divine expression, 68, 83,
    90n54, 90n65, 147, 167n63; Benedict
    on animals sharing in the kingdom,
    173; *Catechism* on animals as divine
    expression, 113; Francis on animals'
    value in the light of Christ, 113;
    Summa Theologica on animals as divine
    expression, 167n63
Sacred Heart Review, 55n198
Safina, Carl, 73
saints: Aquinas on, 13–14, 47n27; devo-
    tion to animals of, 23–24, 26, 51n90,
    129n73, 203
Salt, Henry, 22
salvific economy, 77–78, 80, 85, 136,
    140–43, 155
Sanctus, 160
Sanders, E. P., 79
Schwager, Raymund, 88n4
scientific method, 184–85
Scotus, Duns, 127n7
scriptural citations (Old Testament):
    Genesis, 3, 56, 130n82; Genesis 1:26,

65, 66, 175, 176; Genesis 2:15, 175;
    Genesis 5:1–3, 66; Genesis 9:8–17,
    79–80, 101–2; Deuteronomy 22, 40;
    Job 42:3, 87; Psalms 103:11, 108;
    Isaiah 11:1–9, 5, 99, 102, 156; Isaiah
    55:7–9, 108; Jeremiah 31:31–34, 80;
    Hosea 2:18, 156; Hosea 2:20, 40, 80,
    102; Zechariah 2:8, 102; Zechariah
    8:12, 156
scriptural citations (New Testament):
    Matthew 10:28, 28; Luke 11:13, 108;
    Luke 12:6, 108; Romans 8:18–23, 80,
    103–4, 156; Romans 8:21–22, 26,
    40–41; 1 Corinthians 4:1, 67, 176;
    1 Corinthians 11:25, 79; 1 Corinthi-
    ans 15:44, 28; 1 Corinthians 15:50,
    28; Ephesians 1:10, 80; Colossians
    1:16–17, 80; 1 Timothy 6:16, 28;
    Hebrews 7:22, 79; Hebrews 8:7, 79
self-awareness in animals, 69–72. *See also*
    agency; identity/particularity
self-deception and morality, 34–36
Sideris, Lisa, 58, 107–8
sin and sinfulness: acknowledging,
    34–35; animal mistreatment as, 34,
    37–38, 44; of animals, 53n129,
    63–64; anthropocentrism and,
    85–86; in cultural and social norms,
    182–83; experiments on animals and,
    200; of factory farming, 194–95; the
    fall and, 57, 58, 63–65, 85, 87–88n3,
    88n4, 95; God's foreknowledge of,
    63–65, 90nn49–50; liberation from,
    204; stewardship and, 175, 178; in
    theo-drama of Father/Son, 122, 135,
    136, 140
slaughtering and slaughter-houses, 26,
    37, 43–44. *See also* factory farms
slavery, 35–37, 45, 85
Society for the Prevention of Cruelty to
    Animals (SPCA), 17, 22–25
solidarity, 65, 90–91n67, 145, 146, 155–
    58, 163–64, 186, 205
soteriology: Balthasar on, 135–38, 141,
    158–59, 163; creatures in, 33, 123,
    131n108, 145–46; evolution and, 76;
    human/creation solidarity in, 156–59,

163–64; of *Laudato Si'*, 115; trinitarian framework for, 137–41

souls: of animals vs. humans, 9, 11–12, 27–28, 31–33, 38, 46n2, 50n79, 206; Aquinas on, 9–12, 31, 33, 52n124; Aristotle's hylomorphic theory of, 10; immortality and continuity of, 11, 28–32, 52n120, 52n122; John Paul II on, 52n124

Southgate, Christopher, 58, 88n12, 104, 151

SPCA (Society for the Prevention of Cruelty to Animals), 17, 22–25

sports, 16, 24, 42–43

Stassen, Glen, 207n5

Stegman, Thomas, 92n117

stewardship, 66–67, 84, 157, 164, 206, 208n16; critique and defense of, 174–78

Stillman, J. W., 23, 50n86

Strickland, Lloyd, 54n156

Stubbes, Philip, 16

Suárez, Francisco, 127n7

subject/object bipolarity, 110, 117, 118, 141, 179

Suhard, Emmanuel Célestin, 203

Summa Theologica: on animals as divine expression, 167n63; on body of Christ, 47n30; on charity, 49n37, 49n39; on creaturely diversity, 47n17; on earthly natures, 54n171; on God's plan for creation, 47n14; on *imago Dei*, 90n54, 90n65; on intellect and desire, 132n134; on the soul, 11, 12; on the souls of saints, 47n27; supplement to, 47n10

supralapsarian views, 97, 125, 127n7

Taylor, Charles, 183

technocratic paradigm, 111, 124–25, 200

technology and technological capability, 62, 198

Teilhard de Chardin, Pierre, 57, 60, 110, 130n79

theocentrism, 85–86, 94n138, 105, 111, 113

Theodore of Mopsuestia, 160

theo-drama, 4, 119–23, 125–26, 130n93, 147–50, 166n42, 167n67. *See also* Balthasar, Hans Urs von

Thérèse of Lisieux, 188

Thiel, John, 173

Thigpen, Paul, 46n2

Thomas, Keith, 22

Thomistic framework: animals' souls in, 50n79; Berkman on, 52n126; in Catholic moral thought, 17–19, 33–34; charity for animals in, 15; defined, 3, 15–16; *Laudato Si'* challenging, 113; vivisection debate and, 19–22

Thornhill, Richard, 209n34

Thunberg, Lars, 170n131

Tillich, Paul, 88n4

Tillmann, Fritz, 187

Torrance, T. F., 157

Trent, Council of, 9

Trickett, Rachel, 63

Trinity and trinitarian imprint: agency in, 141–43; animal individuality and, 110, 118–19, 147, 152–55; Balthasar on, 110, 117–18, 121–23, 131n99, 131n113, 131n118, 137–39, 165nn33–35; in the eschaton, 152–53; interconnectivity and, 112; ITC on, 118, 131n101; love and, 4, 48n32, 121–22, 137–43; soteriology of, 134–41; Spirit's role in, 122, 123, 141–46, 163, 165nn33–35, 172–73

"two ways" model, 187–88

Urban VIII, 36

Van Driel, Edward Christiaan, 127n2, 127n6

Vanier, Jean, 188

Vatican II, 3, 31, 173, 174, 187, 205, 212n111

Vaughan, John, 19–22, 37, 39

vegetarianism, 194, 196–97

Victorian Street Society, 51n99

Vischer, Lukas, 94n139

vivisection, 16, 17, 19–21, 24, 28, 49n40, 51n99

Ward, Keith, 165n24
Webb, Stephen, 181
Weld-Blundell, Charles, 19–21,
    49–50n60
Wennberg, Robert, 208n34
Wesley, John, 16, 28. *See also*
    Methodists
Westermann, Claus, 65
whales, 72
White, Lynn, 68, 85
wildlife, 180–81
Williams, Nancy, 210–11n74

Williams, Rowan, 119, 138
Wilson, Kenneth, 207n10
Wollaston, William, 37
wolves, 73, 151
Wright, N. T., 28, 48n32, 52n117,
    92n111, 93n120

Yarri, Donna, 202
Yeago, David, 150

Zizioulas, John, 118, 157, 168n90
Życiński, Józef, 89n30

ABOUT THE AUTHOR

Christopher Steck, SJ, is an associate professor in the Department of Theology and Religious Studies at Georgetown University. His research has focused on fundamental themes in moral theology. His first book, *The Ethical Thought of Hans Urs von Balthasar*, received the College Theology Society's annual book award in 2003. He served as caretaker of the Georgetown mascot, Jack the Bulldog, from 2003 until 2013, and among the courses he teaches are "Dogs and Theology" and "Animal Ethics." He received his PhD from Yale University in 1999.